D1194944

Eucharistic Doctors

Eucharistic Doctors

A Theological History

Owen F. Cummings

Paulist Press
New York/Mahwah, NJ

The scripture quotations contained herein are from the New Revised Standard Version: Catholic Edition, Copyright © 1989 and 1993 by the Division of Christian Education of the National Council of Churches of Christ in the United States of America. Used by permission. All rights reserved.

Extracts from the documents of the Second Vatican Council are from Walter M. Abbott, ed., *The Documents of Vatican II* (New York: The America Press, 1966). Used by permission. All rights reserved.

Cover design by Cynthia Dunne
Book design by Lynn Else

Copyright © 2005 by Owen F. Cummings

All rights reserved. No part of this book may be reproduced or transmitted in any form or by any means, electronic or mechanical, including photocopying, recording, or by any information storage and retrieval system without permission in writing from the Publisher.

Library of Congress Cataloguing-in-Publication Data

Cummings, Owen F.
    Eucharistic doctors : a theological history / Owen F. Cummings.
        p. cm.
    Includes index.
    ISBN 0-8091-4243-0 (alk. paper)
    1. Lord's Supper—History. I. Title.
    BV823.C86 2005
    234'.163'0922—dc22

                                                        2005020578

Published by Paulist Press
997 Macarthur Boulevard
Mahwah, New Jersey 07430

www.paulistpress.com

Printed and bound in the
United States of America

Dedicated to my sons:
Andrew Charles Cummings
Owen Thomas Cummings

Fellow travelers in pursuit of the truth,

And to my grandson
Matthew Bogdan Cummings

Contents

Contents

Introduction

Very few textbooks exist in English that offer the interested student of theology a sense of the richness of the entire Catholic tradition. By the entire Catholic tradition here, I mean not only Roman Catholicism, but also the Orthodox and the Anglican traditions. A comprehensive presentation reflecting with some degree of adequacy all these catholic traditions would be more than a lifetime's work. This book is not comprehensive in that sense. Rather, it represents an accessible, popular introduction to this broad eucharistic tradition, but with sufficient scholarly apparatus for the interested reader to go further. The Latin verb *docere* means "to teach," and it is hoped that the various authors treated in this book will have something to teach us about the Eucharist. Hence the title, *Eucharistic Doctors.* They are certainly not all doctors of the church in the formal sense of that term, but there can be little dispute that they are doctors *in* the church, doctors in the broad Christian tradition of thinking about the Eucharist.

There are many fine expositions of various time periods in the tradition. For the New Testament we have three excellent works of Eugene LaVerdiere: *Dining in the Kingdom of God: The Origins of the Eucharist According to Luke;*[1] *The Eucharist in the New Testament and in the Early Church*[2] and *The Breaking of the Bread: The Development of the Eucharist According to Acts.*[3] LaVerdiere's works, building on the careful New Testament work of earlier scholars, give full play to the unique perspective of the individual New Testament writers, but within a Catholic context of eucharistic appreciation. One constantly hears a Catholic "echo" within his work, an echo that opens up wonderful horizons of sound. *Eucharistic Doctors* does not deal with the New Testament authors as such, but the writer continues to learn much from the model that Eugene LaVerdiere represents. Staying with the New Testament, there is also the helpful book of Francis J. Moloney, *A Body Broken for a Broken People*.[4] Different in approach from LaVerdiere, it is a most useful complement.

For the patristic period we are not as well served. There are various anthologies of patristic texts, some thematically arranged, but not much more than that. The collection of essays by Raymond Johanny and others, *The Eucharist of the Early Christians*,[5] is the only title readily available. However, this excellent collection deals only with pre-Nicene authors and texts. For other authors after the Council of Nicaea one must go to more specialized monographs and studies. The German study of Johannes Betz, *Die Eucharistie in der Zeit der griechischen Vater*,[6] remains untranslated some fifty years after publication, and there is nothing in English to match it.

The medieval period is better served, not least by the first-rate work of Gary Macy. Macy has produced several books. The first I want to mention is *The Theology of the Eucharist in the Early Scholastic Period*,[7] the second, *Treasures from the Storeroom: Medieval Religion and the Eucharist*.[8] A third book by Macy, *The Banquet's Wisdom: A Short History of the Theologies of the Lord's Supper*,[9] is closer in intention to this book, *Eucharistic Doctors*. However, Macy's treatment is more thematic than focused on individual contributions.

There is something faintly absurd and terribly tragic in the writing of this book. There is something absurd in my trying to reach into the minds and hearts of the men represented in these pages, trying to retrieve and express their eucharistic understanding. I am not referring in the first place to the enormous complexity of any hermeneutical retrieval of the Christian past. Rather, I am thinking of what was in the hearts and souls of these men as they celebrated the Eucharist, week after week. I am all too conscious of my failure to grasp how they loved and lived Jesus Christ in the Eucharist. Something of their understanding may be unpacked, but their loving? That is the absurdity in my effort. The tragedy has to do with the splitting of

Christ's Body, the church, that forms the backdrop to several of the chapters. That which of its very nature should have strengthened simultaneously our communion with the Trinity and with one another, the Eucharist, has been fought over, quarreled over and been made privy to our sinful splitting of the church. That is tragedy.

Since the beginning of the Christian tradition, Christ has been understood as present in the Eucharist. Although historical nuance would demand considerable refinement, we may say for the sake of a brief overview that the eucharistic presence of Christ was understood through a variety of terms for the first thousand years. Whether the term was "metamorphosis" or *"metousia"* or whatever, it referred to a change that had taken place in the eucharistic celebration. The eucharistic gifts were no longer bread and wine, but the life-giving body and blood of Christ. This changed in the first half of the second millennium. During those five hundred years the preferred term (but still not the only one), trailing with it a preferred understanding, was "transubstantiation." With the sixteenth century challenges of the Reformation, this term came into dispute, though it will be argued that the belief in Christ's eucharistic presence remained fairly constant. However, the caricature became that Protestants emphasized Word, while Catholics emphasized Eucharist. We will see that, as a consequence of the ecumenical movement, that caricatured contrast no longer stands up to scrutiny. For the first fifteen hundred years of the Christian tradition, the sacrificial dimension of the Eucharist was virtually unquestioned. It was simply there, taken for granted, part of the tradition. With the Reformation, however, that changed, and for the next half millennium, more or less, sacrifice became a contentious issue. Today even that contentious issue is being laid to rest in many Christian traditions and communities.

What we will find in the pages of this book is the centrality of the Eucharist to the church; in the words of Henri de Lubac, "the Eucharist makes the Church." What we will also find is a rich tradition of expressing this fundamental conviction. One objective of *Eucharistic Doctors* is to lead the reader

3

from an appreciation of the theologian or text considered to the actual work of that theologian, or to the actual text itself. But there is a more ultimate objective. It is my hope that readers will feel moved to love the eucharistic Christ more and more, and equally drawn to support in whatever ways they can within their Christian communities the re-establishment of plenary Christian unity around one eucharistic table.

Notes

1. Eugene LaVerdiere, SSS, *Dining in the Kingdom of God: The Origins of the Eucharist According to Luke* (Chicago: Liturgy Training Publications, 1994).

2. ———. *The Eucharist in the New Testament and in the Early Church* (Collegeville, MN: Liturgical Press, 1996).

3. ———. *The Breaking of the Bread: The Development of the Eucharist According to Acts* (Chicago: Liturgy Training Publications, 1998).

4. Francis J. Moloney, *A Body Broken for a Broken People*, rev. ed. (Peabody, MA: Hendrickson Publishers, 1997).

5. Raymond Johanny, ed., *The Eucharist of the Early Christians* (New York: Pueblo Publishing Co., 1978).

6. Johannes Betz, *Die Eucharistie in der Zeit der griechischen Vater* (Basel-Vienna-Freiburg: Herder, 1955).

7. Gary Macy, *The Theology of the Eucharist in the Early Scholastic Period* (Oxford: The Clarendon Press, 1984).

8. ———. *Treasures from the Storeroom: Medieval Religion and the Eucharist* (Collegeville, MN: Liturgical Press, 1999).

9. ———. *The Banquet's Wisdom: A Short History of the Theologies of the Lord's Supper* (New York/Mahwah, NJ: Paulist Press, 1992).

PART ONE:
The Patristic Age

1.

Ignatius of Antioch

Ignatius lived and eventually died
what he would have called a
"eucharistic" life.
—Gary Macy[1]

IGNATIUS OF ANTIOCH
(ca. 35–ca. 107)

Ignatius, bishop of Antioch, was born in Syria probably not more than a few years after the death and resurrection of the Lord. The earliest church historian, Eusebius, tells us that Ignatius was the second bishop of Antioch, succeeding to St. Peter: "Ignatius became famous as the second Bishop of Antioch where Evodius had first established the Church....Ignatius obtained the bishopric of the Church at Antioch second in succession to Peter."[2] If we try to conflate these two traditions from Eusebius, then we have the succession of bishops as Peter, Evodius, Ignatius. However, even to describe Peter as bishop of Antioch is difficult because clear evidence for the development of the episcopal office gets under way only after Ignatius. About Evodius we know nothing. The fact that we lack precise information about Ignatius illustrates the difficulty with so many of the immediately postapostolic Christian authors, that is to say, we simply do not know very much about them. In the last years of the first and the earliest years of the second century what we know of the church in Asia Minor is largely derived from Ignatius' letters and from the correspondence between Pliny the governor of Bithynia and the Emperor Trajan.

Pliny, about 112, asked Trajan for guidance on how to deal with the Christians. Christianity was quite widespread in his province of Bithynia, and, as a result, the pagan temples were emptying and temple butcher shops were unable to sell the meat of sacrificial animals. There was something of an economic crisis in Bithynia. The issue was formally brought to the governor's attention and he dealt with it by executing some Christians who were not Roman citizens, and by holding over for trial in Rome some who enjoyed Roman citizenship. Perhaps to play safe with Trajan, Pliny wrote to him for guidance on the Christian issue. The emperor's reply to Pliny advised him to pay no attention to anonymous accusations that people were Christians, and to follow the normal legal procedures when charges were brought against persons in accord with Roman law and custom.

Clearly, the emperor did not see Christianity as a major threat to the well-being of the empire. Persecution of Christians was neither systematic nor ongoing, even though being a Christian was a capital offense since Christianity was not a legally acknowledged religion under Roman law. If we place the Pliny-Trajan correspondence alongside the information we obtain from the letters of Ignatius, the picture of the church in Asia Minor seems to be something like this: "small beleaguered communities; liable to persecution from the civil authorities; unpopular enough with those outside for some people to inform against them; prone to division within their own ranks on issues of both belief and practice."[3]

Nothing more is known of Ignatius' life other than that he was taken to Rome by a guard of ten soldiers for trial, and ultimately for execution, toward the end of the reign of the Emperor Trajan (98–117). En route Ignatius was received by local Christian communities, and he wrote letters back to them—to the Ephesians, Magnesians, Trallians, Philadelphians, Smyrnaeans and Romans, and one to Bishop Polycarp of Smyrna. Recognizing that the Antiochene Christian community was "prone to division within [its] own ranks," it may be the case that Ignatius' arrest by the Roman authorities was due to some disaffected Christians in his own community. This is of course speculation, but it is quite possible. Ignatius was clearly concerned about the condition of his Church of Antioch, and in a number of letters he asked for prayers for his community. This repeated request for prayer may indicate internal problems in the Antiochene community, perhaps with Docetists (who denied the reality of the incarnation, believing that Christ only seemed to have a human body), and/or perhaps with Judaizers who wished a substantial return to the mother faith of Judaism. Such divisive groups within the community may have been all too happy to delate their bishop to the authorities, particularly when it was a bishop who, from his letters, was equally opposed to Docetism and to Judaizing tendencies.

Whatever the occasion of his arrest, Ignatius was taken to Rome. In his Letter to the Romans, Ignatius asks that the Roman community not try to intercede on his behalf with the imperial authorities, so that he may proceed to his martyrdom without hindrance. This may imply that at least some Christians in Rome had the social rank and status to plead Ignatius' cause with some hope of success. According to church fathers Polycarp and Origen, Ignatius was martyred at Rome.

The Letters of Ignatius

As a literary genre, letters are very self-revealing. Think of what we grasp about St. Paul's life and personality from his letters in the New Testament. We learn from his letters that he was brought up a Pharisee (Phil 3:5), that he persecuted the church (1 Cor 15:9; Gal 1:13), that he had a vision of the Lord Jesus (1 Cor 9:1), that he converted to the way of Christianity (Gal 1–2), that he had a dispute with St. Peter (Gal 2:11–14), that he experienced ecstasy (2 Cor 12:2–4), that he collected money for the poor Jerusalem Church (Gal 2:10; 1 Cor 16:1–4; 2 Cor 8–9; Rom 15:25–31) and so forth. Many details about Paul emerge from his letters. Ignatius in this respect contrasts very favorably with Paul. As one scholar points out, "Even St. Paul does not reveal himself more clearly in his writings."[4] Or, from a modern perspective, one thinks of the famous letters of the Lutheran theologian and martyr Dietrich Bonhoeffer (1906–45), hanged by the Gestapo at Flossenburg. In his posthumously published *Letters and Papers from Prison*, Bonhoeffer is revealed as a theologian of vision, as a deeply prayerful and devout Christian, as one who recognizes the total demand that the gospel lays on the followers of Jesus Christ, and we are given as well many details about his family, friends and relationships.

Our knowledge of Ignatius is meager by comparison, but from his letters we do grasp something of the man. He was passionate in his commitment to Jesus Christ. This emerges particularly in his Letter to the Romans. He tells the Roman Christians that he wants

> to be a libation poured out to God, while there is still an altar ready for [him]. Then you may form a loving choir around it and sing hymns of praise in Jesus Christ to God the Father, for permitting Syria's bishop, summoned from the realms of the morning, to have reached the land of the setting sun. How good it is to be sinking down below the world's horizon towards God, to rise again later into the dawn of his presence![5]

The passage is most interesting. Ignatius desires to be "a libation poured out to God, while there is still an altar ready for [him]." A libation was a drink, usually of wine, poured out on the ground to the gods, often at a drinking party or *symposium,* or at a sacrifice. Ignatius sees his lifeblood as a sacrificial offering poured out before the Father on "the altar" of the arena where he is to be executed. Like the pagan chorus that sings around the altar of sacrifice, the Roman Christian community will form a choir of praise to God the Father, "*in* Jesus Christ." Ignatius, like his Roman sisters and brothers, is *in Christ* through baptism and the Eucharist, but now is entering most profoundly into the movement of Christ's sacrifice through his own sacrifice. He describes himself as "Syria's bishop," the only passage in which he explicitly refers to himself as a bishop. He compares himself to the sun rising in the east ("summoned from the realms of the morning") and setting in the west ("to have reached the land of the setting sun"). He likens his own person to the sun itself making its daily journey across the sky, and sinking from the world to rise again on the morrow. The cosmic analogy of the rising and setting sun becomes the framework for understanding the life and death of a Christian. The sun may die, as it were, in its setting, but it rises again, and so Christians die/set in the Son, but in that same Son will rise again. We get the sense of a man whose trust in God is total, whose love for God is passionate.

In the same Letter to the Romans Ignatius further manifests his desire to be martyred for God. "I am [God's] wheat, ground fine by the lions' teeth to be made purest bread for Christ."[6] This is a famous passage. He is using the analogy of breadmaking here, his body like grain being ground by the teeth of the lions into the flour that will be baked as the purest bread for Christ. The analogy has what one might call a "eucharistic feel" to it, making of Ignatius' martyrdom a kind of eucharistic experience. Some scholars are reluctant to see in Ignatius' words here any eucharistic reference. That seems rather unrealistic. Why would Ignatius use language that suggests eucharistic significance when he could have turned to very different literary expressions? Some eucharistic connection seems intended, especially when one takes into account the fact that he refers to the Eucharist in Ephesians 5 as "the bread of God."

Ignatius' passion for God is well illustrated in these words from Romans 6:

> Leave me to imitate the Passion of my God. If any of
> you has God within himself, let that man understand
> my longings, and feel for me, because he will know
> the forces by which I am constrained.[7]

Not only is Ignatius with the Roman community and, indeed, all baptized Christians "in Christ," but also God-in-Christ is *in* them. The transforming presence of God-in-Christ in the Christian community invites the grace-filled reproduction of the paschal mystery. Here is a man on fire with love for God. Indeed, here is a mystic, and a eucharistic mystic at that, who has a profound experience of union with God-in-Christ through the Eucharist.

Eucharist, Sacrament of Union

The word *Eucharist/eucharistia* occurs four times in Ignatius' letters: Ephesians 13, Philadelphians 4, and Smyrnaeans 7, 8.[8] In Ephesians 13, Ignatius writes: "Do your best, then, to meet more often to give thanks *(eis eucharistian)* and glory to God."[9] The commentators on Ignatius' letters debate the precise meaning of the word *eucharistia* in this passage. Does it mean Eucharist in the specific sense of the sacramental representation of the Lord's Supper, or does it mean, as it can mean linguistically, "thanksgiving"? We follow here the former meaning, so that Ignatius is understood to be commending a more frequent celebration of the Eucharist to the Ephesian community. The normal and regular assembly of Christians at this time would have been for Eucharist, and thus Ignatius seems to be telling the Ephesians that this celebrative act should be central to their self-understanding because:

> When you meet frequently, the powers of Satan are
> confounded, and in the face of your corporate faith
> his maleficence crumbles. Nothing can better a state
> of peaceful accord from which every trace of spiritual
> or earthly hostility has been banished.[10]

The Eucharist strengthens the community to overcome the constant temptation of demonic divisiveness. The words of the Lord from St. Matthew's gospel, which may have been the gospel of the Christian community at Antioch over which Ignatius presided, come to mind: "So when you are offering your gift at the altar, if you remember that your brother or sister has something against you, leave your gift there before the altar and go; first be reconciled to your brother or sister, and then come and offer your gift" (Matt 5:23–24).[11] The Eucharist both effects and expresses the bond of Christian concord ("the face of your corporate faith") and, therefore, merits frequent celebration. This phrase "in the face of your corporate faith" translates a Greek phrase that means literally "in the concord/*homonoia* of your faith." It means "unanimity, concord."[12] It is a favorite word of Ignatius, occurring eight times in his letters: in Ephesians 4 (twice), Ephesians 13; Magnesians 6 and 15; Trallians 12; and Philadelphians 11, and in the inscription. It would seem that for Ignatius authentic participation in the Eucharist engenders that profound communion of heart and mind that should mark those who are "in Christ."

In Philadelphians 4 we read:

> Make certain, therefore, that you all observe one common Eucharist; for there is but one Body of our Lord Jesus Christ, and but one cup of union with his Blood, and one single altar of sacrifice—even as also there is but one bishop, with his clergy and my own fellow-servitors the deacons. This will ensure that all your doings are in full accord with the will of God.[13]

The text is emphatic about the unity of faith and love effected by the Eucharist. Any schismatic, fractious or polarizing tendencies are contrary to the Eucharist. Ignatius is totally opposed to any divisiveness because it fragments the unity of the one Body of Christ, the church. The word "body" he uses in this passage, "for there is but one Body of our Lord Jesus Christ," is in fact the Greek word *sarx*. Strictly speaking this word means "flesh." It is the word used in the prologue to St. John's gospel for the incarnation: "The Word became *sarx* and lived among us" (John 1:14). It is also the word St. John uses in the sixth chapter of his gospel to express the sheer reality of the eucharistic gift of Christ's body.

I am the living bread that came down from heaven.
Whoever eats of this bread will live forever; and the
bread that I will give for the life of the world is my
flesh [sarx]....For my flesh [sarx] is true food and my
blood is true drink. Those who eat my flesh [sarx]
and drink my blood abide in me, and I in them" (John
6:51, 55–56).

The word *flesh/sarx* has a strong material sense to it, a
strong sense of identity between the reality of Jesus Christ and
the eucharistic gift. As Raymond Johanny puts it, "The reality of
Christ's human flesh in his Incarnation and the reality of his
eucharistic flesh are the objects of one and the same faith."[14]

When we come to the phrase "one cup of union with
his Blood," something similar emerges. Just as eating the one
flesh of Christ makes those who eat the one body of Christ, so
with the cup of his blood. "Of union with his Blood" does not
mean "union *with* his blood" so much as "union *from* his blood."
The union of the Christian community, as Ignatius understands
it, comes from Christ's body and blood. It is not a union we
experience and symbolize with Christ. It is a union effected,
brought about by the Eucharist. The church, presided over by
the one bishop, is "the single altar of sacrifice" in which this
unity-making Eucharist is celebrated.

In the seventh chapter of his Letter to the Smyrnaeans,
Ignatius takes issue with those who reject the reality of the
Eucharist, and so stay away from it:

They even absent themselves from the Eucharist and
the public prayers, because they will not admit that
the Eucharist is the self-same body of our Savior
Jesus Christ which suffered for our sins, and which
the Father in his goodness afterwards raised up again.
Consequently, since they reject God's good gifts,
they are doomed in their disputatiousness. They
would have done better to learn charity, if they were
ever to know any resurrection.[15]

Those in the group Ignatius is speaking of are known as the Docetists. This group of Christians was unable to accept the reality of the incarnation, and therefore also could not believe in the reality of the Eucharist, and may have been, as indicated above, responsible for Ignatius' arrest. As Johanny has it, "Having thus done away with the scandal of a God taking flesh, that is, with the scandal of the Incarnation, the Docetists logically proceeded to empty the Eucharist of its meaning: Christ did not take flesh, and therefore his flesh could not be present in the Eucharist."[16] There can be no separation of Christ and the Eucharist. If God did not really become one of us, then not only is the Eucharist "unreal" but so also is our transformation that it is supposed to bring about.

If there is no participation in the real body and blood of Christ in the Eucharist, Ignatius seems to suggest also that the moral life suffers. "They would have done better to learn charity," he writes. The word *charity* is the Greek word *agape,* and some authors think that the reference here is to the love feast, the *agape* meal, which some Christians celebrated at this time. In other words, if Christians absent themselves from the *agape* meal, by that very fact they cannot exercise charity/*agape,* they cannot contribute to the upkeep of the needy in the community. Whether or not the *agape* meal is the specific reference Ignatius is making does not especially matter, because the First Letter of John identifies God with *agape:* "God is love [*agape*] and those who abide in love [*agape*] abide in God, and God abides in them" (1 John 4:16). If we submit to the life-principle of God, that is to love, to the ontological mystery of love through eating the Eucharist, the flesh of God-in-Christ, then we are enabled to perform "love, charity." The word *agape,* "love, charity," is a frequent and favorite word for Ignatius. If we are not performing "charity," Ignatius appears to imply that there is a real deficit in our eucharistic understanding and appreciation. The passage coming immediately before the one just quoted reads: "They have no care for love, no thought for the widow or the orphan, none at all for the afflicted, the captive, the hungry or the thirsty."[17] Absence from the Eucharist, which provides us with the divine life of love, prevents our flourishing as eucharistic people in relation to others

Furthermore the Eucharist must be the *one* Eucharist presided over by the "the bishop himself, or by some person authorized by him."[18] The role of the bishop is to hold this church-communion of love together through celebrating the Eucharist-communion of love. Incarnation, Eucharist and adequate moral performance of Christians are inextricably linked together for Ignatius. What systematic theology separates out into different disciplines—for example, sacramental theology, eucharistic theology, ecclesiology, moral theology—Ignatius sees as held together through *agape*/love. If we are the agapic Body of Christ, made such through baptism and sustained as such through Eucharist, all of which is the action of the God who is *Agape*, then we must act habitually in an agapic manner as befits our identity. That is Ignatius' viewpoint.

Eucharist, Medicine of Immortality

One of the best-known aspects of Ignatius' eucharistic reflection is his notion that the Eucharist is the "medicine of immortality." The passage in question is in the twentieth chapter of his Letter to the Ephesians. There we read that the Eucharist is "the medicine of immortality, and the sovereign remedy by which we escape death and live in Jesus Christ for evermore."[19] "The medicine of immortality" was a technical term used by physicians in the ancient world. It was used for an ointment attributed to the Egyptian goddess Isis, which was believed to have effectiveness over a wide range of conditions. Here Ignatius applies the term to the Eucharist, and it will later be taken up by other patristic writers. Earlier, in the seventh chapter of the Letter to the Ephesians, Ignatius describes Christ as our one *iatros*, our one physician. Again he is the first to use this image for Christ, another image that will become popular throughout the patristic tradition. Christ is both physician as God-in-the-flesh and medicine as Eucharist. The same idea comes to expression in the seventh chapter of his Letter to the Romans: "There is no pleasure for me in any meats that perish, or in the delights of this life; I am fain for the bread of God, even the flesh of Jesus Christ, who is the seed of David; and for my drink I crave that Blood of his which is love imperishable."[20] The eucharistic blood of Christ is *agape aphthartos*, "love imperishable." It can only be described in that fashion if it is really, albeit sacramentally, the real presence of Christ, who is *agape aphthartos*/love imperishable in the flesh. This is the language of mysticism, and should be taken with the utmost seriousness. It is the eucharistic realism of St. John's gospel in Ignatian language. It is the eucharistic realism of the Catholic tradition as it begins to develop in the postapostolic period.

Conclusion

As we begin our treatment of selected eucharistic thinkers and theologians, Ignatius of Antioch provides a solid foundation. All the elements of Catholic eucharistic thought that will be further developed in the tradition are present here: eucharistic presence and sacrifice, the unity of the church effected through the Eucharist, eucharistic eschatology, eucharistic moral performance. Ignatius knew that the Eucharist is the heart of the church. Perhaps we might say he is the founding father of eucharistic ecclesiology.

Notes

1. Gary Macy, *The Banquet's Wisdom* (New York/Mahwah, NJ: Paulist Press, 1992), 27.

2. Eusebius, *The History of the Church*, trans. G. A. Williamson, rev. ed. (Harmondsworth, UK: Penguin, 1990), 22, 36.

3. Maurice F. Wiles, "Ignatius and the Church," in Elizabeth A. Livingstone, ed., *Studia Patristica*, vol. 17, Part Two (Oxford and New York: Pergamon Press, 1982), 750.

4. F. L. Cross, *The Early Christian Fathers* (London: Duckworth, 1960), 16.

5. Ignatius of Antioch, "The Epistle to the Romans," in *Early Christian Writings: The Apostolic Fathers*, trans. Maxwell Staniforth, rev. Andrew Louth (Harmondsworth: Penguin Books, 1987), 85–86.

6. Ibid., 86.

7. Ibid., 87.

8. I am following in the main the excellent outline provided in Raymond Johanny, "Ignatius of Antioch," in Raymond Johanny and others, *The Eucharist of the Early Christians* (New York: Pueblo Publishing Company, 1978), 48–70.

9. Staniforth and Louth, 64.

10. Ibid.

11. For the connections between St. Matthew and Antioch, see Raymond E. Brown and John Meier, *Antioch and Rome: New Testament Cradles of Catholic Christianity* (New York: Paulist Press, 1983), especially 45–72.

12. Geoffrey W. H. Lampe, *A Patristic Greek Lexicon* (Oxford: The Clarendon Press, 1961), 958.

13. Staniforth and Louth, supra, 94.

14. Johanny, *The Eucharist of the Early Christians*, 53.

15. Staniforth and Louth, supra, 102–103.

16. Johanny, *The Eucharist of the Early Christians*, 57.

17. Staniforth and Louth, supra, 102.

18. Ibid., 103.

19. Ibid., 66.

20. Ibid., 87.

2.
Two Roman Theologians: Justin and Hippolytus

Nearly all the Greek Fathers were, consciously or unconsciously, Justin's imitators.
–Hans von Campenhausen[1]

Hippolytus gives a specimen eucharistic prayer which is probably his own composition, but doubtless reflects the pattern with which he was familiar in the Roman Church in his own day.
–Alasdair Heron[2]

JUSTIN (ca. 100–165)

The city of Nablus has been much in the news in recent years as a place of conflict between the Israelis and the Palestinians. The biblical name is Shechem, its ancient name, Flavia Neapolis. It was the birthplace of Justin, often known as Justin Martyr. Though we do not possess a detailed account of his life, he reveals certain biographical details in his own writings. He tells us that he is "Justin, son of Priscus and grandson of Bacchius, of Flavia Neapolis in Syrian Palestine."[3] Probably, Justin was born in the late first century or in the early second, and the Latin form of his name and that of his father and the Greek name of his grandfather, after the god Bacchus, seem to indicate that he was of Roman descent.

He studied philosophy in a personal quest for truth with various teachers at Ephesus, including Stoic, Peripatetic, Pythagorean and finally Platonist. Looking for religious truth,

19

he found a vision of God in Platonism. However, even the transcendent "God" of Platonism left him eventually dissatisfied, and he tells us that one day by the seashore he was led by a wise old man to the truth of the Old Testament prophets and their fulfillment in Jesus Christ.

> My spirit was immediately fired, and a love for the prophets, and for those who are friends of Christ, took hold of me. While thinking about [the old man's] words, I came to see that his was the only sure and useful philosophy. And so now I am such a philosopher.[4]

Justin's conversion experience seems not only to have come about from the guidance of this wise old man, but also from the constancy of Christian witness in the face of persecution and death. The fearlessness of Christians in the face of torture and death further persuaded him of the truth of Christianity.[5] Justin appears to have left Ephesus some time after 135 and found his way to Rome, where he opened a school in his house, probably on the Viminal Hill. Continuing to wear the pallium, the cloak of a philosopher, he taught in Rome during the reign of the Emperor Antoninus Pius (138–61), to whom he addressed his *First Apology*. The purpose of Justin's school was probably to prepare people for becoming Christians, and in all likelihood the content of the *First Apology* reflects the appropriate catechesis.

Rome at this time was an explosive center of philosophical and Christian thought. For Christians, "Rome was a magnet, attracting to itself a stream of provincial elders, scholars and private Christians, eager to see and learn from so ancient a church, above all eager to visit the resting place of the two greatest apostles," Peter and Paul.[6] In terms of the philosophers, Justin found himself in dispute with the Cynic philosopher, Crescens (2 *Apology*, 3). With competing groups of Christians he was no less vigorous, for example with the gnostic Valentinians and the Marcionites, against whom he wrote a treatise, now lost

(*1 Apology*, 26). Valentinus, an Alexandria-educated Egyptian, conducted a school in Rome from about 136 to 165. A speculative gnostic thinker, Valentinus broke away from the main body of the Christian community, distinguishing a three-tiered church. It was composed of the hylics—the unredeemable, material, worldly mob; the psychics—those Christians who had been "merely" baptized; and the pneumatics—the spiritual ones, who had been fully redeemed and were full of the Spirit.

The crisis provoked by gnosticism was widespread, and one of its consequences, and a most understandable one at that, was that its adherents became utterly skeptical of the value of philosophy and speculation for the understanding of the Christian faith. Marcion—son of the bishop of Pontus, and named the "sea-captain," suggesting a somewhat itinerant lifestyle—taught a theology that despised the Creator God of the Old Testament, and indeed, the Old Testament as such. Justin shared none of the presuppositions of either the gnostics or Marcion. Of all the earliest Christian theologians, he is the most hopeful in terms of seeing a relationship between philosophy and the Christian faith. While completely opposed to pagan worship and cults, Justin was very open to the philosophers, especially Plato. Justin virtually makes Socrates a Christian and Christ a philosopher, a teacher of the way toward wisdom and happiness. At the same time, Justin recognizes in the scriptures the criterion with which to judge philosophy and philosophers. It is the biblical doctrine of God and his relation to the world that enables him to discern in philosophy what is true and congruent with Christianity. In this respect, the value Justin places on scripture far exceeds that of Marcion and his followers, who disallow those parts of the Bible that are in conflict with their predetermined positions.

In making the bridge between Greek philosophy and Christian faith, Justin uses the doctrine of the Logos, the Word of God. He understands that the Logos appeared in all its fullness only in Jesus Christ. Nevertheless, there was a "seed of the Logos" scattered among all of humankind long before the historic advent of Jesus. Every human being, in virtue of being human, possesses in some degree, through his reason, a seed of the Logos. Every human being, if you will, has a natural orientation toward God and Christ, a theology reminiscent of Karl Rahner's theory of the "anonymous Christian." This is how Justin puts it:

> We have been taught that Christ is the firstborn of God, and we have acknowledged that he is the Logos. The human race partakes of the Logos, and those who lived according to the Logos are Christians, even though they have been considered atheists, as among the Greeks, Socrates and Heraclitus, and thinkers like them.[7]

Justin espouses no sectarian view of Christianity, but a Christianity that is truly Catholic, reaching out in God's grace to touch the soul of every person.

Justin's *Second Apology* was addressed to the Roman Senate, and it was probably this that brought him into open collision with the state. According to reliable tradition (the *Acts of Justin*), in about 165, during the reign of the Emperor Marcus Aurelius, he was reported to the city prefect, Junius Rusticus, and was martyred for his faith by being beheaded.

Church and Sacraments

Exact figures are unavailable, but it is clear from Justin's writing that the church was undergoing considerable expansion during his lifetime. He tells us that as the Christian faith was expanding, Gentile Christians were becoming more numerous than Jewish Christians.[8] This is a universal church. Justin does not present us with a developed ecclesiology, but rather approaches the church through a range of biblical images—for example, the true Israel, the vine planted by God and Christ.[9]

His description of the sacraments of baptism and the Eucharist provides the most detailed account we possess in the pre-Nicene church. This is especially intriguing, given that the accounts occur in Justin's public apologies for the church. Why did he make so public such details of the Christian rites? The answer can only be that he wished to put to rest pagan fears about these rites, that they were cannibalistic, "eating flesh," or in some sense undermining the imperial peace.

Justin implies that baptism took place at some distance from the church's regular meeting place.

> Then we *lead* [those to be baptized] to a place where there is water, and they are reborn in the same manner in which we ourselves were reborn. In the name of God, the Father and Lord of all, and of our Savior, Jesus Christ, and of the Holy Spirit they receive the washing with water....After baptizing the one who has believed and given his assent, we take him back to the place where the brothers are assembled, to offer up prayers in common for ourselves, for the baptized person, and for all other persons wherever they may be, in order that, since we have found the truth, we may be judged fit through our actions to be regarded as good, law-abiding citizens, and so attain eternal salvation.[10]

Baptism for him is a washing with water in the name of the Trinity. Where was the water? Where did baptism occur? Since Christianity was still a proscribed religious movement, and so there could not yet be church buildings for worship, baptism would have taken place discreetly where there was a body of water—a pool or water coming from an aqueduct, perhaps even at the public baths. Then the newly baptized would have made their way back to the full assembly of Christians for the celebration of the Eucharist.

Eucharist

The Eucharist is thanksgiving for both creation and redemption in Justin: "For all the favors we enjoy we bless the

Creator of all, through his son Jesus Christ and through the Holy Spirit."[11] His emphasis on blessing the Creator is at least implicitly an anti-gnostic comment, reflecting Justin's constant struggle against the gnostic community in Rome, and we shall come across it again later in his writings. The primitive liturgy began with selected readings from the prophets and apostles, and there was a sermon—an early version of our Liturgy of the Word. There were various prayers of petition, and the kiss of peace. Then the president of the assembly was given bread and wine mixed with water, and prayed a longer prayer of thanksgiving.

There are a number of interesting things in Justin's description. The "president of the assembly,"—in Greek, *ho proestos ton adelphon*, literally "he who presides over the brothers"—refers to the bishop. Why did Justin refer to the "presider" and not to the "bishop" (*episkopos*)? There is no clear answer to this question, but it may have to do with the fact that, although "bishop" is a term being used in other parts of the Christian world, it is not at the time of Justin used of the bishop of Rome.[12] An entirely clear organizational picture of the church of Rome at this time is not available. The mixing of wine with water probably reflects both the ancient custom of mixing, and also the desire to counter pagan gossip about drunkenness among Christians. The deacons then distribute the Eucharist to the community, and also take it to those members unable to be present.

Justin also tells us about the charity and social concern for others occasioned by the celebration of the Eucharist:

> The wealthy who are willing make contributions, each as he pleases, and the collection is deposited with the president. He aids orphans and widows, those who are in need because of ill-health or some other cause, those who are in prison and visiting strangers—in short, he is the guardian of all in need.[13]

Made and sustained as the Body of Christ through the Eucharist, the community of the church takes seriously the practical social and moral obligations flowing from this sacrament. The sick, the poor and the marginal in the community are assisted. One author phrases it very nicely: "The collection is understood as a fruit of communion: God's gift to us turns us into givers to others."[14] The fruit of communion in social concern flows directly from what the Eucharist is. If, as Justin avers, there is a parallel between the incarnation and the Eucharist— the Word of God gave flesh and blood to Christ, and so the Word of God transforms or eucharistizes the bread and wine— the Eucharist is the God-given, divinizing bond that makes us gifts to one another.[15] In his *Dialogue with Trypho the Jew,* a book designed to refute Jewish objections to Christianity, we are provided with additional insights into Justin's eucharistic theology:

> The offering of fine flour that was prescribed for those cleansed of leprosy prefigures the bread of the eucharist which our Lord Jesus Christ commanded us to offer in memory of the passion he underwent for the sake of those whose souls are cleansed of all evil.[16]

Here he refers to a small detail in the ritual for the cleansing of lepers in Leviticus 14:10. The flour mentioned in the Leviticus reference becomes a type of the Eucharist. Where the former cleansed from leprosy, so the Eucharist cleanses from all evil. Similarly he turns to the famous passage in Malachi 1:11, a favorite passage of writers in the patristic period for underscoring the sacrificial dimension of the Eucharist. That passage reads: "For from the rising of the sun to its setting, my name is great among the nations, and in every place incense is offered to my name, and a pure offering; for my name is great among the nations, says the Lord of hosts." He sees in Malachi the divine command that a pure sacrifice be offered to the Lord, and in the Eucharist the execution of that command "among the nations." This theme "among the nations" is important to Justin not only in terms of his debate with Trypho's Judaism, but also in relation to his theology of the Logos. The universality of the church centered in the Eucharist finds an echo in the universality of the Logos, seminally present in all human beings.

HIPPOLYTUS (ca. 170–ca. 236)

Like Ignatius of Antioch and Justin of Rome, we have very little information about the life of Hippolytus of Rome. He must either have known Justin or known about him. He was a well-known presbyter in the city, a theologian of repute and a good preacher. The great Origen of Alexandria heard Hippolytus preach in Rome about 212. He seems to have had difficulties with the popes of the time. He attacked Pope Zephyrinus (198/9–217) on the grounds that he was a modalist, that is to say one who believes that the Father, Son and Holy Spirit are just temporal modes of the one God. He also opposed Zephyrinus' successor, Callistus (217–22). He had himself elected bishop in opposition to Callistus, thus becoming the first antipope. Cardinal Jean Danielou, SJ, believed that this authority problem of Hippolytus "represents the resistance of the ancient Roman system of government by presbyters to the development of monarchical episcopacy."[17] During the first century, or so it seems, the Roman Church had no single dominant official or bishop, governance being shared by a group of elders/presbyters. In Danielou's judgment, Hippolytus reflects this older, and in that sense, more conservative position. In this regard it may be of interest to note that Hippolytus wrote in Greek, opposed perhaps to the use of the Latin language then being encouraged by the bishops of Rome.

Because he was schismatic and the last significant writer of the Roman community to use Greek, the transmission of his works has been patchy. His most important work is the *Refutation of All Heresies*. His treatise, *The Apostolic Tradition*, written about 215, provides us with information on the liturgy of the Roman Church, and it is in this book that we shall find his thinking about the meaning of the Eucharist. Hippolytus also shares the purist rigorism of Tertullian, the North African father who espouses a strong, robust Christianity that refuses to yield to human weakness and sin. Hippolytus, like Tertullian, wanted a church that was a community of saints. Yet, having said that, it needs equally to be stated that "the Church of *Lumen Gentium* [The Constitution on the Church of Vatican II] would recognize itself in the picture given to us in Hippolytus' *Apostolic Tradition*."[18] In that document we find a treatment of the Roman liturgy, but also norms and rules to govern Christian behavior and church order, in intention and sometimes in expression not dissimilar to those in *Lumen Gentium*.

Hippolytus recognizes the centrality of the Word and the Eucharist. A major concern for Hippolytus was exegesis, that is, the meaning and interpretation of holy scripture. He is the first Christian writer whose continuous commentaries on scripture we have: the *Commentary on Daniel*, the *Blessings of Isaac and Jacob* and the *Commentary on the Song of Songs*.[19] Noting Hippolytus' interest in the interpretation of scripture is not simply a matter of information, but of formation. Vatican Council II talks of our being fed by the Word made flesh at the Table of the Word (the Liturgy of the Word) and the Table of the Eucharist (the Liturgy of the Eucharist). In the *Constitution on Divine Revelation*, paragraph 21 we read: "The Church has always venerated the divine scriptures just as she venerates the body of the Lord, since…she unceasingly receives and offers to the faithful the bread of life from the table of both God's word and of Christ's body." Hippolytus understood this. His concern with the Word in holy scripture was to make it live for the people of his day in Rome. It was not some kind of archaeological interest in ancient texts that generated his commentaries on scripture. It was Hippolytus' desire to hear the sound of the Word, the voice of God, today in the words of holy scripture.

Hippolytus is interested in eschatology, the doctrine of the last things, his earliest work being a discussion of the Antichrist.[20] He wrote a book on the Apocalypse, the eschatological book *par excellence* of the New Testament, and his *Commentary on Daniel* demonstrates his interest in eschatological speculation, though he rejects the idea that the End is imminent.[21] Eschatological speculation may have been fueled in part by the ongoing but sporadic persecutions to which the church was subject. One can imagine a persecuted community laboring with the question, "Are these deaths and exiles and losses of property which we are experiencing signs that the End is nigh?" Holding oneself in readiness for the End is one of Hippolytus' motivations for espousing a strict, rigorist ethic. If judgment may come and soon, one should always be ready.

Hippolytus and Callistus

The thought of a third-century theologian, Sabellius, had gained ground in Rome during the lifetime of Hippolytus. We know very little about Sabellius, but it seems that he taught a doctrine of God in which there was no distinction between Father, Son and Spirit. "They" are simply modes of one and the same being that is God. At the opposite end of the spectrum stood Hippolytus, who believed strongly in the distinct "persons" of the Father and the Logos. In between these two positions stood Callistus, a deacon of the Roman Church.

Hippolytus did not see eye to eye with Callistus. As a young man Callistus had been the slave of a wealthy Christian in the imperial household named Carpophorus, and had been responsible for a bank that was used by Christians. Callistus was accused of financial mismanagement by his master, but Roman Christians, despite serious financial losses, took his part, saving him from severe punishment. However, as a result of a prank in a Jewish synagogue—described by one author as "brawling in a synagogue on the Sabbath"[22]—Callistus was hauled before the city prefect and exiled to the mines of Sardinia. He was emancipated as the result of the intercession of Marcia, a Christian and the concubine of the Emperor Commodus. Then Pope Zephyrinus put the deacon in charge of a new cemetery on the Appian Way near the place known as Catacumbas, now the catacombs of S. Callisto. He was to become a force to be reckoned with in the Roman Church.

In the debate about God, according to Hippolytus, Callistus acknowledged the distinctiveness of Father and Son, but the difference was that the "Father" was the name for the divine Spirit indwelling the "Son," which blurs a strong Trinitarian sense. For Hippolytus, this did not sound too far removed from the heretical position of Sabellius. Callistus responded to Hippolytus by suggesting that he believed in two-Gods-ism, ditheism. Matters came to a head when Callistus was elected bishop of Rome after the death of Zephyrinus. Pope Callistus went on to enact legislation that was totally unacceptable to the rigorist Hippolytus. Comparing the church to Noah's ark into which entered both clean and unclean animals, Callistus decreed that the church should reconcile to itself Christians who had fallen into serious sin after baptism, including sexual sin. As modern commentators have said, "Honor is due to the Pope who in the face of certain opposition from the zealots first formulated gentleness with sinners into the Church's rule."[23] But Hippolytus saw things differently. Hippolytus was a zealot and could not abide what he considered to be a backsliding innovation. Further, Callistus went on to recognize marital unions between free women and male slaves, unions frowned upon in Roman law.[24] As a result, Hippolytus had himself elected as rival bishop of Rome, becoming the first antipope. There were, then, serious disagreements and differences between Hippolytus and Callistus, but it seems to have been the personal factor, the social and temperamental factor that ultimately brought them into schism.[25] A sad comment. The sadness of the comment does not rest in the historical judgment, but in the recognition that that is how we are as human beings. Our flawed nature gets in the way of Christian witness.

The schism was to continue throughout the reigns of Popes Urban (222–30) and Pontian (230–35). The new emperor in 235, Maximinus Thrax, began a persecution of the church in which both Pontian and Hippolytus were to fall victim. They were both exiled to the mines of Sardinia, and died thereafter, probably after being reconciled. Pope Fabian (236–50) brought both their bodies back to Rome in 236 or 237.

The Ordination Eucharist

One scholar in the Reformed tradition has recently described Hippolytus in these terms: "[He] reflects the kind of churchmanship that is overly concerned with how cheese, olives, and oil are to be blessed at the Eucharist and how the evening lamps are to be lit at vespers. He goes into great detail, for example, on what kind of people can be admitted to the catechumenate—are they respectable? The ruling principle for Hippolytus seems to be propriety."[26] Now, it is true that Hippolytus is concerned with the range of things listed here, but to reduce his concern to the level of the socially conventional is not only to misjudge Hippolytus, but to view him through a rather bare lens of mechanical, sacramental participation. He is interested in all these things, but that is because his spirituality is not gnostic, but fundamentally sacramental. In other words, for Hippolytus these things matter because matter matters! Despite his partially sectarian ecclesiology Hippolytus cannot help being Catholic.

Though there have been caveats and criticisms brought by scholars to the Hippolytan authorship of *The Apostolic Tradition*, the majority of scholars have supported the position that this document originates from Rome and is the genuine work of Hippolytus, written about 215. *The Apostolic Tradition* provides us with the earliest eucharistic prayer in the Christian tradition, a eucharistic prayer described as "a venerable monument of the past, but also a vivid and brilliant exposition of eucharistic thought at the start of the third century."[27] However, not only is the eucharistic prayer of *The Apostolic Tradition* of importance in the historical scheme of things, it also provides the basis for the second of our modern eucharistic prayers. In point of fact, Hippolytus describes two Eucharists, one after an ordination, which provides us with the eucharistic prayer, and the other after baptism. So, what we find in Hippolytus is not a systematic treatise on the Eucharist, but an insight into how it was celebrated and understood.

After the ordination of a bishop, preparations for the Eucharist are made, with the deacons bringing forward the eucharistic gifts, known as the "oblation," on which the bishop and the presbyters are to lay their hands (iv.2). The very term used, "oblation," manifests the ongoing tradition of understanding the Eucharist in sacrificial terms. Then the eucharistic prayer begins, which is meant to figure as a model for a bishop:

> *The Lord be with you.*
> And the people shall say: *And with your spirit.*
> [And the bishop shall say:] *Lift up your hearts.*
> [And the people shall say:] *We have them with the Lord.*
> [And the bishop shall say:] *Let us give thanks unto the Lord.*
> [And the people shall say:] *It is fitting and right* (iv.3).

The introduction to the eucharistic prayer here is virtually identical to our own.

Then the bishop proceeds with the eucharistic prayer itself. The prayer opens thus:

> We render thanks to You, O God, through your Beloved Child Jesus Christ, whom in the last times You sent to us to be a Saviour and Redeemer and the Angel of your will; who is your inseparable Word, through whom you made all things...(iv.4).

The prayer continues with the eucharistic words: "He took bread and gave thanks to You, saying, 'Take, eat; this is my body, which is broken for you.'" Likewise also the cup, saying: "This is My Blood which is shed for you; when you do this, you make my remembrance" (iv.9–10). After the consecration the prayer is said for the sending of the Holy Spirit:

> And we ask that you would send your Holy Spirit upon the offering of your holy Church; that, gathering her into one, you would grant to all who receive the holy things to be filled with the Holy Spirit for the

> strengthening of faith in truth; that we may praise and
> glorify you through your Child Jesus Christ (iv.12).

At the beginning of the eucharistic prayer, Christ is described as "Child" and "Angel of your will," descriptions that may seem somewhat strange to our ears. The title "Child" for our Lord occurs in early Christian literature of the first two centuries. In all probability it refers to the "Servant of God" passages in Isaiah 53, where the Greek (Septuagint) translation has the word *pais*/child for "servant of God." It thus becomes one of the oldest and most important interpretations of Christ, perhaps going back ultimately to Jesus' own self-understanding. Jesus is the suffering "Servant of God." It is probably this early understanding that lies behind Hippolytus' usage here. Talking of Christ as the angel of the Father's will is also a very early interpretation of Christ. If these were the only titles given to Christ in the eucharistic prayer, they would reflect what is known as "low christology," that is to say an understanding of Christ lacking specific reference to his divinity. However, the prayer continues by describing the Lord as the "inseparable Word" of the Father, and since the word is the very expression of the person, so the Father's Word is his own very self-expression.

If earthly food is to become "spiritual" food, then the Father must send the Spirit on it, and not only on the food but also on those who, by eating this food, are to become spiritual members of Christ's Body. As the Holy Spirit transforms the gifts so the same Holy Spirit is asked to transform those who receive the gifts. The strong realism underlying the Eucharist trails into an equally strong realism of the church as the Body of Christ. Eucharist and ecclesiology go hand in hand.

The Baptismal Eucharist

In his account of Christian initiation, the ritual sequence is very clear: after renouncing Satan the candidates were anointed with the oil of exorcism. Then there was baptism in water, with little children being baptized first. After baptism there was a second anointing with the oil of thanksgiving (chrism). This second anointing is equivalent to our sacrament of confirmation. The celebration of the Eucharist then followed. Hippolytus thus witnesses to the integrity of the rites of initiation in the ritual sequence of baptism, confirmation and Eucharist. In the Eucharist that follows upon baptism, we read:

> Then the offering shall be brought up by the deacons to the bishop. He shall give thanks over the bread, which the Greeks call the antitype [*antitypon*] of the Body of Christ; and the cup of mixed wine, which is the antitype, which the Greeks call "likeness," [*homoioma*] of the Blood which was shed for all who believe in him, and the milk and honey mixed together in fulfillment of the promise which was made to the fathers, in which he said, "a land flowing with milk and honey," which Christ indeed gave, his Flesh, through which those who believe are nourished like little children, making the bitterness of the heart sweet by the gentleness of his word, and water also as an oblation to signify the baptism, that the inner man also, which is the soul, may receive the same thing as the body. The bishop shall give an explanation concerning all these things to those who receive.
>
> And when he breaks the bread, in distributing to each a fragment he shall say: "The bread of heaven in Christ Jesus." And he who receives shall answer "Amen."
>
> And if there are not enough presbyters, the deacons also shall hold the cups, and stand by in good order and with reverence: first, the one who holds the water; second, the one who holds the milk; third, the one who holds the wine. They who receive shall taste of each. And he who gives shall say, "In God, the Father almighty." And he who receives shall say, "Amen." (xxiii.1–8)

The words "antitype" and "likeness" are used of the eucharistic gifts to signify the realism of the identity between the bread and the wine and the body and blood of Christ, but avoid any crude literalness. The language is not intended to be a fully thought out articulation of the meaning of sacrament. It is for Hippolytus a "good enough" language to express his traditional eucharistic faith.

We know from both Tertullian (*Against Marcion*, 1.14) and Clement of Alexandria (*Pedagogue*, 1.6) of the custom of giving newly baptized Christians milk and honey, testifying to a widespread practice. It would seem that after communion of the bread and before communion of the cup there took place a drinking of water and then of milk mixed with honey. The water recalls the baptismal washing and regeneration that has just taken place. Milk and honey were the food of the newborn, appropriate for those newborn in Christ. Milk and honey also suggest, as Hippolytus notes, the promised land, and the new Christians have entered into that promised land through the sacraments of initiation. Hippolytus goes on to add his own contribution to the symbolism of the milk and honey: the milk represents the Christ's flesh and the honey his gentleness.

Care for the reserved Eucharist comes to expression later in *The Apostolic Tradition*, where Hippolytus instructs the faithful:

> Let all take care that no unbaptized person taste of the Eucharist, nor a mouse or other animal, and that none of it fall and be lost. For it is the body of Christ to be eaten by them that believe and not to be thought of lightly. (xxxii.2)

Here Hippolytus reflects the custom of taking communion home either to communicate those who were unable to be present for the eucharistic celebration, or for oneself until the next Eucharist. Behind Hippolytus' admonition lies a strong sense of eucharistic presence, the same kind of presence noted in Ignatius of Antioch.

Conclusion

Justin of Rome stands in the tradition of eucharistic realism that we have seen in chapter one, in Ignatius of Antioch. He adds to Ignatius' rich theology a further dimension, that of bridge-building between ordinary "reasonable" people, seeded by the Logos, philosophy and Christian faith. Although he does not develop systematically the connection between the Logos—seminally present in everyone—and the Eucharist as *the* sacrament of the Logos Incarnate, that development could be made. If the Logos in some degree is present in all, uniquely and fully present in Jesus Christ, and if the Eucharist is the sacramental presence of Jesus Christ, surely we must conclude that each person in principle shares a eucharistic orientation. Just as in the natural order a seed flourishes as a full-grown plant, so the seeds of the Logos find their full and final flourishing in Christ. At the center of that flourishing is the gift of the Eucharist. Perhaps we might say that Justin provides us with the foundations of a eucharistic metaphysics.

If Ignatius and Justin witness the major eucharistic doctrines to be more fully developed in the subsequent tradition, Hippolytus, especially in *The Apostolic Tradition*, gives us insights into two important things. First, that scripture is essential to the Catholic understanding of the Eucharist, that Christ is present when the Word that he is, is proclaimed in the Liturgy of the Word. It is this implicit understanding that underpins Hippolytus' commentaries on scripture. Second, that the shape of the eucharistic prayer as we now know and pray it, is in fundamental continuity with the faith of the early Christians. The recognition of that continuity gives an added dimension to the communion of saints. Among the great cloud of witnesses stands Hippolytus, "warts and all." His eucharistic witness invites us to become "the apostolic tradition" to the coming generations of Christians.

Notes

1. Hans von Campenhausen, *The Fathers of the Church*. Combined edition of *The Fathers of the Greek Church* and *The Fathers of the Latin Church* (Peabody, MA: Hendrickson Publishers, 1998), 15.

2. Alasdair Heron, *Table and Tradition: Towards an Ecumenical Understanding of the Eucharist* (Edinburgh: The Handsel Press, 1983), 62.

3. Justin, *1 Apology*, 1. Translations from Justin are my own.

4. ———. *Dialogue with Trypho the Jew*, 8.

5. ———. *2 Apology*, 12.

6. Eamon Duffy, *Saints and Sinners, A History of the Popes* (New Haven and London: Yale University Press, 1997), 9.

7. Justin, *1 Apology*, 46.

8. ———. *1 Apology* 32, 53, 56.

9. ———. *Dialogue with Trypho*, 63, 110.

10. ———. *1 Apology* 61, 65.

11. ———. *1 Apology*, 67.

12. See Leslie W. Barnard, *Justin Martyr, His Life and Thought* (Cambridge: Cambridge University Press, 1967), 132–33. For a thorough understanding of the complexity of Christianity, including the structures of the church, in Rome at this time, see the outstanding work of Peter Lampe, *From Paul to Valentinus: Christians at Rome in the First Two Centuries* (Minneapolis: Fortress Press, 2003).

13. Justin, *1 Apology*, 67.

14. Maurice Jourjon, "Justin," in Willy Rordorf and others, *The Eucharist of the Early Christians* (New York: Pueblo Publishing Company, 1978), 75.

15. Ibid., 76.

16. Justin, *Dialogue with Trypho*, 41.

17. Jean Danielou, Arthur H. Couratin and John Kent, *Historical Theology*. Vol. 2 of *The Penguin Guide to Modern Theology*. (Harmondsworth, UK: Penguin Books, 1969), 73.

18. Aime-Georges Martimort, "Nouvel examen de la 'Tradition Apostolique' d'Hippolyte," *Bulletin de litterature ecclesiastique* 88 (1987), 7.

19. See Jean Danielou, "Hippolytus and the Extension of Typology," in his *Gospel Message and Hellenistic Culture*, trans J. A. Baker (Philadelphia: Westminster Press, 1973), 257–72.

20. Hippolytus, "On Christ and Antichrist." An English translation

can be found in Alexander Roberts and James Donaldson, eds., *The Ante-Nicene Fathers* (Grand Rapids: Eerdmans, 1990), vol. 5.

21. David G. Dunbar, "The Delay of the Parousia in Hippolytus," *Vigiliae Christianae* 37 (1983), 313–327.

22. John N. D. Kelly, *The Oxford Dictionary of Popes* (New York and Oxford: Oxford University Press, 1986), 13.

23. Gregory Dix and Henry Chadwick, eds., *The Treatise on the Apostolic Tradition of Hippolytus of Rome* (London: The Alban Press, 1992), xvii. All subsequent references in this chapter to *The Apostolic Tradition* are taken from Dix and Chadwick.

24. See Lampe, *From Paul to Valentinus*, 118–22.

25. Stanley L. Greenslade, *Schism in the Early Church* (London: SCM Press, 1953), 49.

26. Hughes O. Old, *The Reading and Preaching of the Scriptures in the Worship of the Christian Church*, vol. 1, *The Biblical Period* (Grand Rapids: Eerdmans, 1998), 274.

27. Josef A. Jungmann, *The Early Liturgy* (Notre Dame: University of Notre Dame Press, 1959), 73.

3.

The Syriac and Greek Churches: Ephrem of Nisibis and Cyril of Jerusalem

Ephrem was the greatest poet of the patristic age, and perhaps the only theologian-poet to rank beside Dante.
–Robert Murray[1]

The most imaginative inclusion of the moral life is found in the work of Cyril. For him, in the baptismal act the faithful die and rise with Christ, not in reality (aletheia) but in mystery (mysterion). This is then the basis for participation in the Eucharist and eucharistic nourishment is nourishment of this new life in Christ.
–David N. Power[2]

EPHREM OF NISIBIS
(ca. 306–373)

Ephrem of Nisibis is a representative of Syriac Christianity. Syriac as a language is a branch of Aramaic and was spoken in and around Edessa from shortly before the beginning of Christianity. It is a language very close to the language Jesus himself would have spoken. Active Christians in the area led to its extensive use in the early church. One of the outstanding literary genres in Syriac is liturgical poetry, and Ephrem is its finest exemplar. Until about 400 CE, Syriac Christianity was at its most Semitic in character, not greatly influenced by Hellenistic thought patterns.

According to Syriac sources, Ephrem was the son of a pagan priest at Nisibis, his hometown. Most scholars today, however, believe that from his own writings there is enough evidence to indicate that his parents were Christian. He was ordained a deacon, probably by Bishop Hames of Nisibis. He seems to have been a teacher of theology, perhaps a catechist in a catechetical school established by the bishops of Nisibis. Such a position would provide a likely context for his many commentaries on scripture, as he attempted to form his catechumens in and through the books of the Bible. In addition to this, Ephrem seems to have had a responsibility for choirs in the community that supported the celebration of the liturgy throughout the year. Many of his works are hymns he composed for the liturgical year, for example, the "Hymns on the Nativity."[3]

In 363 the Emperor Julian ("the Apostate") was defeated in battle and met his death at the hands of the Persian armies, a constant menace on the easternmost borders of the far-flung Roman Empire. As a result of the peace treaty signed after the defeat, the city of Nisibis was ceded to Persia. In a series of hymns, Ephrem lamented the fall of Nisibis to the non-Christian Persians—a defeat he saw as a result of the folly and sin of the apostate Julian. After the cession of Nisibis, Ephrem, along with most of the Nisibene Christian community, went to live in Edessa, which was in the Roman Empire and was, therefore, safe for Christians. As one author notes, "these Syriac speaking Christians accepted it as axiomatic that because of the providential relationship between the church and the Roman Empire, to be Christian was to be Roman. Consequently, it was unacceptable to them to live under Persian rule."[4] And so Ephrem offered his services to Barses, the bishop of Edessa.

In order to counter approaches to and interpretations of Christian faith that were perhaps antagonistic to women, Ephrem taught choirs of women at Edessa his liturgical compositions. Jacob of Serugh (ca. 451–521), an influential Syriac bishop-theologian, makes a point of commenting on Ephrem's concern for women in his choirs, referring to him as a "Moses for women," a liberator of women.[5] He spent the last ten years of his life there, dying in 373, perhaps as a result of contracting an illness while nursing the sick during an epidemic.

As a church father, Ephrem is much less well known than most others. There are at least two reasons for this. First, the fact that he wrote in Syriac makes him much less accessible to Western readers and students unacquainted with the language, but this in no way means that Ephrem and his Syriac-writing colleagues are less valuable in Christian theology. One important Syriacist writes: "If these Oriental fathers are very little known to Western Christians, this is due not to any intrinsic inferiority on their part, but to the heavenly Eurocentric character of the academic study of church history and doctrine."[6] Insofar as ancient languages are still required in seminaries and divinity schools, it is usually Latin and Greek (and perhaps Hebrew) that get attention. This is what is meant by "Eurocentric."

Second, the fact that Ephrem was essentially a poet renders him somewhat suspect, even though he was considered the greatest poet of the patristic age, and perhaps the only poet-theologian who could stand beside Dante. Preference seems to be given to architectonic systematic theologies in which philosophy is often given the dominant role in the shaping of theology. Western analytic and systematic thinkers have not tended to take with great seriousness those whose theological vision is mediated through poetry. St. Ephrem was proclaimed a doctor of the universal church by Pope Benedict XV on October 5, 1920.

The Inaccessibility of God

A major and perduring theme in Ephrem's theological poetry is the inaccessibility of the divine to human reason. That God exists is knowable, but the nature of God remains impenetrable to human intelligence.[7] Only the Son can comprehend the Father because they are of the same nature. It is not, however, the case that while God remains opaque to our human intelligence and inquiry, we on the other hand are quite transparent to ourselves. If we are mysteries to ourselves, *a fortiori* God is mysterious to us. If, as Ephrem has it, the servant seldom reaches a real knowledge of self, how can he even begin to probe into the nature of his Master?[8] Interestingly, Ephrem describes the Arians as rationalistic, and as the ones who "scrutinize," because of the basic implication that they "know" the nature of God.[9] The Arians imply that they have a complete knowledge of God since, in principle, they disallow Jesus' divinity. Their comprehensive divine knowledge thus leads them to rule out the orthodox christological tradition. Robert Murray comments: "Ephraem refuses to answer the Arians by developing speculative theology on the orthodox side, as both Athanasius and the Cappadocians did; he sticks to his symbolism and demands that the mystery remain veiled. Not *fides quaerens intellectum* (faith seeking understanding) but *fides adorans mysterium* (faith adoring the mystery)."[10] This attempt to penetrate and even exhaust the mystery of God is condemned also when it makes an impact on other mysteries. For example, Ephrem is just as deeply opposed to attempts to grasp comprehensively the meaning of the Eucharist:

> Our Lord has become our living bread,
> and we shall delight in our new cup.
> Come, let us then eat it without investigation,
> And without scrutiny let us drink his cup.
> Who disdains blessings and fruits
> And sits down to investigate their nature?
> A human being needs to live.
> Come, let us live and not die in
> The depth of investigation.[11]

Undoubtedly, this theme of Ephrem's finds at least some of its roots in the notion of God in the Old Testament. One thinks of those passages where God's nature remains unknowable and even hidden to human beings, for example, Isaiah 55:9: "As the heavens are higher than the earth, so are my ways higher than your ways."

If God remains radically inaccessible to human reason and inquiry, if we ought not to "scrutinize" God after the Arian fashion, the question emerges logically, "How can we know anything about God?" For Ephrem, the intellect has its own proper role. It can inquire into those places where God has revealed himself in creation. Real knowledge of God unfolds in creation, grows in scripture and reaches its climax in the incarnation. Divine love for humankind is the motive that leads God to bridge the ontological chasm between Creator and creation in a process of self-manifestation.[12]

Knowledge of God consists in a progressive revelation of God's own self. "Ephrem considers revelation as a process of engaging God himself in a sort of progressive incarnation," says one commentator. "In imprinting in nature and sacred scripture the signs which reveal him, it is as if God were preparing to put on the human body of Jesus."[13] This connection of the revelation in creation and the revelation in Christ is integral for Ephrem: creation is revelatory because it comes from the Word himself:

> Wherever you look, the symbol of Christ is present. And where you read, you find his types. For it is by him that creatures have been made, and he has marked all his works by his symbols, since he created the world.[14]

If nothing can exhaust the mystery of God, then human language is necessarily inadequate in attempting to speak the mystery. A particularly beautiful and paradoxical image has to do with the womb of the Father. Addressing Christ, Ephrem writes:

> If anyone seeks your hidden nature, behold it is in heaven in the great womb of divinity. And if anyone

seeks your revealed body, behold it rests and looks
out from the small womb of Mary![15]

By divinity in this passage Ephrem intends the Father. The
Father in heaven has a "great womb," which eternally generates
the Son. The incarnation of the Son takes place in the "small
womb" of Mary.

A Western systematic thinker might be inclined to fault
Ephrem here, in that from an analytic perspective it is clearly
incongruous to talk about fathers having wombs, especially the
eternal Father. Poetry, however, does not operate in unambigu-
ously lucid, analytic terms, but by way of allusion, heaping up
images and metaphors, and making at least an implicit affirmation that logical analysis does not have the last word on human
meaning. Perhaps poetic paradox is the best we can do in speaking of the things of God. Where the logically apparent discord
is prematurely resolved, theological imbalance occurs. One
might say that this perennial temptation of theologians to reach
beyond the "discord" of paradox is what causes the pendulum to
swing constantly between affirmations of God's utter transcen-
dence, and his total immanence. For Ephrem, God permeates
the created order with his presence and with signs of his presence so as to reveal himself and to make himself in that sense
accessible to us.[16]

Eucharist

"In the florid diction of Ephrem's images, the eucharist
emerges as a complex reality that can never be reduced and
exclusively equated with any one of its aspects," says Joseph
Amar.[17] This is what one would expect from a poet-theologian.
Nonetheless, we can focus on some aspects of this rich
Ephremite tradition. Ephrem describes Christ as the "medicine
of life which flew down from on high."[18] At the Last Supper, "the
Lifegiver of all blessed the food, and it became the medicine of
life for those who ate it."[19] In similar fashion about the eucharis-

tic cup, he writes: "The grape of mercy was pressed, and gave the medicine of life to the peoples."[20]

The idea of the Eucharist as the medicine of life (or eternal life, immortality, resurrection) was quite common in Christian antiquity, the phrase being noted for the first time, as we have seen, in Ignatius of Antioch. At a time when life was constantly threatened by pestilence, natural disasters, disease and the ever-present power of the demonic, the Eucharist as the medicine of life spoke readily to the experience of early Christians.

Ephrem seems to envisage daily communion—which is not, of course, daily *celebration* of the Eucharist—when he writes: "The assembly of the saints bears resemblance to paradise: in it *each day* is plucked the fruit of him who gives life to all."[21] The return to the paradise forfeited by Adam and Eve is a favorite image for the sacrament of baptism in the Syriac fathers. By allowing the work of the Holy Spirit to transform one, one moves out of fallen creation into the state of paradise.

The baptismal paradisiacal motif is further developed by Ephrem in relation to the Eucharist:

> The spiritual bread of the Eucharist
> makes light and causes to fly:
> the peoples have been wafted up
> and have settled in paradise.
> Through the Second Adam who entered paradise
> Everyone becomes an eagle who reaches as far as
> paradise.
> Whoever eats the living bread of the Son
> flies to meet him in the very clouds.[22]

The Eucharist is heaven on earth, by anticipation and pledge, not by final realization. In the hymn also, the Pauline theme of the First Adam/Second Adam is allied to the Johannine theme of Christ as the living bread come down from heaven to give paradisiacal life to all who receive it. Ephrem's eucharistic theology is saturated in scripture.

Probably because martyrdom was largely a thing of the past when Ephrem was writing—the "peace of Constantine" is now a reality for Christians—the notion of sacrifice applied to the Eucharist is not so prominent in Ephrem. It is not, however, absent. In "Hymns on the Nativity" we read:

> Blessed is the Shepherd who became a lamb
> for our atonement.
> Blessed is the Vine that became a chalice
> For our salvation.[23]

The Shepherd becomes the sacrificial lamb, so prominent in the Gospel of John and the Book of Revelation. The true Vine, also a Johannine theme, becomes the chalice of salvation, outpouring Christ's precious blood for our salvation. More often than, however, his biblical usage tends toward the affirmation of a more intimate, organic link between the Christian and Christ through reception of holy communion.

Nor is there any lack of what we might call eucharistic realism in the mystical theology of Ephrem. This realism is finely brought out in a hymn in which he describes the eucharistic Christ as the "coal of fire" in Isaiah's prophetic vision:

> The seraph could not touch the coal of fire with his
> fingers, and the coal merely touched Isaiah's mouth:
> the seraph did not hold it, Isaiah did not consume it,
> but our Lord has allowed us to do both.[24]

In the prophetic vision of Isaiah 6, there is a "coal of fire" symbolizing God's majestic presence. The seraph takes a coal with tongs from the altar and merely touched Isaiah's mouth. In holy communion, however, the same divine majesty is both touched and handled, and enters into the communicant.

This eucharistic realism is developed even more when Ephrem describes how Christian life is to be lived in greater and

45

ever greater conformity with Christ as we are assimilated to him in holy communion:

> Christ's body has newly been mingled with our bodies,
> his blood too has been poured out into our veins,
> his voice is in our ears,
> his brightness in our eyes.
> In his compassion the whole of
> Him has been mingled
> In with the whole of us.[25]

CYRIL OF JERUSALEM
(ca. 315–386)

It is extremely difficult to sort out truth and slander in the controversies of the period between the Councils of Nicaea (325) and Chalcedon (451).[26] This is certainly true when we attempt to learn about the life of St. Cyril, bishop of Jerusalem. During his time and well into the fifth century the church suffered from Arianism, a heresy taking its name from Arius (ca. 260–336), a priest and theologian of the important Egyptian city of Alexandria. The complex debate associated with Arius is beyond the scope of this chapter. Suffice it to say that, for Arius, Jesus Christ was not "one in being with the Father," but a creature, albeit the best creature God made or could make. What made Arius' position attractive to so many was its apparent rational simplicity, the rationalism to which Ephrem took exception. If Christ is a creature, then the straightforward simplicity of monotheism—belief in one God—is not muddied by the doctrine of the Trinity.

The popularity of Arianism divided the church and not only theologically. Successive pro-Arian emperors entered the lists, often using their political power to appoint or to depose bishops whose theology was "Catholic" or anti-Arian. It was in this dangerous and divisive environment that Cyril was called to be bishop of Jerusalem, and, while holding that office, he was exiled and restored three times. "At the time, which party represented 'orthodoxy' was not by any means obvious," one author notes. "In all probability Cyril found himself caught in the cross-currents of contemporary ecclesiastical politics without being doctrinally committed to any particular party."[27]

So, who was Cyril? As is the case with so many other fathers of the church, we lack detailed information. He came from a Christian household, and was probably born in Jerusalem. Appointed bishop of Jerusalem in 350, he fell into difficulties with his superior, Acacius, bishop of Caesarea. The issue that brought the men into dispute concerned church property. After the Edict of Toleration (313), the city of Jerusalem became a center of pilgrimage and the Emperor Constantine and other prominent Christians had lavished many rich gifts on the Church of Jerusalem. During the decade between 350 and 360 there had been famine in the area, and to alleviate distress Cyril had sold church treasures to feed the hungry. According to the church historian Sozomen:

> Jerusalem and the neighboring country was at one time visited with a famine, and the poor appealed in great multitudes to Cyril, as their bishop, for necessary food. As he had no money to purchase the requisite provisions, he sold for this purpose the veil and sacred ornaments of the Church. It is said that a man, having recognized an offering which he had presented at the altar as forming part of the costume of an actress, made it his business to inquire whence it was procured; and ascertained that a merchant had sold it to the actress, and that the bishop had sold it to the merchant. It was under this pretext that Acacius deposed Cyril.[28]

That was probably in 357. In 359 Cyril was reinstated, only to be sent into exile again in 360. Reinstated in 361, he was exiled yet again in 367, returning to his see in 378. He attended the Council of Constantinople in 381, the council that defined the divinity of the Holy Spirit. He died in 386.

The Catechetical Orations

One of the major responsibilities of a bishop at the time was to prepare candidates for Christian initiation. Cyril's addresses to the catechumens of Jerusalem have come down to us, "an invaluable liturgical legacy, the earliest complete set of extant baptismal instructions in ancient Christianity."[29] There is no exact and accurate evidence for the precise length of the catechumenate in the fourth century, and it is unclear in Cyril when the course of catechetical lectures is finished, except when he indicates that the feast of Easter, the Pascha, is at hand. What follows in description here is but an approximation.

After the inaugural catechetical class that corresponds to the taking down of names (see the Procatechesis), five addresses were given to the congregation on each of the first five Sundays of Lent, which at that time in the East lasted eight weeks. Then followed twelve catechetical lectures, each one providing a commentary on the creed, and these twelve lectures corresponded to the daily meetings of the sixth and seventh weeks of Lent. And finally, the "Mystagogical Catecheses" were delivered after the neophytes, the newborn Christians, had been initiated during the Easter Vigil celebration. These catecheses gave an explanation of the sacramental rites.

At the end of the fifth lecture, the creed is given to the elect: "In learning the faith, and in professing it, acquire and keep that only, which is now delivered to you by the Church, and which has been built up strongly out of all the Scriptures" (Procatechesis 5.12). There is no conflict or tension for Cyril between the doctrines of the creed and the scriptures because essentially he views the former as a digest of the latter. Ordinary folk would not, of course, have had their own copies of the scriptures, and so the elect are to learn the creed by heart, as a scriptural summary of Christian belief.

After the handing out of the creed, lectures six to eighteen provide commentary on the creed. Whatever topic Cyril deals with is always consistently and thoroughly based on scripture as the source of information. Without developing the point in great detail, he contrasts what he considers the proper approach to scripture, the "believing" approach, with the "speculative" approach: "...for we are met together, not now to make a speculative exposition of the Scriptures, but rather to be certified of the things which we already believe" (Procatechesis 13.9). It is neither difficult nor fanciful to see in Cyril's distinction between a speculative and believing approach to scripture, one of the theses of postliberal theology. Before the onset of the modern age, most Christians read the Bible as a sort of realistic narrative, from creation to the last judgment. They located their own individual stories within the framework of that larger story.[30] Scripture is absorbed, not beginning with contemporary human experience and then making connections with the Bible, but rather by laying out the narrative that is the Bible, and inviting identification, ownership, performance. As the Eucharist shapes us to Christ, so does the Word as we come to know it, make it our own, and attempt to live by it.

As an interesting aside, one might note that in his catecheses Cyril provides us with the earliest evidence in antiquity for reading silently.[31] The ancients normally read aloud, and not silently as we do. Instructing the catechumens how to behave while they awaited their individual exorcisms before baptism, he tells the men to sit together reading aloud: "Let the men when sitting have a useful book; and let one read, and another listen: and if there be no book, let the one pray, and another speak something useful" (Procatechesis 14). The young women catechumens are to conduct themselves differently, so that they may read but silently, unlike the men: "Let the part of young women be so ordered, that they may either be singing or reading, but without noise, so that their lips may speak, but others may not hear." The silent reading of the young women is based, of course, on 1 Corinthians 14:34: "Women should be silent in the churches." Cyril reflects the attitudes of his day here, but far more interesting is not so much the fact of the *silent* reading, which was unusual, but the very fact that these young men and women waiting for exorcism were reading at all. It indicates that Cyril's congregation included educated men and women, literate men and women.

Eucharist

It is in the Mystagogical Catecheses that Cyril's eucharistic theology is found.[32] In Mystagogical Catechesis IV, Cyril takes as his point of departure the realism of the words of our Lord at the Last Supper: "Take, eat, this is my body...take, drink, this is my blood" (IV.1). The body and blood of Christ are given to us "in the figure" of bread and wine. The word Cyril uses for "figure" is the Greek word *typos*, our closest English equivalent being "sacrament." Type or figure for Cyril means that this *is* Christ's body and blood, thought not obviously so. Though he would not have put it like this, Cyril means that the type is the efficacious sacramental sign of Christ. It is truly and really the reality of Christ, or everything else Cyril has to say about the issue is meaningless. As a result of eating and drinking the body and blood of Christ, Cyril tells us that we become of "the same body and the same blood with him...we become partakers of the divine nature" (IV.3). That phrase, "the same body and the same blood with him," in Greek is actually two words, *syssomos* and *synaimos*. In English it takes nine words to translate the idea, but the mere two Greek words are more powerfully suggestive of the dynamic union that occurs between the believer and Christ through the Eucharist. The words say something like "Christ bodies us with himself, bloods us with himself." That sounds cumbersome, but it captures something of the profound union between Christ and the church. This eucharistic union renders us *koinonoi* with the divine nature. "Partakers" sounds much too bland to communicate this. Something like "communioned in and with God" is more literal and better. Though our human senses see and taste bread and wine, faith assures that it is the very body and blood of Christ (IV.6, 9). Cyril has a lovely word for the communioned Christian, *christopheros*, a *christopher*, one who bears Christ. We are *christified* through the sacraments, centered on the Eucharist. In fact, what Cyril is talking about is what western Christians call "grace," the life of God communicated to us to enfold us in that life. To be divine is to be God, and if God is communicating himself then that communication is divinization. God reaches out from himself to place us within himself. However it is expressed, God reaches out to embrace us through the incarnation and the Eucharist, so that the one reality is dependent upon the other. This is how a recent commentator on Cyril puts it: "Defense of Christ's incarnation, a proper christology, and the reality of Christ's bodily presence in the eucharist cannot be divided from one another. Defending Christ's presence in the eucharist entails defending the incarnation of the only-begotten Son of God."[33]

Mystagogical Catechesis V proceeds to provide a commentary on the rite of the Mass, and so reveals to us the shape of the celebration in Cyril's time in Jerusalem. The deacon gives the priest water to wash his hands, symbolizing his purity from all that is sinful and unlawful (V.2), after which the deacon cries aloud, "Receive ye one another; and let us kiss one another" (V.3). The kiss is the kiss of reconciliation, and here Cyril calls to mind the words of our Lord in Matthew 5:23: "So when you are offering your gift at the altar, if you remember that your brother or sister has something against you, leave your gift there before the altar and go; first be reconciled to your brother or sister, and then come and offer your gift." Paragraphs four and five of the catechesis launch the eucharistic prayer in a way that recalls the rite of Hippolytus of Rome described in the last essay in the last chapter:

> Priest: *Lift up your hearts.*
> People: *We lift them up unto the Lord.*
> Priest: *Let us give thanks to the Lord.*
> People: *It is meet and right.*

Then Cyril describes a preface, involving all creation in the glory and praise of God, and ending with the Sanctus: "Holy, holy, holy, Lord God of Sabaoth" (V.6). This is the song of the seraphim in Isaiah 6:1–4, and by means of it Cyril connects our earthly liturgy with the worship of the heavenly hosts. The Holy Spirit is invoked on the gifts to change them into the body and blood of the Lord. "Then having sanctified ourselves by these spiritual hymns, we call upon the merciful God to send forth his Holy Spirit upon the gifts lying before him; that he may make the bread the Body of Christ, and the wine the Blood of Christ; for whatsoever the Holy Spirit has touched, is sanctified and changed" (V.7).

The word "change" is significant. The Holy Spirit brings about a real change in the elements so that we may be really changed, that is become *syssomos* and *synaimos*, "one body and one blood" with Christ. Cyril acknowledges that this is a "spiritual sacrifice...a sacrifice of propitiation" (V.8). The word for "propitiation" is *hilasmos*, the word used in 1 John 2:2 and 4:10 for Christ's once-for-all sacrifice on the cross. The unique *hilasmos* of Christ is represented in the Eucharist. Intercession is then made with God for the church, the world, rulers, the sick and all standing in need of God's help (V.8). Commemoration is made of "Patriarchs, Prophets, Apostles, Martyrs...Fathers, Bishops...and all who in past years have fallen asleep among us" (V.9–10).

The curious thing is that in his description of the eucharistic prayer Cyril does not actually mention the narrative of the institution of the Eucharist. He does describe the narrative of the institution in Mystagogical Catechesis IV, but not in this catechesis where he describes the actual rite of the Eucharist. How is this to be explained? It is an issue on which the scholars differ, but the solution that makes most sense to the author is that Cyril did not include mention of the institution narrative here because he had just dealt with it in the previous catechesis and what he had said did not require repetition.[34]

The Lord's Prayer is then prayed. In fact, Cyril's writings are the first evidence for the use of the Lord's Prayer after the eucharistic prayer, and he also gives us his commentary on it. Commenting on "Our Father who art in heaven," Cyril points out that "they too are a heaven who bear the image of the heavenly, in whom God is, dwelling and walking in them" (V.11). As Christians are enabled to call God "Father," bear God's image, their filiation makes them heavenly, "like" God. "Give us this day our daily bread" picks up the meaning of the word "daily," in Greek *epiousios*, not an easy word to translate. Nonetheless, the meaning is clear. This is the daily bread that takes those who eat it into the very heart and reality of God. Finally, the "evil" from which we ask deliverance is clearly for Cyril "the Wicked Spirit who is our adversary" (V.18).

After this the priest says, "Holy things to holy people" and Cyril indicates the meaning: "the holy things correspond to the holy persons," but we are holy by participation, not by nature. The communion now takes place, and Cyril provides us with two splendid passages about its meaning, deserving of quotation in full:

> Approaching, therefore, come not with thy wrists extended, or thy fingers open; but make thy left hand as if a throne for thy right, which is on the eve of receiving the King. And having hollowed thy palm, receive the Body of Christ, saying after it, Amen. Then after thou hast with carefulness hallowed thine eyes by the touch of the Holy Body, partake thereof; giving heed lest thou lose any of it; for what thou losest is a loss to thee as it were from one of thine own members. For tell me, if any one gave thee gold dust, wouldest thou not with all precaution keep it fast, being on thy guard against losing any of it, and suffering loss? How much more cautiously then wilt thou observe that not a crumb falls from thee, of what is more precious than gold and precious stones? (V.21).

> Then after having partaken of the Body of Christ, approach also to the Cup of His Blood; not stretching forth thine hands, but bending and saying in the

way of worship and reverence, Amen, be thou hallowed by partaking also of the Blood of Christ. And while the moisture is still upon thy lips, touching it with thine hands, hallow both thine eyes and brow and the other senses (V.22).

After receiving the Eucharist, the final prayer of the liturgy is prayed.

Conclusion

Both Ephrem and Cyril are of the East, the one Syriac, the other Greek. Cardinal Yves Congar, after fifty years of ecumenical labor and cooperation, concluded: "at the sacramental level, i.e., where the supernatural mystery is expressed in our world, East and West are the same Church."[35] At the same time, Congar acknowledged that there are real differences between East and West. There is no room for complacency as both traditions seek to rediscover each other and, as they succeed in doing so, find their long-lost unity. There is a basic need for each to know about the other, and find personal and ecclesial transformation in that knowledge. In his apostolic letter *The Light of the East*, Pope John Paul II makes this point well when he remarks: "Since, in fact we believe that the venerable and ancient tradition of the Eastern Churches is an integral part of the heritage of Christ's Church, the first need for Catholics is *to be familiar with that tradition*, so as to be nourished by it and to encourage the process of unity in the best way possible for each."[36]

In this context of striving for unity between East and West through a growing rapprochement based on knowledge of the other, Ephrem of Nisibis is a powerful focus for unity. His eucharistic theology faces both East and West, and resonates with both traditions. For Cyril, one might say that his two foundational resources are the Word and the Eucharist, the scriptures and the body and blood of Christ. Ephrem and Cyril help western Christians to become familiar with the great eastern tradition of eucharistic reflection.

Notes

1. Robert Murray, *Symbols of Church and Kingdom: A Study in Early Syriac Tradition* (Cambridge: Cambridge University Press, 1975), 31.

2. David N. Power, *The Eucharistic Mystery* (New York: Crossroad, 1992), 148–49.

3. See Sidney H. Griffith, "Ephraem the Syrian's Hymns: 'Against Julian.' Meditations on History and Imperial Power," *Vigiliae Christianae* 41 (1987), 238–66.

4. ———. "'Faith Seeking Understanding' in the Thought of St. Ephraem the Syrian," in George C. Berthold, ed., *Faith Seeking Understanding: Learning and the Catholic Tradition* (Manchester, NH: St. Anselm College Press, 1986), 36.

5. ———. "Images of Ephraem: The Syrian Holy Man and His Church," *Traditio* 45 (1989–90), 15.

6. Sebastian P. Brock, "The Oriental Fathers," in Ian Hazlett, ed., *Early Christianity: Origins and Evolution to AD 600* (London: SPCK, 1991), 163.

7. Ephrem, "Hymn on the Nativity, # 14," in A. Edward Johnston, trans., *Nicene and Post-Nicene Fathers*, second series, vol. 13 (Grand Rapids: Eerdmans, 1964), 251–52.

8. ———. "Hymns on Faith," # 1, in Sebastian P. Brock, *Harp of the Spirit* (Oxford: Fellowship of St. Alban and St. Sergius, 1975), 7.

9. ———. "Hymns on Faith," # 19, in Sebastian P. Brock, *The Luminous Eye: The Spiritual World Vision of St. Ephrem* (Kalamazoo, MI: Cistercian Publications, 1992), 104.

10. Murray, *Symbols of Church and Kingdom*, 89.

11. Ephrem, "Hymns on Virginity," 16.5, in Kathleen McVey, ed., *Ephrem the Syrian, Hymns* (Mahwah, NJ: Paulist Press, 1989), 330.

12. ———. "Hymns on Faith," 51.2–3, in Brock, *The Luminous Eye*, 28.

13. Seely J. Beggiani, *Early Syriac Theology* (Lanham, MD: University Press of America, 1983), 25.

14. "Hymns on Virginity," 20.2, in Beggiani, *Early Syriac Theology*, 25.

15. "Hymns on the Nativity," 13.7, in McVey, *Ephrem the Syrian, Hymns,* 138.

16. Paul S. Russell, "St. Ephraem, The Syrian Theologian," *Pro Ecclesia* 7 (1998), 89.

17. Joseph P. Amar, "Perspectives on the Eucharist in Ephrem the Syrian," *Worship* 61 (1987), 444.

18. "Discourse 3," cited in Brock, *The Luminous Eye,* 99.

19. "Unleavened Bread," 14.16, in Brock, supra, 101.

20. "Hymns on Virginity," 31.3, in McVey, *Ephrem the Syrian, Hymns,* 99.

21. "Hymns on Paradise," 6.8, in Brock, *The Luminous Eye,* 100.

22. "Unleavened Bread," 17. 8–12, in Brock, supra, 101.

23. "Hymns on the Nativity," 3.15, in McVey, *Ephrem the Syrian, Hymns,* 79.

24. "Hymns on Faith," 10.10, in McVey, supra, 104.

25. "Hymns on Virginity," 37.2, in McVey, supra, 105–6.

26. Frances M. Young, *From Nicaea to Chalcedon* (London: SCM Press, 1983), 311.

27. Ibid., 125.

28. Sozomen, *History of the Church,* 4.25.

29. Thomas M. Finn, *From Death to Rebirth: Ritual and Conversion in Antiquity* (New York/Mahwah, NJ: Paulist Press, 1997), 194.

30. Owen F. Cummings, "Cyril of Jerusalem as a Postliberal Theologian," *Worship* 67 (1993), 155–64.

31. Michael Slusser, "Reading Silently in Antiquity," *Journal of Biblical Literature* 111 (1992), 499.

32. The edition followed here is Frank L. Cross, ed., *St. Cyril of Jerusalem's Lectures on the Christian Sacraments* (London: SPCK, 1951).

33. Kent J. Burreson, "The Anaphora of the Mystagogical Catecheses of Cyril of Jerusalem," in Paul F. Bradshaw, ed., *Essays on Early Eastern Eucharistic Prayers* (Collegeville, MN: The Liturgical Press, 1997), 135.

34. See John Baldovin, SJ, *Liturgy in Ancient Jerusalem* (Bramcote, Notts: Grove Books, 1989), 25–27.

35. Yves Congar, *Diversity and Communion* (London: SCM Press, 1984), 73.

36. John Paul II, *The Light of the East [Orientale Lumen]* (Washington, DC: United States Catholic Conference, 1995, 1.

4.

East and West: John Chrysostom of Constantinople and Ambrose of Milan

John's sermons reflect something of the authentic life of the New Testament, just because they are so ethical, so simple, and so clear-headed.
−Hans von Campenhausen.[1]

Ambrose was the first Latin Church father to be born, reared, and educated not as a pagan, but as a Christian. He was likewise the first descendant of the Roman high aristocracy to have found in the Church his life-work.
−Hans von Campenhausen[2]

JOHN CHRYSOSTOM
(ca. 347–407)

John Chrysostom is esteemed as the greatest preacher of the ancient church and the saintly teacher of Eastern Orthodox Christianity. He was born in Antioch, Syria, about 347. His father, Secundus, a civil servant, died when John was a child. He was reared by his mother, Arthusa, who had been widowed at just twenty years of age. The whole burden of his upbringing and education as well as the administration of the household now fell upon this relatively inexperienced woman. Arthusa faced these difficulties with courage and she brought John up a gentleman. He studied with Libanius, the most distinguished rhetorician of his day. John's success seemed to promise a career in the civil service, but his passion lay with the church.

John was baptized in 368, and, beginning the serious study of holy scripture under Melitius, bishop of Antioch, soon was immersed not only in the sacred text but also in the realist school of Antiochene exegesis. He went through a period of discernment, trying to decide whether his vocation lay in the call of the desert as an ascetic or in public life. Consequent upon Arthusa's death about 374/5, John became a monk in the communities of hermits south of Antioch, and virtually ruined his health with his austerities. Ordination to the priesthood by Bishop Flavian followed in 381, and John's main business now was preaching, for which he was eminently well prepared. The next decade proved to be the most productive of his life, as he wrote homilies on Genesis, Matthew, John, Romans, Galatians, First and Second Corinthians, Ephesians, Timothy and Titus.

In 387 he gave the famous "Homilies on the Statues." Due to the Emperor Theodosius I's serious fiscal problems, taxes had been raised very steeply, provoking in Antioch an adverse reaction in which statues of the imperial family were smashed. This was tantamount to treason, and while Bishop Flavian was in the capital, Constantinople, pleading to Theodosius for mercy for his people, John preached a series of twenty-one sermons, the "Homilies on the Statues," correcting the people for what they had done and trying to console them in the face of the consequences. Other collections of homilies followed including homilies *On the Incomprehensible Nature of God*, preached against the Arians in Antioch, whose Christology taught that God was rationally comprehensible. During this time he also preached a series of homilies against Judaizing Christians, who were attracted to certain Jewish observances, such as the weekly Sabbath and the annual Rosh Hashanah and Yom Kippur. Robert Wilken, who has studied these homilies and John's language about the Jews in detail, comments: "When these sermons were copied or translated in medieval Europe, a society in which Christianity was the dominant religion, their defamatory and abusive language helped foster anti-Jewish attitudes among Christians."[3]

In 398 John was forced to accept appointment as bishop of Constantinople—"New Rome" as it was then known. Preaching became the most conspicuous part of his episcopal ministry. Often John did not preach from the bishop's throne in the cathedral, but, in order better to be heard by his congregation, from the ambo in the middle of the nave.[4] People flocked from far and wide to hear John preach. We are told that on one occasion, when John invited an elderly Galatian bishop to preach on a particular Sunday, the congregation streamed out of the church with loud complaints.[5]

Unfortunately his preaching skills were not matched by his diplomatic skills, and John soon found himself in difficulties with the imperial administration in the city. His very ascetic, personal lifestyle and his disdain for a life of luxury and ease made him enemies at court. His enemies were not only prominent civic functionaries but also important churchmen, perhaps less zealous than himself. The net result of the very considerable intrigues was a synod at "The Oak," near Chalcedon, southeast of Constantinople across the Bosphorus, in 403. John was summoned to answer a list of charges, and, when he refused to appear, was deposed. The deposition would have been ineffective if John had been on good terms with the Empress Eudoxia and the Emperor Arcadius, but he was too much at odds with the royal family and their lifestyle. Arcadius ratified the decision of the synod at the Oak and John was to be exiled. However, as he left for exile at a town on the Black Sea, there was an earthquake, seen popularly as God's judgment against the judgment of John, and he was recalled.

Matters did not rest there. Some months later, the Empress Eudoxia had a silver statue of herself erected near John's cathedral of Holy Wisdom in Constantinople. This met with his most articulate disapproval, and again he was deposed and sent into exile where he lived out his final days. John died in 407, and his remains were returned to Constantinople some thirty years later.

Eucharist

About the year 390 John delivered some ninety homilies in Antioch. In Homily 82 on St. Matthew's gospel he comments on the figure of Judas and the question of his reception of holy communion—an issue that would continue to perplex Christians in the Middle Ages, such as Hugh of St. Victor, as we shall see. John acknowledges that Judas received communion, but was convinced that it did him no good. Judas did not respond to the gift given. No doubt John was also speaking to members of the congregation at Antioch, speaking to their blindness and the failure to follow the Lord, even as they received his body. Judas becomes a type of the nondisciple, and so John can write, "Let there be no Judas present, no one avaricious. If anyone is not a disciple, let him go away. The table does not receive such ones."[6]

John, as is the case with most of the fathers of the church, is always addressing pastoral issues in his congregation even as he comments on the sacred text. Again, in the same homily for example, he picks up the scandal in St. John's gospel, Chapter 6, overeating Christ's body and drinking his blood. He is sensitive to this question, but his solution is to show the Lord himself leading the way, and so taking away the scandal: "And he himself drank of it…lest they should be similarly troubled then, he did this first himself, leading them to a calm participation in the mysteries. For that reason he himself drank his own blood."[7] In this same homily, John takes up the pastoral-liturgical abuse of people leaving the liturgy before it is over. He challenges the liturgical minimalists in his congregation with very strong language: "Let all those who hear this who, like browsing swine, rudely abuse the ordinary table, and rise up drunk. For it is proper to give thanks, and to end with a hymn. Hear this, all you who do not wait for the final prayer of the mysteries, for this is a symbol of it. He gave thanks before giving the Eucharist to his disciples, that we may also give thanks. He gave thanks, and sang a hymn after giving the Eucharist, that we too may do this very thing."[8] If Christians pattern themselves after the Lord Jesus, their liturgical participation should be so patterned too.

Chrysostom has, as one would expect, a strong sense of Christ's self-gift in the eucharistic elements for the purpose of sharing the divine life with the communicants. In a homily on the sixth chapter of St. John's gospel, again probably given in Antioch, he writes:

> In order, then, that we may become of his flesh, not by charity only, but also in very fact, let us become commingled with that flesh....It is for this reason that he joined himself to us, and has brought his body down to our level, namely, that we might be one, just as a body is joined with the head.[9]

In another homily he emphasizes the importance of having one's whole life comport with the Eucharist, with no excesses of eating and drinking and pleasure-seeking. John is perhaps temperamentally opposed to such good things as a result of his love of asceticism, but it is the excess that he condemns. The reality of Christ's eucharistic presence should deter us from excessive self-indulgence:

> You do these things when you have enjoyed the table of Christ, on the very day on which you have been counted worthy to touch his flesh with your tongue! To prevent this, each one of you should make your pure right hand, your tongue and your lips which have become a threshold for Christ to walk upon.[10]

Absorbed into Christ, into divinity, the ordinary rituals and customs of human life should signal that absorption. However, it is not only a matter of personal discipline as we grow more fully into Christ. There are other eucharistic demands.

In a homily on First Corinthians, John picks up the moral consequences of receiving communion, and thus being in communion with the whole Christ, head and members, and most especially with the neediest members of his body.

> You are not fed from one body, and the next person from another, but all from the very same one. And so, the apostle [Paul] adds "For we all partake of the one bread." Now if from the same bread, and we all become the same, why do we not also exhibit the same love, and become one in this respect also? …Many and various are the contentions between all, and we are disposed worse than wild animals towards the members of one another….If, therefore, you come to the Eucharist, do not do anything unworthy of the Eucharist. Do not shame your brother, or neglect him in his hunger. Do not be intoxicated, do not insult the Church. You come giving thanks for what you have enjoyed, so give back something in exchange and do not cut yourself off from your neighbor.[11]

Eucharistic realism for John does not stop with the recognition of the unique divine gift on the altar, but moves on to the recognition and moral performance that this divine gift, shared in and with the whole body, including its very poorest members, demands.

AMBROSE OF MILAN
(CA. 339–397)

In a recent essay devoted to St. Ambrose of Milan, Mary C. Murray comments on the fact that too many studies of the saint have concentrated on his role as a churchman and a politician, and have insufficiently adverted to his other contributions, including his theology. "The habit of viewing [Ambrose's] personality always from the standpoint of politics means that we have to some extent been deprived of knowledge of one of the most engaging personalities of the ancient church," she writes.[12] Ambrose's standing up to the Emperor Theodosius I is frequently commented on in the standard works. His political savvy is an established fact. But, what do we know of this engaging personality? What do we know of him as a bishop and shepherd of his flock?

Some biographical information may be extracted from Ambrose's corpus of writings. We are also well served by a *Life of Ambrose* written by Paulinus, a deacon of the Church of Milan, probably about 412. Murray tries to piece together what Ambrose would have looked like from the mosaic portrait in the Chapel of St. Victor in the Basilica of St. Ambrose in Milan. Her description is quite long but is worth quoting in full to get an appreciation of Ambrose:

> He was a small man, five feet four inches in height, and with the physical characteristic of a slight depression in the right cheek, which must have given the impression, when he was alive, of his having one eye slightly higher than the other. This peculiarity is found in the mosaic which dates from the beginning of the fifth century, just after his death. From the portrait with the somewhat weary look in the large eyes, it is not hard to infer that he suffered from ill health. And that this was so we know from his letters, in which he refers to his sickness, which seems to have been a permanent state, and which he seems to have accepted as an inevitable fact. Paulinus too mentions his illness and Augustine adds that when Ambrose spoke his voice easily grew hoarse. This was why, contrary to the custom in antiquity of reading aloud, Ambrose read silently to himself. This throat problem must have been a constant trial to one who had a career of preaching and public speaking.[13]

Murray's engaging but accurate description is clearly based on an intimacy with this mosaic of Ambrose.

Ambrose was born in the city of Trier (now in modern Germany) about 339 AD. His father, also Ambrose, had a major position in the administration of the Roman Empire, being prefect of the Gauls. He and his wife (whose name never appears in any text touching upon Ambrose) had three children: a daughter, Marcellina, and two sons, an older son Satyrus and Ambrose. The family relocated to Rome, probably after the elder Ambrose's death. Marcellina committed herself to a life of virginity, probably continuing to live at home with her family but with a higher degree of asceticism and regular prayer. A book later written by Ambrose, *On Virgins* (3.1.1), reveals that she made her profession of virginity in the presence of Pope Liberius in the Basilica of St. Peter on Christmas day (probably between the years 352–54). Both Ambrose and Satyricus studied the liberal arts and law in Rome, perhaps with a view to following in their father's footsteps as civil servants. Ambrose ended up in 370 as governor of Liguria and Aemilia in the north of Italy, a position of considerable importance and responsibility. The center of his administration was the city of Milan.

During the fourth century this city was engulfed in the conflict throughout the Christian world between pro- and anti-Arian factions in the church, often aided and abetted by imperial policies and interference. When the Arian bishop of Milan, Auxentius, died in 373, Ambrose was involved in maintaining the peace between the Arians and the orthodox Christians who had accepted the christological formula of the Council of Nicaea (325), that Jesus Christ was "one in being" with the Father. Impressed with the way Ambrose was fulfilling his civil administrative duties, the Christian population of Milan chose him as successor to Bishop Auxentius, even though Ambrose was still a catechumen—that is, as yet unbaptized. The new bishop was baptized, ordained and consecrated very quickly, and threw himself into his studies, both exegetical and theological, in order to minister to his new diocese. His career in civil administration would have brought clearly to his attention the plight of the poor in the empire. As a bishop, Ambrose determined that the poor would be one of his greatest concerns, and he gave his wealth to the poor.

In Letter 71 we are given an insight into the practical workings of Ambrose's life as bishop. The letter is addressed to Eusebius, a layman from Bologna whose son Faustinus was in Milan:

> Little Faustinus is suffering from a cough....He thinks that I am a doctor and looks to me for his meals. So he gets his medicine here twice a day and has begun feeling fairly well, but when, out of excessive love, they hold off the doses, his stomach cough begins worse than before, and if he does not return to his medicines, he will continue to suffer.[14]

The image of a bishop, ministering to a sick child, trying to get him to eat is not only attractive in itself, but reveals so much about the personality of Ambrose. Ambrose also had a nice sense of humor. In Letter 3, written to his friend Felix, he thanks him for his gift, even as he chides him for failing to visit:

> The truffles you sent me are of extraordinary size, so large as to cause amazement. I had no desire to hide them, as they say, in the fold of my toga, but I preferred showing them also to others. As a result, I shared some with friends, some I kept for myself. Your gift is most agreeable, but is not weighty enough to still in me the complaints rightly caused by the fact that you never come to see me....[15]

The weight and size of the truffles do not compensate for Felix's absence from Ambrose's life. The presence of Felix is the "truffle" he desires!

Paganism, of course, was still widespread in the Roman Empire at the time of Ambrose. He showed no compromise in defending the new order of Christianity against this lingering paganism. For example, in the senate house in Rome there was a statue and an altar of Victory. Ambrose was involved in debate with the pagan senator Symmachus, who had contested the removal of the altar by the Emperor Gratian. Gratian was resolutely opposed to paganism and refused as emperor to accept the pagan title of *pontifex maximus* or high priest. Ambrose, in debate with Symmachus and his religiously conservative paganism, was both gentlemanly and courteous. He detested paganism but not the pagans, and he freely admitted liberty of conscience to Symmachus and spoke well of him. Until his death in 397, it would be accurate to regard Ambrose as the most important western bishop.

Eucharist

"In Ambrose and Augustine we meet two writers whose works contain within themselves in embryo not only the teachings but the controversies which are to mark the history of the Western Eucharist," one commentator has said.[16] If one were to consult the details of eucharistic controversy and debate in the early medieval period—for example between Paschasius and Ratramnus or Berengar and Lanfranc—the stamp of Ambrose and Augustine is obvious. The influence of Ambrose is to be found especially in two features: his emphasis on the conversion of the elements of bread and wine into the body and blood of Christ, and his emphasis on the eucharistic words as bringing about this change. These two aspects of eucharistic theology were to figure prominently in the tradition at least until the time of St. Thomas Aquinas' treatment of the doctrine of transubstantiation, and even beyond. Ambrose's eucharistic reflection is found principally in his treatises *On the Sacraments* and *On the Mysteries*—the former to be dated between 380 and 390, the latter perhaps in the early 390s They consist of a series of talks or instructions delivered by Bishop Ambrose to those who had been recently received into the church at Easter. The content of the instructions is given over to baptism, anointing with oil or what Ambrose called "the spiritual seal," and the Eucharist. Here we shall examine Ambrose's *On the Sacraments*, Books IV-V[17]

He contrasts Christian sacraments with what he calls "the sacraments of the Jews" and judges the former to be "more godly."[18] Behind his judgment lies a contrast in salvation history that was common in the patristic period, beginning in the Letter to the Hebrews, a contrast that shows the figures and the "sacraments" of the Old Testament to be shadows of the fullness to come in Jesus Christ. The really-real order, established through the event of Jesus Christ in the New Testament, finds its ultimate expression in the future, in heaven. Just as the various Jewish "sacraments," the signs and rituals of the Old Testament are but a shadow of the good things to come in Jesus Christ, so our empirical world is but an "image" of the fullness of reality that will come to be when God-in-Christ is all in all at the Parousia. The Eucharist is real, but yet an image of the fullness of divine reality to occur at the end.

If the newly made Christians are inclined to think that the eucharistic bread looks like ordinary bread, and perhaps just is ordinary bread, Ambrose is quick to point out that:

> That bread is bread before the words of the sacraments. When consecration has been added, from being bread it becomes the flesh of Christ.[19]

Consecration for Ambrose means the "word of Christ." Immediately, one thinks of the eucharistic words of the Lord at the Last Supper. Ambrose, however, goes on first to describe the "word of Christ" by which creation came into being. Having drawn attention to this powerful word, he concludes:

> If, then, there is so great a power in the word of the Lord Jesus that things which were not began to exist, then how much more effective that those things previously existing should, without ceasing to exist, be changed into something else?[20]

If creation emerges through the word of Christ, creation that was not in some fashion pre-existent but simply came to be through the divine speaking, how much easier it is to acknowledge the transformation of what already is into the new creation. In *On the Mysteries*, Ambrose continues:

> The Lord Jesus himself cries, "This is my body." Before the blessing of the heavenly words another kind of thing is named, after consecration it is designated "body." He himself speaks of his blood. Before consecration it is spoken of as something else, after consecration it is named "blood." And you say, "Amen," that is, "It is true." What the mouth speaks let the mind within confess; what the speech utters let the affections feel.[21]

This is something novel in the history of eucharistic reflection. From Ambrose onward, the words of consecration become all-important and significant in the history of eucharistic theology. There is no concern in the treatise *On the Sacraments* for an epiclesis, an invocation of the Holy Spirit to effect the transformation of the eucharistic gifts, something normal in the churches of the East. This is probably due to the fact that in the actual eucharistic prayer that Ambrose knows and upon which he comments—something very close textually to the Roman Canon—there was no epiclesis or specific invocation of the Holy Spirit.

If the intellectually curious neophyte were to persist, maintaining that what he sees is wine and nothing more, Ambrose has an answer:

> For just as you took on the likeness of death (Rom. 6.4), so too, you drink the likeness of the precious blood, that there may be no horror of blood, and yet the price of redemption may be effective.[22]

In other words, God has designed the eucharistic gifts, especially the blood of Christ, in terms of "likeness"—he also uses the word "figure"—so that human sensibilities will not be offended. In many ways in these reflections, Ambrose is the forerunner of the doctrine of transubstantiation, avoiding both a crude physicalism and a naïve symbolism about the eucharistic presence of Christ.

Reflecting on the mixture of water with wine in the chalice, Ambrose offers a number of thoughts juxtaposing the Old Testament with the New. For example, the water that flowed from the rock in Exodus 17 and Numbers 20 is connected with First Corinthians 10:4, in a way that is typical of biblical interpretation at the time. Then he comes to the root issue, that the water has a sacramental significance connected to the piercing of the dead Christ's side with a lance, whence flowed blood and water (John 19:31–34): "Why water? Why blood? Water to cleanse, blood to redeem."[23]

Ambrose next takes up the issue of communion. Citing the Song of Songs 1:1, "Let him kiss me with the kiss of his mouth," he applies this beautiful text to eucharistic communion. The altar is "an image of the body of Christ" and eucharistic communion is the kiss of Christ.[24] The sheer intimacy of the kiss gives us an indication of the spiritual and ontological intimacy/union with Christ brought about and sustained in the Eucharist. He interprets Psalm 23, "The Lord is my shepherd," as applying to the Eucharist: "The Lord feeds me and nothing will be lacking to me."[25] Nothing can be lacking since the Lord feeds us with himself.

Conclusion

Both Ambrose and Chrysostom led their congregations into the eucharistic mystery in season and out of season. They preached continuously. Their commitment to preaching, their passion for the body of Christ on the altar and in the poor and marginal continues and strengthens our eucharistic concern today to be both inclusive and morally and liturgically integrated. East and West find in both of them true eucharistic doctors of the church and models of episcopal ministry.

Notes

1. Hans von Campenhausen, *The Fathers of the Church: Combined* edition of the *Fathers of the Greek Church* and *the Fathers of the Latin Church* (Peabody, MA: Hendrickson Publishers, 1998), 157.

2. Ibid., 89.

3. Robert L. Wilken, "John Chrysostom," in Everett Ferguson, ed., *Encyclopedia of Early Christianity* (New York and London: Garland Publishing Co., 1990), 496. See also Robert Wilken, *John Chrysostom and the Jews* (Berkeley: University of California Press, 1983).

4. Wendy Mayer and Pauline Allen, *John Chrysostom* (London and New York: Routledge, 2000), 26.

5. John N. D. Kelly, *Golden Mouth* (Ithaca, NY: Cornell University Press, 1995), 131.

6. Daniel Sheerin, ed., *The Eucharist*, in vol. 7, *Message of the Fathers of the Church* (Wilmington, DE: Michael Glazier, 1986) 291.

7. Ibid., 197.

8. Ibid., 198.

9. Ibid., 204–5.

10. Ibid., 217.

11. 210–14.

12. Mary C. Murray, "They Speak to Us Across the Centuries: Ambrose," *The Expository Times* 109 (1998), 228.

13. Ibid., 228. A clear reproduction of the mosaic of St. Ambrose appears on the cover of Boniface Ramsey, *Ambrose* (New York and London: Routledge, 1997).

14. Ambrose, *Saint Ambrose Letters*, trans. Sister Mary Melchior Beyenka, in vol. 26, *The Fathers of the Church: A New Translation* (Washington, DC: Catholic University of America Press, 1954), 414.

15. Ibid., 102.

16. Raymond Moloney, *The Eucharist* (Collegeville, MN: The Liturgical Press, 1995), 102.

17. Sheerin, *The Eucharist*, 74–85.

18. Ibid., 76.

19. Ibid., 77.

20. Ibid., 78, adapted.

21. Ambrose, *On the Sacraments* and *On the Mysteries*, trans. T. Thomas, ed. J. H. Strawley (London: SPCK, 1950), 148, adapted.

22. Daniel Sheerin, *The Eucharist*, 79.

23. Ibid., 82.

24. Ibid., 83.

25. Ibid.

5.

West and East: Augustine of Hippo and Maximus the Confessor

The first thing to be noted about Augustine is the ecclesial perspective within which he preaches about or discusses the Eucharist. The sacrament is the sacrament of the Body of Christ and is intended for the communion of the one Christ, head and members, a holy communion in the love of God.
–David N. Power[1]

Maximus sees the greater part of the liturgy as a pre-enactment of the final drama of the Parousia and the entry into the life of heaven.
–Geoffrey Wainwright[2]

AUGUSTINE OF HIPPO
(354–430)

Whatever one thinks of him, Augustine is probably the most influential thinker of the patristic period, making an impact on every generation since his own. He is the father about whom more tends to be written than any other, and he is undoubtedly the best-known Latin father of the church.

The life of Augustine is well known because he left us that superb biography, his *Confessions*, and so in the context of this essay on his eucharistic theology, all that needs to be done is to sketch in the merest outline of his life and career.[3] Born at Tagaste, North Africa, in 354 of a pagan father, Patricius, and a

Christian mother, Monica, he received a Christian education and went for further studies to the great center at Carthage. Gradually falling away from his minimal appreciation of Christianity, Augustine took a mistress, to whom he remained faithful for fifteen years. Beginning in 373 he developed an acute interest in philosophy and, in pursuit of truth, became a Manichaean. A gnostic and dualistic religious system, Manichaeism taught that the object of religious commitment was to release the particles of light in the human person, "liberating the light," so to speak. Disillusioned by this system, Augustine moved to Rome, and then later to Milan, where he came under the influence of Bishop Ambrose, the subject of the previous chapter. Absorbing a Neoplatonist philosophy, he found himself moving ever closer to Christianity. He was attracted by Ambrose's sermons, but the one basic obstacle in his path toward baptism was his inability to live a chaste life. Eventually, he was baptized at the Easter Vigil in 387 by Ambrose. He returned to Tagaste in 388, establishing a kind of monastery with some friends. While on a visit to the town of Hippo Regius, the people suddenly presented him to their aging bishop, Valerius, for ordination. It may be argued that ordination for Augustine represented a conversion-like experience every bit as decisive as his experience at Milan when he prepared for baptism. He became a priest in 391 and then bishop of Hippo in 396, presiding over the Church of Hippo until his death in 430, as the barbarian Vandals were storming the gates of the city.

Eucharist, an Overview

First, using the magisterial work of Frederik Van der Meer, let us describe what a Sunday would have been like in Augustine's church. It is impossible to have an exact record of the eucharistic liturgy as it would have been celebrated by Augustine, but from the many allusions and references in his written work it is possible to re-create the basic lineaments of the liturgy, and this is what Van der Meer has done. Here is a wonderfully imaginative but accurate description in Van der Meer of a Sunday morning in Hippo:

> It is a cool Sunday morning; a continuous muffed noise echoes through the white capital city, for except for the ascetics and for those who are both free and well-to-do, there is little in the nature of Sunday rest from servile tasks. Slaves trot through the back streets, the shops are open and the market gardeners and muleteers watch the faithful go up to the great church. The faces of these dark-eyed people seem strangely pale in the sunlight and contrast with their light and usually colourful clothing. People of rank, with their clients about them, bring up the tail of the procession and often come too late. Around the fountain under the parched plane trees there squat the everlasting idlers of this country, who in those days sat near the church as today they sit near the mosque, while high above, on the top of the coping of the basilica, there gleams the golden emblem of the Lord Jesus Christ....Bishop Aurelius Augustinus, with his flaming dark eyes and shaven head, is at this moment sitting in the *secretarium* surrounded by his clergy, and is just concluding his short morning audience, which he is in the habit of giving before Mass....Then Augustine follows a long row of assistants,...passes under the updrawn curtain between two pillars and ascends the apse....The doors still stand open and still the people stream in, but now there is a sudden silence, and from the steps of the apse Augustine greets his people. "The Lord be with you." "And also with you."[4]

The Liturgy of the Word—what Van der Meer calls "the instructional service"—then took place. As the lector ascended the ambo for the readings, the people would have greeted him with the words, "Peace be with you." There is no clear evidence of a gospel procession. After the deacon had finished reading the gospel, Augustine preached for about an hour, the entire worship lasting for about an hour and a half. He would have preached seated on his *cathedra* or chair, with one of the books of scripture open on his knees for commentary and explanation.

After the catechumens had been dismissed, the "sacrifice of the faithful" commenced. It seems that the order of penitents—those who had formally been cut off from receiving holy communion until their period of penance was complete—remained at the back of the church. Augustine now moved with his priests down the steps of the apse to the chancel. The people thronged around him, but outside the chancel or sanctuary. No one knelt (except during Lent) because it was the Lord's Day, commemorating the resurrection, and the fitting posture is standing. After a litany of prayers of petition for all the various ranks of the church, for the emperor and the empire, for the catechumens and the congregation, the sacrifice began.

The altar was prepared by the deacons with the offerings of bread and wine that the faithful had brought. Then Augustine prayed the eucharistic prayer, at the center of which come the words of our Lord at the Last Supper. The living church was prayed for, as were the dead and the martyrs. Once the Lord's Prayer had been completed, the presider introduced the kiss of peace, which the faithful would have exchanged probably on the lips. Communion was distributed first to the children, then to the men, and last of all to the women. The remaining eucharistic elements from the celebration were carried into the *secretarium*, the prayer after communion was prayed and the deacon pronounced the dismissal, "Go in peace."

Augustine did not leave us a treatise on the Eucharist, but rather made reference to the sacrament often in his sermons and writings. For the sake of overview, Augustinian specialists divide his reflections into three periods, periods defined by the major controversies with which he was engaged: 391–400, the Manichaean controversy; 400–12, the Donatist controversy, and 412–30, the Pelagian controversy. Using this schema, let us proceed to make some general remarks about Augustine's eucharistic theology before going to deal in more detail with some of his texts.

The Manichaean Period

Augustine, at the request of friends, replied to a Manichaean pamphlet of a certain Faustus about 398-400—his response, *Against Faustus the Manichee* being his longest anti-Manichaean writing. Faustus and Augustine met, probably toward the end of 382, and it may be that the book Faustus wrote was written against Augustine, who had abandoned Manichaeism. Faustus' object was to demonstrate that Manichaeism was the purest form of Christianity. Against Faustus' rejection and ridicule of the Old Testament, which was in line with gnostic movements generally, Augustine argued for the unity of the Old and New Testaments. He recognized the cult of the Old Testament as a prophecy fulfilled in Christ. The sacrifices of the old Law are taken as figures of the unique sacrifice of Jesus Christ, and of the Eucharist as the sacramental celebration of that sacrifice.

The Donatist Period

Donatism was a religious movement whose origins lay in the persecutions of the church in North Africa. The Donatists separated themselves from the Catholics through their refusal to accept Caecilian, who had been ordained bishop of Carthage in 311. The reason for their refusal to accept Caecilian had to with the fact that his consecrator had been Bishop Felix of Aptunga who had been a *traditor*, one who had handed over the sacred books of scripture for public destruction during the last great persecution of the church under the Emperor Diocletian in 303 and 304. The bishops of Numidia consecrated a rival to Caecilian, a "real" bishop who had stood fast during the persecution, and he in turn was succeeded by Donatus from whom the schism is named.

For the Donatists, the Holy Spirit was present only in their church, which they believed had preserved intact the purity of the Christian faith. They held that there was no valid celebration of baptism or the Eucharist outside of their pure church. Against the Donatists, Augustine explained the validity of the eucharistic sacrifice by the presence of Christ, the unique priest and author of the sacraments. Augustine recognized that the root issue was ecclesiology, the meaning of the church, and so he emphasized the Eucharist as not only the sacrifice of Christ but also the sacrifice of the church. Because the church is the *totus Christus*, the whole Christ Head and members, the Christians can see themselves on the altar.

The Pelagian Period

Pelagius (ca. 350–ca. 425) was probably a British ascetic and theologian who arrived in Rome about 390 and became the leader of a reformist, ascetic group of Christians. In his anti-Pelagian writings Augustine considers the issues of grace, original sin, freedom and predestination. These issues are not on the immediate horizon of eucharistic theology, but, in response to Pelagian theology, Augustine presumes the axiom *lex orandi, lex credendi*, the rule of worship is the foundation of the rule of faith—or, as it might be put today, liturgy is *primary theology*. If liturgy is *primary theology*, then the Eucharist, the very heart and soul of Christian worship, must be the grace-giving center of Christian life.

Eucharistic Texts

Augustine's most important reflections on the Eucharist are to be found in his Easter sermons, and so let us begin with Sermons 227, 228, 228B.[5] Sermon 227, coming in the Pelagian period, is dated Easter, 414–15. The sermon was preached to those who were baptized and received their first communion the night before. Augustine says to them:

> I haven't forgotten my promise. I had promised those of you who have just been baptized a sermon to

explain the sacrament of the Lord's table, which you can see right now, and which you shared in last night.

The sanctified bread and wine are the body and blood of Christ and, affirms Augustine, "If you receive them well, you are yourselves what you receive." These neophytes, just received into the church, are provided with the most profound Christian identity. As the eucharistic elements are the very presence of Christ, so are they, if they receive the elements well. This is the heart of eucharistic ecclesiology, that is, that the Eucharist makes the church. Augustine, going on to comment on the order of the celebration, comes to the introduction to the eucharistic prayer and the words, "Lift up your hearts...."

> If you have become members of Christ, where is your head? Members have a head. If the head hadn't gone ahead before, the members would never follow. Where has our head gone?...So our head is in heaven....[6]

Their union with Jesus Christ, their head, is absolutely real, and that is the reason why they are invited in the liturgy to lift up their hearts and to reply, "We have lifted them up to the Lord." The implication would seem to be that where Christ the head is they are to follow. Christ's grace is pulling them up, as it were, into the heaven where he dwells with the Father and the Spirit.

In Sermon 228, preached perhaps at Easter 420, Augustine uses the powerful metaphor of birth-rebirth to speak of baptism and the Eucharist. Addressing the faithful who have been baptized some time, he tells them that their Christian lives should be examples of faith to the newly born in baptism.

> What ought to be growing strongly in you has been started afresh in them; and you that are already the faithful must set them good examples which can help them to make progress....Being newly born, you see,

they look to you to observe how to live, who were
born a long time ago.[7]

If the faithful are not living as Christ's body, fed and nourished
through the Eucharist, what realistic hope can there be for the
infants of the Easter Vigil? In Sermon 228B Augustine returns to
the change effected in believers through eating the Eucharist:

> And therefore receive and eat the body of Christ,
> yes, you that have become members of Christ in the
> body of Christ; receive and drink the blood of
> Christ....So then, having life in him, you will be one
> flesh with him.[8]

Augustine was fascinated by the dual meaning of Paul's "body of
Christ." It referred to the eucharistic gift and the ecclesial
people. In Sermon 272 he can say to the neophytes, "The mystery that you are lies on the table; it is your own mystery that
you receive."[9]

There emerges throughout all these sermons the strong
sense of union with Christ as his body, and, therefore, an
equally strong sense of union with one another through eating
the eucharistic body. Throughout these three sermons, as well
as in other places, Augustine uses the image of the many grains
of wheat gathered into/made into the one loaf of bread offered
at the Eucharist. This is an image in the Christian tradition that
goes back to the *Didache* (Chapter 9), perhaps later first century.
Eating the one sacramental body of Christ, the believers
become one in the ecclesial Body of Christ.

Moving from the sermons to *City of God*, Book 10,
Chapter 6, we find further treatment of the Eucharist; in fact, it
is Augustine's most comprehensive treatment of the Eucharist as
sacrifice. Augustine begins this section of his book with the
words, "Thus the true sacrifice is offered in every act which is
designed to unite us to God in a holy fellowship...."[10] Here we
have a fine understanding of sacrifice as communion with God.
It is followed by Augustine's elucidations of St. Paul in Romans

12:1: "I appeal to you, therefore, brothers and sisters, by the mercies of God, to present your bodies as a living sacrifice, holy and acceptable to God, which is your spiritual worship." Here is Augustine's comment on the verse:

> If then the body, which the soul employs as a subordinate, like a servant or a tool, is a sacrifice, when it is offered to God for good and right employment, how much more does the soul itself become a sacrifice when it offers itself to God, so that it may be kindled by the fire of love and may lose the "form" of worldly desire, and may be "re-formed" by submission to God as to the unchangeable "form," thus becoming acceptable to God because of what it has received from his beauty.[11]

He takes for granted that along with the body the soul is one of the two constituents of a human being. But he also accepts the Platonic view of the soul, that is to say, that it is a rational, incorporeal substance ruling the body—hence, the body is a subordinate tool or servant of the soul. Body and soul may both be understood as sacrifice. Finally, he comes to the heart of the matter, the proper sacrifice of Christians:

> This is the sacrifice of Christians, who are "many, making up one body in Christ." This is the sacrifice which the Church continually celebrates in the sacrament of the altar, a sacrament well-known to the faithful where it is shown to the Church that she herself is offered in the offering which she presents to God.[12]

Once again we meet the strong realist sense of our union with God in and through the Eucharist. The sacrifice offered to God, the Eucharist, is at the same time the sacrifice of the church, because the church can never be anything other than the whole Christ, head and members. Thus, in this passage from the *City of God*, Augustine considers sacrifice as the entire movement of humankind toward God, and at the heart of this movement stands the Eucharist, in and through which we are "one-d" with the unique sacrifice of Christ. In Book 10, Chapter 20 he says:

> Being the body of which he is the head [the Church] learns to offer itself through him. This is the true sacrifice; and the sacrifices of the saints in earlier times were many different symbols of it.[13]

Finally, let us look at two of Augustine's letters, Letters 54 and 55, written to Januarius, whom he addresses as "most beloved son" but about whom we know nothing. The letters date from about 400, and deal with liturgical matters, especially the date of Easter. In Letter 54 Augustine makes some distinctions about liturgical customs. First, there are those customs that can be found clearly in scripture. They are

> very few in number, very easy of observance, most sublime in their meaning, as, for example, baptism, hallowed by the name of the Trinity, Communion of his Body and Blood, and whatever else is commended in the canonical writings.[14]

Here he is recognizing the two dominical sacraments of baptism and the Eucharist, the notion of seven sacraments coming later in the Middle Ages. In addition to these, one may point to the customs that have come from the apostles themselves or from various church councils—Augustine does not distinguish as we might between ecumenical councils and local or regional synods—such as the "annual commemorations of the Lord's Passion, Resurrection and Ascension into heaven." All of the above are celebrated by the universal church, but there are also customs to be found that are local. Here he points to fasting, which differs from place to place, and the Eucharist:

> Some receive daily the body and blood of the Lord, others receive it on certain days; in some places no

day is omitted in the offering of the holy sacrifice, in others it is offered only on Saturday and Sunday, or even only on Sunday.[15]

Frequent, even daily communion, was customary in the churches of Africa, but not in the eastern Greek-speaking churches. In the longer Letter 55, Augustine is concerned with the date of Easter. He is replying to the question why Easter is not celebrated on the same date every year as Christmas is. The birthday of the Lord at Christmas is celebrated simply as memory, he says, "a recalling of the fact that He was born...."[16] Easter, on the other hand, is not a mere memorial, but is a celebration "in sacrament." He continues:

> We celebrate Easter, so as not only to call to mind what happened—that is, that Christ died and rose again—but we do not pass over the other things about Him which bear witness to the significance of sacraments.[17]

What does he mean by "the other things"? The key lies in his citation of Romans 4:25: "[He] was handed over to death for our trespasses and was raised for our justification." Jesus died to remit our sins, and rose to give us "justification," new life, his own divine life. The passage of Christians to new life occurs at the time of Christ's passage from death to life. Easter is the time for baptism and Eucharist, when people are initiated into the new life that is Christ. The sacraments of initiation enfold them in the paschal mystery of Christ, and so Easter is celebrated "in sacrament."

We cannot leave Augustine's theology of the Eucharist without turning to his account of his mother Monica's burial rites. This occurs in the *Confessions*, 9.13.32. He informs us that the Eucharist was celebrated at her graveside before she was buried. This appears not to have been the practice everywhere, the Eucharist being celebrated after burial rather than as a constitutive part of the burial rites themselves. Monica apparently had asked for the celebration of the Eucharist for the forgiveness of her sins before she died, asking that "we should remember her at your altar, where she had been your servant day after day."[18] David Power comments: "In this way, the prayer that the Church makes for her is based on her own reception of the sacrament. It is a pleading that what Christ guaranteed her in sacramental communion should be efficacious against any onslaughts of Satan that may follow death."[19] She died at Ostia, on her way back to Africa with her now-Christian son, but her concern was not for the place of her burial. Her concern was for eucharistic remembrance. Perhaps Augustine had this memory of Monica in mind when he penned that wonderful passage in the *City of God*, Book 20, Chapter 9, about the place of the dead in the church:

> For the souls of the pious dead are not separated from the Church, which is even now the Kingdom of Christ. Otherwise they would not be commemorated at the altar of God at the time of the partaking of the body of Christ....Why are such steps taken, unless it is because the faithful are still members of this body, even when they have departed this life?[20]

In the Eucharist, Augustine knew himself to be in communion with Monica and all the sainted dead who have gone before us marked with the sign of faith.

MAXIMUS THE CONFESSOR
(580–662)

While most Christians will have heard of St. Augustine of Hippo, not too many will be aware of Maximus the Confessor. Even though it is true that little was known about Maximus the Confessor before the second half of the nineteenth century (though his work was known to students of theology long before this), the same cannot be said of the twentieth century. Many careful studies of Maximus have appeared in recent years.

Maximus was born in Constantinople in 580, just ten years before the great prophet of Islam, Muhammad. He received an excellent education and entered the imperial service, becoming first secretary to the Emperor Heraclius. Shortly thereafter, about 613 or 614, he left the service of the emperor to enter a monastery at Chrysopolis. In 624 he moved to the monastery of St. George at Cyzicus. In 626, as a result of the Persian advance toward Constantinople, Maximus, like many other monks, fled to Crete, and then later about 628 to Carthage in North Africa, where he remained until 645. He was well-known as an adversary of heresy, especially the heresy of monothelitism, the heresy acknowledging only one will in Jesus Christ. His opposition to this heresy was based on the teachings of the Council of Chalcedon, where it was clearly affirmed that Christ is both divine and human. To be human is to have a will, and therefore Christ had a human will and not only a divine will. Maximus' opposition to this heresy did not stem only from a concern for orthodox theological doctrine; he also recognized that if Christ had no human will, then he would have been less than completely human, and this deficit would have implications for salvation. "What is unassumed is unhealed" was the patristic adage about salvation. If no human will is assumed by the Word made flesh, the flawed human will remains unhealed.

Maximus moved to Rome in 645, where he had a considerable influence on the deliberations of the Lateran Council of 649. This was the council that condemned the heresy of monothelitism. The heresy was favored by the imperial authorities, mainly for political reasons, and in 653 Maximus was arrested in Rome, along with Pope Martin I, for his continued opposition to it. Along with the same pope, he was brought to trial in Constantinople for his staunch defense of orthodox Christology, as it had been defined at the Council of Chalcedon in 451. Martin was tried, condemned and sent into exile into the Crimea where he died in 655. Maximus was first tried and exiled, while influence was brought to bear on him to adopt monothelitism. When this failed, he was condemned in 662. He was flogged, his tongue was cut out and his right hand cut off when he continued to refuse to assent to monothelitism. Later that year he died in exile in the Caucasus, at Lazica, on the southeastern shore of the Black Sea.

In this chapter we shall be paying particular attention to Maximus' book the *Mystagogia*, which is his commentary on the Eucharist. He was responsible for two other important works: *Ambigua*—the word means "difficulties"—a series of responses to problems raised by the theology of St. Gregory of Nazianzus; and a series of responses to sixty-five questions mainly concerning the interpretation of scripture. He is certainly no systematic theologian in the contemporary sense. His theology, as described by Andrew Louth, is "tentative, exploratory, meditative, and open to different approaches. It has a certain unity, but it is the unity of vision, with the certitude of being on a pilgrimage, rather than an exclusive, dogmatic certainty."[21]

Theology

Central to Maximus' theology is his understanding of creation and especially of the human person. Creation is a free act of God, an act of love, literally an *ekstasis*, a "standing-out" from God. Commenting on a passage from the *Ambigua* (which is a series of theological soundings on Maximus' part, in response to Gregory of Nazianzus as we have noted), Metropolitan John D. Zizioulas (of Pergamum) writes:

> The idea of *ekstasis* signifies that God is love, and as such he creates an immanent relationship of love *outside himself*. The emphasis placed on the words "outside himself" is particularly important, since it signifies that love as *ekstasis* gives rise not to an emanation...but to an *otherness* of being which is seen as responding and returning to its original cause.[22]

There is no absolute necessity to the fact of creation. Creation need not exist. It exists as an act of love on God's part, but an act of love that come from/stands out from God who is Love, and the final goal of creation is to return to that Love from which it came. God had thus arranged for the entire cosmos out of love, planning to unite this being other than himself in his own divine life, again out of love. However, man turned away from God's plan, throwing this ecstatic ("ek-static") act of love into disarray. Splintering and division were the cosmic results of man's fall. George Maloney describes the fall in these terms:

> All existence is splintered into antipodes of the cre-
> ated world and the uncreated God, the sensible and
> the intelligible, earth and heaven, the world and
> Paradise, masculine and feminine. Instead of unity as
> willed by God, the cosmic reality of death that so
> graphically separates man's soul from his body reigns
> over the universe, separating and dividing what was
> meant to be united.[23]

This helpful summary of Maximus' view by Maloney clearly indicates that man is at the heart of creation in more ways than one. He was intended to be the very vital center of creation by God, but through sin he infected not only himself in relation to God's plan, but also all of creation. What God intended to be concordant harmony has become through human sin discordant, divisive diversity. Louth notes that Maximus perceived that, after the fall, "humankind no longer holds together the diversity of the cosmos. The glory of the cosmos, the reflection of God's own glory, is no longer evident."[24] So, what is this creature "man," and what is his definition and responsibility vis-à-vis the rest of creation?

Maximus, like all the patristic writers before him, develops his anthropology from holy scripture and from Greek philosophical thought. He interweaves these two sources of scripture and philosophy with such ease that it seems the one was made for the other. At the very center of creation is the human person. Man is psychophysical, that is to say, a being composed of body and soul, and the soul of man is tripartite: *nous*, the intellect; *thymos*, the passionate part; *epithymia*, the desiring part of man.

This concept is not particularly new. One will find similar approaches in Origen of Alexandria and Evagrius Ponticus, foundational thinkers for the eastern Greek tradition. What is far more interesting about Maximus' understanding of the person-in-creation is his notion of man as a microcosm and cosmic mediator.[25] It is in this respect that humankind has the responsibility and role, in Christ, of restoring concordant harmony to creation.

In *Ambigua* 10, man is said to be the last-made of all creatures because he was to be their natural link, their *syndesmos*, summoned to bring into unity that which was by nature differentiated, but not divisive.[26] Man preferred darkness over the light and abandoned his link-role with and for creation. It was Jesus Christ, as God-man, who fulfilled man's unifying and mediating role, becoming the divine *syndesmos*, the one man in true relationship with God and with the cosmos. Jesus Christ, to use the Pauline term, is the Second Adam, since he is Adam as God intended him to be and as man's true aspiration. Inserted into Christ, humanity shares by grace in this new Adamic form, participates in Christ's mode of existence. The linking and healing of creation thus begins with Christ and ends at the Parousia. Between the incarnation/resurrection stands the church as God's healing agency. At the heart of this ongoing transfiguration that is the church is the Eucharist. This is how Maloney puts it:

> It is the Church that exposes to us the Incarnate Christ, living in his glorious resurrected life to be encountered by us through the sacraments. Baptism administered by the Church opens to us the fruit of the Incarnation. But it is especially in the reception of the Divine Logos and High Priest in the Holy Eucharist that man is deified and is able to fulfill his priestly function of making all things holy.[27]

Let us now turn to Maximus' understanding of the Eucharist as the healing center of man and, therefore, of creation.

Eucharist

The principal text with which we will be concerned is *The Church's Mystagogy*. The text contains Maximus' explanation of the symbolism of the divine synaxis, that is, the entire celebration of the Eucharist.[28] Right away in Maximus we get a sense of the liturgy, not as an intramural exercise of the church to satisfy the religious-ritual needs of its members, but of something that is sheerly cosmic in scope. Through this action, the divinization, the completion-in-God of the cosmos is being both signified and effected.

As Maximus proceeds, he refers constantly to "a certain grand old man" whose reflections on the liturgy he cherishes. Scholars continue to try to establish his identity; for example, some make the case for St. Sophronius who had been Maximus' religious superior when he was in Carthage. Others feel it is a reference to Denys the Areopagite, who was a profound influence on Maximus' theology. We simply do not know who he is, and, indeed, it may be a literary fiction, an expression of modesty on Maximus' part.

His theology of the church, as one would expect from a Byzantine theologian, is very high:

> All are born into the Church and through it are reborn and recreated in the Spirit. To all in equal measure it gives and bestows one divine form and designation, to be Christ's and to carry his name.[29]

All in the church have equally received the divine form and designation; all are Christ's. This is important in Maximus, because, as he makes his way through the various parts of the liturgy, he duly acknowledges the role and function of the bishop, the high priest, but also emphasizes that the entire church has been remade in Christ's Spirit, and is equally Christ's. Different roles, but the one divine calling for all. The liturgy of the church is cosmic because the church itself is cosmic:

> It possesses the divine sanctuary as heaven and the beauty of the nave as earth. Likewise the world is a church since it possesses heaven corresponding to a sanctuary, and for a nave it has the adornment of the earth.[30]

Implicitly, all of creation, the entire cosmos, is involved in the Divine Liturgy. The world looks like a church, with the sky as its sanctuary, and the earth as its nave. Within the church building itself this cosmic symbolism is continued, the sanctuary or chancel is heaven and the nave is earth. This cosmic-liturgical arrangement of the church reflects the human person:

> Holy Church is like a man because for the soul it has the sanctuary, for mind it has the divine altar, and for body it has the nave. It is thus the image and likeness of man who is created in the image and likeness of God.[31]

When worship occurs, when the divine Eucharist is being celebrated, this is no isolated action of the disciples of Jesus, but rather these disciples give voice to the whole of creation, the cosmos, acknowledging its divine origin and goal.

One may think of the holy scriptures in a similar fashion.

> The entire holy Scripture taken as a whole [is like] a man with the Old Testament as body and the New Testament as spirit and mind....The historic letter of the entire holy Scripture, Old Testament and New, is a body while the meaning of the letter and the purpose to which it is directed is the soul.[32]

Comparing the scriptures to a human being is not new with Maximus, and may be found in other writers since the time of Origen. The purpose of scripture, for Origen, is to make known the hidden doctrines that will enable the soul to make progress toward perfection. One might put it like this: that the physical text of scripture is the secondary narrative husk within which may be found the primary kernel of spiritual truth. Maximus shares Origen's perspective.

Thus far, Maximus has been providing general guidelines for understanding what the liturgy is about. Now we approach the entrance rites.

> The first entrance of the bishop into the holy church
> for the sacred synaxis is a figure and image of the first
> appearance in the flesh of Jesus Christ the Son of
> God and our Savior in this world.[33]

Although the bishop shares with his people the equal measure of the Holy Spirit, nevertheless, he images the Christ of the incarnation in his entrance into the church. He is a sacrament of the incarnate Christ, and just as Christ preached conversion to the people of old, now the people, in their physical entrance into the church building, symbolize their conversion to Christ.

> The entrance of the people into the church with the
> bishop represents the conversion of the unfaithful
> from faithlessness to faith and from sin and error to
> the recognition of God as well as the passage of the
> faithful from vice and ignorance to virtue and
> knowledge.[34]

The Liturgy of the Word now takes place, climaxing in the reading of the gospel, after which the bishop preaches. The bishop's task in preaching is to take the kernel of scripture out of the husk, so as to present it to the faithful, enabling their spiritual progress. That for Maximus is "gnostic contemplation," the kind of gnosis/knowledge that characterizes the spiritually mature.

The catechumens are now dismissed as the Liturgy of the Eucharist, "the nuptial chamber of Christ," is prepared. The spiritual kiss, the kiss of peace, is exchanged. Maximus describes its meaning in beautiful terms:

> The spiritual kiss which is extended to all prefigures and portrays the concord, unanimity, and identity of views which we shall all have among ourselves in faith and love at the time of the revelation of the ineffable blessings to come.[35]

The kiss anticipates the Parousia, "the ineffable blessings to come," when God is all in all. That will be a time of concord, heart with heart, unanimity and identity of views, but Maximus implies that if the spiritual kiss now anticipates this final consummation, then something of this concord and unanimity should be a present experience among worshippers. The Trisagion, that is, the thrice Holy of the Sanctus, reminds the congregation of that "union and equality of honor" that will be theirs with all the angels at the End.

Maximus proceeds to comment on holy communion without any word on the eucharistic prayer. This is passed over in silence. Since at this time the eucharistic prayer was recited silently in the Byzantine liturgy, perhaps Maximus thought it appropriate to pass over it with due respectful silence in his liturgical commentary. Be that as it may, Maximus is outstanding in his words on holy communion:

> After this, as the climax of everything, comes the distribution of the sacrament, which transforms into itself and renders similar to the causal good by grace and participation those who worthily share in it. To them is there lacking nothing of this good that is possible and attainable for men, so that they also can be and be called gods by adoption through grace because all of God entirely fills them and leaves no part of them empty of his presence.[36]

Behind these words lies a powerful sense of the metamorphosis that the Eucharist brings about, and, therefore, of what we have come to call the "real presence." Those who receive the Eucharist worthily "can be called gods by adoption through grace." The Eucharist divinizes those who receive it; they share in the very life of the Trinity by grace, because "all of God entirely fills them and leaves no part of them empty of his presence."

Conclusion

Arguably, it is Augustine's doctrine of the Eucharist—about which he never wrote an entire treatise—that is at the heart of our tasting and enjoying God, and our being healed. His great speculative work on the Trinity, the thirteen-years-in-the-making *City of God*—indeed, all Augustine's works find their divinizing focus in this ritual of sharing the blessed bread and cup. Through this ritual we, too, stand in the same tradition of Catholic eucharistic faith—that is to say, that in the Eucharist Christ is not changed into us as is ordinary food, but we are changed into him. Augustine's great contribution and emphasis lies in our being changed into Christ by the eucharistic gifts, and our being communioned one with one another here and now.

A Maximian eucharistic spirituality speaks especially to our times with the concern today for relationality, for the environment, for the healing of relationships between men and women. The Eucharist as the heart of the person-in-the-church is the healing link with the cosmos. This eucharistic healing, "this cosmic liturgy," as Andrew Louth has it, "is the reality of the humblest celebration of the divine liturgy."[37] The healing, begun and advanced here and now in every celebration of the Eucharist, reaches its finale at the Parousia, when God-in-Christ-through-the-Spirit is all in all.

Notes

1. David N. Power, *The Eucharistic Mystery* (New York: Crossroad, 1992), 151–52.

2. Geoffrey Wainwright, *Eucharist and Eschatology*, 2nd ed. (London: Epworth Press, 1978), 73.

3. See Peter Brown, *Augustine of Hippo: A Biography* (Berkeley and Los Angeles: University of California Press, 1967).

4. Frederik Van der Meer, *Augustine the Bishop* (London: Sheed and Ward, 1961), 388–89.

5. Following the order and translation of Edmund Hill, in St. Augustine, *Sermons on the Liturgical Seasons*, vol. 6 (184–229Z), in *The Works of St. Augustine: A Translation for the Twenty-first Century*, trans. Edmund Hill, OP, ed. John E. Rotelle, OSA (New York: New City Press, 1993), 254–72.

6. Both quotes are from St. Augustine, *Sermons on the Liturgical Seasons*, vol. 6: 254.

7. Ibid., 257.

8. Ibid., 262.

9. Ibid., vol. 3: 258.

10. St. Augustine, *Concerning the City of God Against the Pagans*, trans. Henry Bettenson (Harmondsworth: Penguin Books, 1984), 379.

11. Ibid.

12. Ibid., 380.

13. Ibid., 381.

14. St. Augustine, *Letters 1–82*, trans. Wilfred Parsons, in *Fathers of the Church*, vol. 12 (Washington, DC: Catholic University Press, 1951), 252.

15. Ibid., 253.

16. Ibid., 261.

17. Ibid.

18. See St. Augustine, *Confessions*, trans. Henry Chadwick, IX.13.36 (Oxford and New York: Oxford University Press, 1998), 177.

19. Power, *The Eucharistic Mystery*, 156.

20. St. Augustine, *Concerning the City of God Against the Pagans*, 916.

21. Andrew Louth, "They Speak to Us Across the Centuries: 4, St. Maximos the Confessor," *The Expository Times* 109 (1998), 101.

22. John D. Zizioulas, *Being as Communion* (Crestwood, NY: St. Vladimir's Seminary Press, 1985), 93.

23. George Maloney, *The Cosmic Christ: From Paul to Teilhard* (New York: Sheed and Ward, 1968), 169.

24. Louth, "They Speak to Us Across the Centuries," 102.

25. See Lars Thunberg, *Microcosm and Mediator: The Theological Anthropology of Maximus the Confessor*, 2nd. (Chicago: Open Court Publishing Company, 1995).

26. An English translation of this Maximian text may be found in Andrew Louth, *Maximus the Confessor* (London and New York: Routledge, 1996), 94–154.

27. Maloney, *The Cosmic Christ*, 177.

28. I am following the text as it appears in George C. Berthold, ed., *Maximus Confessor: Selected Writings* (Mahwah, NJ: Paulist Press, 1985), 183–225.

29. Berthold, *Maximus Confessor*, 187.

30. Ibid., 189.

31. Ibid., 189–190.

32. Ibid., 195.

33. Ibid., 198.

34. Ibid.

35. Ibid., 202.

36. Ibid., 203.

37. Louth, *Maximus the Confessor*, 77.

PART TWO:
The Middle Ages

6.

The Celtic Witness and John Scottus Eriugena

One way in which Celtic texts are important is that they alert us to possibilities of Christian existence subtly different from our own, which are both ancient and new.
–Oliver Davies[1]

Johannes Scottus Eriugena has a good claim to be considered the greatest Celtic thinker who ever lived.
–John Macquarrie[2]

The last quarter century has witnessed a renaissance of interest in all things Celtic, not least in Celtic Christianity and theology. The fundamental question is, "What is Celtic Christianity?" The scholars warn against the attempt to posit a distinctive Celtic church over against the Western church as such: "In truth…the Western Church was united as one Church until the Reformation, and what might be construed as a conflict between the 'Celtic Church' and the 'Roman Catholic Church' was in fact competition between different trends and traditions within a single and still united Church," says Oliver Davies.[3] Although "Celtic" may be applied variously and legitimately to a diverse number of peoples and languages and geographical locations, in this presentation it will be taken in a narrow sense to refer to the church and Christian culture of Ireland, Scotland and Wales. The liturgical interest, however, will be exclusively Irish because our major liturgical source is Irish.

Ireland, never conquered by the Romans, never part of the Roman Empire, had a Christian presence prior to the arrival of the missionary St. Patrick, but the new faith began to take root far and wide on the island after his death. Unlike the countries of "Roman" Europe, the evangelization of Ireland was marked by the spread of monasticism, in contrast to the large urban, episcopal centers of the Mediterranean world. From the sixth century onward monasteries became the center of Irish Christianity. Oliver Davies and Fiona Bowie, scholars of Celtic Christianity, draw attention to four major characteristics of Celtic Christianity, traditional characteristics from which contemporary Christians may also learn.

The first is the physical dimension of Celtic Christianity, its penitential tradition in particular. This is a self-imposed discomfort and deprivation as a way to God. While penance may be out of favor among many contemporary Christians, Davies and Bowie argue that it is "a way of including the body in our dialogue with God."[4]

Second is the Celtic emphasis on the place of nature within the Christian revelation. The natural world has come from God and is, therefore, a place where God may be found. There is no principled dichotomy between nature and supernature, the world of nature and the world of grace, but rather they are best seen as a continuum. This attitude gives rise to a permeative sense of God's presence so that "the Celt was very much a God-intoxicated man whose life was embraced on all sides by the divine Being. But this presence was always mediated through some finite, this worldly reality so that it would be difficult to imagine a spirituality more down to earth than this one."[5] For the Celt, there is no distance from the Divine.

The third characteristic has to do with art, much valued by the Celts. "The place of the scribe within early Irish society and the belief of Welsh poets that the Holy Spirit was their direct inspiration remind us that the creative arts stood not at the margins of the Church but at its very centre," note the authors of *Celtic Christian Spirituality*.[6]

Finally, there is the spirit of community. Celtic Christianity was a communal Christianity, expressed in its monastic form, but also in the close-knit fabric of Celtic society. Ultimately, this sense of community(-ion) is rooted in the Divine Communion, the Trinity, which held a special place in Celtic thought and art.

The Lord's Day

Three catecheses from the ninth century provide us with a sense of what the Lord's Day meant at this time in Celtic Christianity.[7] What is immediately striking about the theology of Sunday is its broad richness. Here is no narrow construal of Sunday along Sabbatarian lines, but a stimulating, many-faceted, patristic approach to Sunday. Sunday is the day of the paschal mystery, of the resurrection, the day of Pentecost, the day of many other well-known themes in Christian literature. Perhaps less well-known is the notion of Sunday as the great day of creation:

> Now it is impossible to doubt that the Lord's day is the first day, for it is written that in six days the world was made and God rested on the seventh day; this seventh day is called the Sabbath. Now as the Mother of the Lord holds the first place among all women, so among the rest of the days of all the days, the Lord's Day is greatest; thus we do not call the Lord's Day the eighth day, but the first day.[8]

The Lord's Day is, so to speak, the "mother" of days, because this day saw God's act of creation, beautifully described by Thomas O'Loughlin as "the primordial miracle in that it is the primordial free act of divine love."[9]

From our perspective of eucharistic theology it is note-worthy that the three catecheses, while they are resonant of various eucharistic themes such as the manna in the desert and the miraculous feeding of the multitude with loaves and fishes, do not mention the actual celebration of the Eucharist as such. True, one of the catecheses says that the Lord's day is the day "on which the people come together to the church," but it does not go on to enunciate the purpose, "to celebrate the Eucharist." A curious omission! O'Loughlin surmises, and this seems borne out by the Stowe Missal, as we shall see, that the Celtic emphasis is on what God has done for us in creation and redemption, rather than on what *we* do, our human response.[10] The utter priority of God's grace is the meaning of the Lord's Day, and so, therefore, of the Eucharist.

Eucharist: The Stowe Missal

The eschatological sense of the Eucharist, that it is our participation in the heavenly liturgy of the Jerusalem above, remained a constant feature of eucharistic theology throughout the first millennium. It fell into the background in western eucharistic theology some time between the eleventh and thirteenth centuries.

Attention is now drawn to the Stowe Missal, named as such because it once belonged in the personal collection of the Marquis of Buckingham, of Stowe House, Buckinghamshire.[11] In all likelihood, this missal originated from the monastery of Tallaght in County Dublin, in the late eighth or early ninth centuries. Monasteries then were not quite what we think of monasteries as being now. The Celtic monastery was a huge complex—for all practical purposes, a small town and college and center of religious devotion. It was far from being, in simplistic terms, a retreat from the world, but much more like an incarnational embracing of the world, with the requisite balance between prayer and action. The Tallaght monastery represented a reform movement within Irish monasticism that had the name of the Celi De, the "clients of God," sometimes put into English as "Culdee." The reform of the Celi De may have risen to counteract what was perceived as a growing laxity among the older churches of the country. The Stowe Missal came out of this context of renewal and, says O'Loughlin, represents "the energy of a young community with a clear image of itself as leaders and exemplars of the monastic life."[12] Though it exemplifies essentially the Roman rite, there are aspects of the eucharistic celebration in the Stowe Missal that are worthy of comment in their own right.

The Litany and the Communion of Saints

The Eucharist begins with a Litany of the Saints, a litany that is very revealing of this community. The litany takes the place, pretty much, of the penitential rite at the beginning of Mass. The community assembles to celebrate the Lord's Supper, recognizes its profound unworthiness and calls upon the saints to intercede for them. The litany itself is too long to cite here, but we will focus on its more interesting inclusions. It begins with a basic confession of sin:

> We have sinned, O Lord. We have sinned.
> Spare us from our sins. Save us.[13]

The first in the list of saints who are asked to pray for the community is our Lady, and next are the apostles. Mary was present at the birth of the church at Pentecost with the apostles (Acts 1:14), and the Twelve themselves were present at the Last Supper. Who better than these original eucharistic ecclesial Christians to be with the community as it repeats this foundational action of the Eucharist! Then follow the Irish saints: Patrick, Brigit and Columba, and the many lesser-known Irish monastic saints. "These are the intercessors that we should expect....These were the actual intercessors whom in their everyday lives they were seeking to follow and be in communion with; these were the saints whose power they had heard of not just in books, but from stories 'down the road,'" O'Loughlin notes.[14] Asking the saints in litany for assistance had more than simply a penitential meaning. This was the family to which the worshippers belonged through grace, to which they were moving throughout life, to be fully joined with after death. This eucharistic litany of the saints tells us that we are never alone, and more: "To truly be and become yourself, you need the ancient radiance of others."[15]

One Bread, One Cup, One Body

Nor can you be yourself without the others who are here and now in the terrestrial Body of Christ. Their contemporary radiance is no less necessary for the Christian. The Stowe Missal seems to assume one large eucharistic bread that was broken for the communion of the congregation. The symbolism is expressed in First Corinthians 10:17, where St. Paul writes: "Because there is one bread, we who are many are one body, for we all partake of the one bread." In the Irish homily in the missal, the bread was broken symbolically into five, seven, eight, nine, eleven, twelve and thirteen pieces. Here is a portion of the text:

> The confraction is of seven kinds, that is, five pieces of the common Host as a figure of the five senses of the soul; seven of the Host of saints and virgins, except the chief ones, as a figure of the seven gifts of the Holy Spirit; eight pieces of the martyrs' host as a figure of the eight sections of the New Testament; nine of the Host of Sunday as a figure of the nine households of heaven and the nine grades of the church.[16]

The eight sections of the New Testament are the four gospels plus Acts, the Catholic epistles, the Pauline epistles and the Book of Revelation. The nine households of heaven are the nine ranks of angels, made popular through the work of the Pseudo-Dionysius. Thus, the reason for this complicated fraction was catechetical, reminding people of various aspects of Christian doctrine. As O'Loughlin further points out, "All these breakings taken together allowed the loaf to be broken into 65 pieces which [the Missal] says is the number for Christmas, Easter and Pentecost. So here we have a possible number for the expected congregation at the Eucharist on the great feasts."[17]

While the fraction of the consecrated bread was taking place—because it would have taken some time to complete—there was an interesting prayer inserted, both to fill up the time of the fraction and to explain its meaning to the assembly:

> They knew it was the Lord. Alleluia;
> In the breaking up of the loaf, Alleluia.
> The loaf we break is the body of Jesus Christ, our
>   Lord, Alleluia;
> The chalice we bless is the blood of Jesus Christ, our
>   Lord, Alleluia;
> For the remission of sins, Alleluia.
> Lord, let your mercy rest upon us, Alleluia.
> They knew it was the Lord, Alleluia;
> In the breaking up of the loaf, Alleluia.
> O Lord, we believe that in this breaking of your body
>   and pouring out of
> your blood we become your redeemed people;
> We confess that in taking the gifts of this pledge
>   here, we lay hold in hope
> of enjoying its true fruits in the heavenly places.[18]

No doubt the prayer was repeated over and over until the fraction was complete. We notice immediately the eschatological emphasis of the prayer. The Eucharist anticipates the reality of the Parousia.

St. Paul in the same Corinthian passage seems to intend one eucharistic cup when he says: "The cup of blessing that we bless, is it not a sharing in the blood of Christ?" (1 Cor 10:16). The Derrynaflan Chalice, discovered in 1980 and dated to about the late eighth or early ninth centuries, like the Stowe Missal, may well be the "one cup" used for the Eucharist. Its handles easily allow it to be passed from the minister to the communicant, and it might have held somewhere in the region of 1.5 liters of wine. It provides about the same number of mouthfuls as the altar bread assumed for communion, enough for about 65 people.[19]

Communion with Christ

The duration of time needed for the distribution of communion (and the clearing away of the vessels afterward) would have varied, depending on the number of communicants. The Stowe Missal provided for this time period with a catena of "eucharistic" texts, principally from the gospels and from the Psalms. The thrust of the biblical texts is on the person being taken into communion with Christ; that is to say, on the divine movement in the action, rather than on the assembly's taking of communion.

JOHN SCOTTUS ERIUGENA
(ca. 810–ca. 870)

The dates of Eriugena's birth and death are uncertain, as are so many other aspects of his life. He was certainly born in the first quarter of the ninth century, and arrived at the court of the Carolingian Emperor Charles the Bald in the 840s, where he taught at the palace school. There is no reference to his being a cleric, and in all likelihood he was just an ordinary monk. He was able to read Greek with ease, a skill not shared by many of his peers, and, at the Emperor Charles' request, translated the influential works of Pseudo-Dionysius into Latin. His most important personal work is probably his *Periphyseon*, in which he sets out the main lineaments of his thinking about God and reality.

Traditionally, Creator and creation are understood as quite discrete and separate in Christian theology. In the strict sense of the word, God is uncreated, and yet, for Eriugena, in the very act of creating God creates God's own self, as it were. "This means that God, as cause, is the essence of all things; outside of God there is nothing," he wrote.[20] Everything has the same beginning in God, and everything will have the same end in God. In creation God becomes "not-God," through a process of going out from God. All being, therefore, is from God and in

God.[21] Although it may sound like it, this is not a version of pantheism, but the traditional doctrine that everything that is exists by participation in the divine, for Eriugena the super-essential being of God. This emphasis on the divine immanence in all creation harmonizes in general with the themes of Neoplatonic philosophy, but it may also find its source in the immanence of God that is characteristic of Celtic spirituality, already noted above.[22]

God-in-Christ-through-the-Spirit is everywhere, and everywhere is in the Triune God. Eriugena has a strong sense of the Trinity, not only from revelation, but also from reason. Everything in the created order, through its divine origin and the divine presence, has the capacity to be a theophany of God. A theophany is not merely some passive sign, as it were, of God in creation, but rather an active communication and invitation from God to humankind to move in the direction of God, toward deification. The entire universe is sacramental.[23] This is how Eriugena himself puts it:

> Love is a bond or chain by which the totality of all things is bound together in ineffable friendship and indissoluble unity....Rightly, therefore, is God called Love since he is the Cause of all love and is diffused through all things and gathers all things together in one and involves them in himself in an ineffable return, and brings to an end in himself the motions of love of the whole creation.[24]

Eriugena's theophanic sacramental perspective may superficially seem to dispense with the need for sacraments. If nature is sacramental in and of itself, what need is there for specific ecclesiastical sacraments? Though he does not put it this way, Eriugena would probably have replied that the sacramentality of creation is for the sacramentality of the church, especially as expressed in *the* sacramental actions. The church is the vanguard of the *reductio* of everything to God. The sacramentality of the church expresses here and now, and promotes the final, that is the eschatological sacramentality of the creation. The church is formed by the sacraments that flowed from the pierced side of the Lord, "the blood for the consecration of the chalice, the water for that of baptism."[25] Here, too, we find the motif of God's ecstatic love. Eriugena writes: *"Propter ecclesiam venit, ut haberet sponsam venit,* He comes on account of the church, he comes so that he may have her as his spouse."[26]

Eriugena himself composed a treatise on the Eucharist, a treatise that has been lost. Putting together eucharistic fragments from other Eriugena writings, one Eriugena scholar offers us something of a synthesis:

> He could say that believers are crucified with Christ when they enter into his mysteries, and immolate him spiritually, and receive him not with the mouth but with the mind. To the outward senses of carnal men the sacrament remains ordinary bread; but for those who can ascend to the height of spiritual understanding, it is transfigured into a spiritual morsel, abiding eternally, made into the mystery of the Lord's body and blood.[27]

The "spiritual" nature of the eucharistic presence underscored here reflects in general Eriugena's sense that the process of deification is a process of spiritualization, but it may also respond to the "physicalist" understanding of Paschasius of Corbie, an understanding of eucharistic presence that was fast gaining ground at this time.[28] At the time when Eriugena was at the court of Charles the Bald in the mid-ninth century, Charles had received Paschasius' treatise, *On the Body and Blood of Christ.* It may be that Eriugena was instrumental in surfacing the questions about this "physicalist" treatise that led to Paschasius' fellow-monk Ratramnus' more "symbolist" response.

Conclusion

The Celts did not produce a eucharistic doctor like those we have been looking at in this book, not even in John Scottus Eriugena. However, they give witness to a eucharistic Christianity with its own particular emphases. While theology on mainland Europe began to move into a phase of eucharistic exploration, it seems fair to say that the Celts, exemplified mainly in the Stowe Missal, evince a eucharistic practice, within a distinctive spirituality, that was far from narrow. It was rooted and founded in a communal and eschatological vision. And, finally, the backdrop to this eucharistically present Christ was the presence of God in all of creation. Perhaps we might say that the Celtic genius was to hold together simultaneously a "macro-eucharistic" picture with a "micro-eucharistic picture."

Notes

1. Adapted from Oliver Davies, with Thomas O'Loughlin, ed., *Celtic Spirituality* (New York/Mahwah, NJ: Paulist Press, 1999), 25.

2. John Macquarrie, *In Search of Deity: An Essay in Dialectical Theism* (London: SCM Press, 1984), 85.

3. Oliver Davies and Fiona Bowie, *Celtic Christian Spirituality: An Anthology of Medieval and Modern Sources* (New York: The Continuum Publishing Company, 1995), 3.

4. Ibid., 20.

5. John Macquarrie, *Paths in Spirituality*, 2nd ed. (Harrisburg, PA: Morehouse Barlow, 1992), 156.

6. Davies and Bowie, *Celtic Christian Spirituality*, 20.

7. Thomas O'Loughlin, "The Significance of Sunday: Three Ninth-Century Catecheses," *Worship* 64 (1990): 533–44.

8. Ibid., 536.

9. Ibid., 542.

10. Ibid., 543.

11. A selection of texts from the Stowe Missal may be found in Davies, *Celtic Spirituality*, 311–18.

12. Thomas O'Loughlin, *Celtic Theology: Humanity, World and God in Early Irish Writings* (New York and London: The Continuum Publishing Co., 2000), 130.

13. Ibid., 137–39.

14. Ibid., 140–41.

15. John O'Donohue, *Anam Cara: A Book of Celtic Wisdom* (New York: HarperCollins, 1997), 85.

16. Cited in Davies, *Celtic Spirituality*, 312.

17. O'Loughlin, *Celtic Theology*, 135.

18. Ibid., 142.

19. Ibid., 136.

20. John Scottus Eriugena, *Periphyseon* 454A and 452C, cited in Deirdre Carabine, *John Scottus Eriugena* (New York and Oxford: Oxford University Press, 2000), 34.

21. *Periphyseon* 683A-B.

22. See Macquarrie, *In Search of Deity*, 85.

23. G. S. M. Walker, "Eriugena's Conception of the Sacraments," in Geoffrey J. Cuming, ed., *Studies in Church History*, vol. 3 (Leiden: E. J. Brill, 1966), 154.

24. *Periphyseon* 519B and D, cited in Macquarrie, *In Search of Deity*, 96.

25. *Periphyseon*, 836D, cited in Walker, "Eriugena's Conception of the Sacraments," 155.

26. In his [Eriugena's] *Commentary on John*, 326C.

27. Walker, "Eriugena's Conception of the Sacraments," 158.

28. See Owen F. Cummings, *Eucharistic Soundings* (Dublin: Veritas Publications, 1999), 30–40.

7.

Two Parisian Professors: Hugh of St. Victor and Cardinal Robert Pullen

Hugh of St. Victor was the most influential of the several scholars of this period who labored to recover the teaching of earlier centuries on the Eucharist.
—Gary Macy[1]

The evidence taken together permits the tentative hypothesis that the term "transubstantiation" was first introduced at Paris around 1140, and that Robert Pullen was its inventor.
—Joseph Goering[2]

HUGH OF ST. VICTOR
(1096–1142)

The Abbey School of St. Victor in Paris produced two very fine theologians in the twelfth century: the Scotsman Richard of St. Victor, and his older contemporary, Hugh, perhaps from the Low Countries. This house of Augustinian canons was founded by William of Champeaux (ca. 1070–1121), the philosopher who taught in various Paris schools until humiliated by his most famous student, Peter Abelard, in 1108. Abelard claimed to have put William to flight from the schools to seek refuge in the clois-ter. Whatever the truth of that claim, William set out to pursue a life of contemplation and teaching at a deserted chapel on the

Left Bank, just outside the walls of Paris. The foundation was named after St. Victor, the martyr of Marseilles. The abbey school received its charter from King Louis VI in 1113, and soon grew into a significant center of cultural and intellectual life. It was here that Hugh entered about the year 1115. Little is known of his life. It would seem that, once he entered the abbey, Hugh never left it, with the one exception of a visit to the court of Pope Innocent II. He remained at St. Victor until his death in 1142.

From about 1120 onward, Hugh was the leading theologian of the school of St. Victor. The medievalist David E. Luscombe remarks that "unlike Abelard, [Hugh] gained no known enemies."[3] This was quite an accomplishment at a time when reputations and enemies were rapidly made and easily broken. It is certainly interesting that when Abelard was condemned at the local Synod of Sens, Hugh took no part in that condemnation.

Theology

Hugh's written work covers a very wide field: the arts, theology and commentaries on Holy Scripture. He told his students: "Learn everything; you will see afterwards that nothing is superfluous and that there is no joy in a knowledge that is cramped and narrow."[4] His principal philosophical work, the *Didascalion*, is composed of seven books in which he treats of the liberal arts (three books), theology (three books), and religious meditation (one book). Yet all of the arts and all of learning serve to promote a greater understanding of scripture and theology. His work is pervaded by the spirit of the fathers, especially St. Augustine, so much so that he has been described as "the second Augustine."

For centuries western scholars and theologians had sought out the mystical or spiritual sense of scripture, but with Hugh the literal sense of the text comes into its own. He taught that "history is the beginning and foundation of sacred doctrine."[5] Hugh was not opposed to the spiritual meaning of scripture, nor to its use in doctrine, but held that the foundations must first be laid. The foundations have to do with the literal or historical meaning of the text. At that time French Jews were experiencing something of a renaissance in biblical studies, due in no small part to the great Rabbi Solomon ben Isaac, better known from the initials of his name as Rashi (1040–1105). Rashi, appointed rabbi in his home city of Troyes, set out to ascertain the literal meaning of the text of the Old Testament, and his commentaries were used in the school of St. Victor. It may have been that Hugh consulted Jewish rabbis on the meaning of the Hebrew text.

In the second half of the 1120s one of his students named Lawrence wrote down Hugh's lectures. Once a week Hugh personally reviewed Lawrence's work as it was proceeding, and these lectures were the basis of Hugh's *On the Sacraments of the Christian Faith*, written about 1130–37. What Hugh means by "sacraments" in this text is much broader than our modern understanding. It includes all the holy things spoken of in scripture and revelation, the history of salvation and also what we normally mean by "sacrament."

Hugh's theology stands in sharp contrast with other institutions of Christian learning at the time. His theology was christocentric, ecclesial and sacramental, in contrast to theology that was metaphysical, anthropological, psychological and moral. It is tempting to see the philosopher-theologian Peter Abelard as representing the schools and universities, and Hugh as standing for the more monastic and contemplative practice of theology. If Hugh encouraged his students to learn everything, it was because of his strong christocentric vision. If everything came to be through the Word, then the study of anything has the potential to lead us to the Word. The Word is written in nature and scripture. Philosophy is concerned with nature, which reflects the perfections of God. Theology is concerned with scripture, the sacred page, and neglects neither reason nor faith. The ultimate goal is the union of the soul with God, and if nature and scripture are read correctly, they will lead the Christian soul to prayerful understanding of and union with

God. It is from Hugh's lectures, *On the Sacraments of the Christian Faith*, that we shall be presenting Hugh's eucharistic theology.[6]

Eucharist

Gary Macy writes that "of all the masters of the twelfth-century schools, none produced a theology of the Eucharist as rich and consistent as that of Hugh."[7] This is high praise indeed from the foremost English-language interpreter of medieval eucharistic theology, especially when one recognizes that the twelfth century witnessed a great renaissance of letters and thought, with almost every Parisian master of theology writing a summa on the sacraments, and particularly on the eucharist.

From the sacrament of the Eucharist, says Hugh, comes "all sanctification."[8] The Eucharist is for Hugh not simply one among other sacraments, but rather is the center of the sacraments, being instituted by Christ at the Last Supper. The bread and wine were changed into his body and blood "by divine power." This seems to suggest that Hugh was not interested in futile debates about *how* the transformation of the eucharistic gifts takes place. Like St. Ambrose of Milan, it is enough to believe that it does, through the power of God.

Immediately Hugh is led to a discussion of the nature of Christ's body given in the sacrament. Is this a passible or an impassible body, capable of real human suffering or not? Is it a mortal or an immortal body? Hugh's approach to such questions bears a certain impatience: "I think, as I have professed also in other places, that divine secrets of this kind are more to be venerated than to be discussed."[9] Reverence before the mystery of God's self-donation in the Eucharist is what counts, not philosophical speculation for its own sake.

He picks up on the question whether Judas received the body of Christ at the Last Supper. The natural Christian response would probably be in the negative, that communion in Christ's body and betrayal of his person could not so closely follow. Hugh's response is interesting. Judas did receive holy communion, he says:

> For it must be understood that [Christ] had already distributed the sacrament of his body and blood to all these [apostles], where even Judas himself was, just as holy Luke very clearly relates.[10]

However, he makes the point that the purely physical reception of the body of Christ may lack spiritual fruits. Hugh accepts what the gospel text actually says, in line with his historical approach to exegesis, but, at the same time, he has a theological perspective that enables him to recognize the important and necessary role of cooperation with God's grace.

When he comes to explicate the meaning of holy communion, this "second Augustine" has absorbed the Augustinian emphasis on incorporation into Christ:

> Elsewhere what is eaten is incorporated. Now when the body of Christ is eaten, not what is eaten but he who eats is incorporated with Him whom he eats. On this account Christ wished to be eaten by us, that he might incorporate us with Him.[11]

This is the same Augustinian insight that in the Eucharist Christ is not changed into us as is the case with ordinary food, but rather we are changed into him. We are the Body of Christ through eating the body of Christ. The Eucharist "makes people divine and makes those participants in divinity who partake of it in a worthy manner."[12]

Hugh is aware of the already existent quests for an understanding of eucharistic truth. He says:

> There are those who think that they have drawn a defense of error from certain passages in the Scriptures, saying that in the sacrament of the altar the body and blood of Christ do not truly exist but [are] only an image of this and an appearance and a figure.[13]

This is the question that began in the ninth century with Paschasius and Ratramnus, on whether the eucharistic gifts represented the body and blood of Christ *in figure* or *in truth*. On an obvious commonsense level the bread and wine look and taste like bread and wine. This would suggest that they are figurative of Christ's presence. On a deeper level the church's tradition maintained that, despite appearances to the contrary, the eucharistic gifts *are* the body and blood of Christ. The tradition had continually insisted on the ontological reality of the Eucharist, and moved away from more epistemological concerns. This was Hugh's perspective also:

> Why can the sacrament of the altar not be a likeness and truth? In one respect, indeed, a likeness; in another, truth.[14]

In a chapter of the section "On the Body and Blood of Christ" in *On the Sacraments of the Christian Faith*, Hugh proceeds to elaborate this further by making a clear-cut distinction between the appearance/image/figure of bread and wine and the reality/truth of the body and blood of Christ:

> Thus the sacrament of the altar and the Divine Eucharist in the true body and blood of Our Lord Jesus Christ is an image according to the appearance of bread and wine, in which it is perceived, and the thing is according to the truth of its substance, in which it is there believed and perceived. And again, that we now take Christ on the altar visibly, according to the appearance of the sacrament, and corporally, according to the truth of the body and blood of Christ, is the sacrament, and the image is that we should take the same Himself in the heart invisibly and spiritually according to the infusion of grace and the participation of the Holy Spirit.[15]

The language is somewhat cumbersome, but perhaps we may schematize it in this way for the sake of clarification:

Perception = appearance of bread and wine = image.

Belief and perception = the truth of the body and blood of Christ = sacrament.

In other words, in the Eucharist there is *figure* inasmuch as there are the appearances of the bread and wine, but the *reality*, perceived through faith, is that of the body and blood of Christ. The third aspect of the Eucharist is the spiritual grace, the invisible and spiritual participation in Jesus Christ that comes about through holy communion. This is the really central aspect of the sacrament. These distinctions of Hugh's were to influence subsequent scholars.

In his very fine book *The Theologies of the Eucharist in the Early Scholastic Period*, Gary Macy appears to suggest that Hugh had a more individual than ecclesial approach to the sacrament.[16] The outward sign in the sacramental mystery points to and draws to the inner, spiritual reality of mystical union with Christ. That is a key aspect of Hugh's theology. This seems difficult to sustain, however, as the major emphasis in Hugh's *On the Sacraments of the Christian Faith*. There we find unmistakably ecclesial emphases, as well as passages that are more individual in emphasis. It would be very problematic to consider the strong Augustinian influence on Hugh evacuated of the central points of Augustine's eucharistic theology, namely, our corporate unity in Christ. For example, again under Augustinian influence, Hugh has a strong ecclesial sense of the Eucharist. This is how he puts it:

> For the entire Church is the body of Christ, namely, the head with its members, and there are found in that body, so to speak, three parts of which the whole body consists. One part is the head itself....Another part of the body consists of those members which immediately followed the head, and they are together with the head itself, where the head itself is.[17]

Christ is the head of his body, and the members who have immediately followed him are the sainted dead. These two parts of the church are represented by the consecrated hosts. The faithful in this world are represented by the chalice. They "still live in suffering until they themselves also go out of this life and pass over to their head where they neither may die nor suffer more."[18] The soul never loses its essential quality of being a member of Christ and the church. Certainly, as Macy schematizes the eucharistic insights of this period, Hugh is a powerful example of the individual-mystical approach to the Eucharist. At the same time, it does not seem to make marginal his ecclesial sense of the sacrament.

> After receiving the sacrament of the Eucharist, what happens to it? As long as the sense is affected corporeally, his corporeal presence is not taken away. But after the corporeal feeling in receiving fails, then the corporeal presence is not to be sought but the spiritual is to be retained; the dispensation is completed, the perfect sacrament remains as a virtue; Christ passes from mouth to heart.[19]

On this issue Gary Macy is certainly correct when he says that "Hugh of St. Victor eloquently drew his students away from a useless concern with the physical presence of Christ on the altar."[20] The presence of Christ in the Eucharist is to bring about the spiritual transformation of the communicants.

CARDINAL ROBERT PULLEN
(ca. 1080–ca. 1146)

The first canon of the Fourth Lateran Council in 1215 reads:

> [Christ's] body and blood are truly contained in the sacrament of the altar under the forms of bread and wine, the bread and wine having been changed in substance by the divine power [Latin = *transubstantiatis pane in corpus et vino in sanguinem potestate divina*] into his body and blood, so that in order to achieve this

> mystery of unity we receive from God what God
> received from us.[21]

It is a most important and clear statement of belief in the eucharistic presence of Christ, using a word from what we might call "the family of transubstantiation," but it seems not in fact to be a formal definition of transubstantiation as such. Very soon this term, transubstantiation, became "the preferred terminology and a touchstone of orthodoxy."[22]

Where did the term "transubstantiation" come from? Norman Tanner proposes Peter Damian as the first to use the word. A much stronger case, however, can be made for Robert Pullen as the inventor of the term.[23]

Robert Pullen was an English theologian and cardinal—in fact, the first English cardinal, made such by Pope Lucius II (1144–45). Exact and precise biographical details are not available, but he seems to have been born about 1080, and studied at Paris under the famed William of Champeaux. Returning to England, he taught at Exeter, and then in 1133 he came to Oxford to lecture on scripture in a school attached to one of the churches of the city, since the university had not yet been founded. He remained there for about five years.

He then taught in Paris where the medieval humanist John of Salisbury (ca. 1115–80) was one of his pupils. Robert probably journeyed to Rome about 1142. When St. Bernard's disciple, Bernardo Pignatelli of Pisa, became the new Cistercian Pope, Eugenius III, Bernard exhorted Pullen to advise and offer support to him. Robert probably died at Viterbo in 1146. His extant writings include some sermons and the *Sententiarum Theologicarum*, the "Eight Books of Sentences," written in Oxford, probably before 1142, and described as "the earliest comprehensive theological work to be produced by an English writer."[24]

Eucharist

St. Bernard describes Robert Pullen's theology as "sane." The term seems to have been used by the saint not only of Pullen, but also of Anselm of Laon, the teacher of William of Champeaux, and of the Abbey of St. Victor in Paris, founded by William. What St. Bernard meant was that Robert stands in a sound tradition. It may be the case that Robert went to Paris at the suggestion of St. Bernard to fill the theological gap left by the death of Hugh of St. Victor in 1142, or perhaps Hugh and Robert both taught there briefly at the same time.

Book VIII of the *Sentences* provides, among other topics, Robert's account of the Eucharist. Fifty years ago Francis Courtney remarked, at the outset of his treatment of Pullen's eucharistic theology: "He does not use the term transubstantiation, but clearly holds this doctrine."[25] Far from that being the case, it now seems that Robert Pullen is the first to use the term, and to use it in a slightly different form, *transubstantio*. Researching medieval, particularly twelfth-century manuscripts, Joseph Goering found one in Corpus Christi College, Oxford, and one in Peterhouse, Cambridge, both using the term *transubstantio*. The details of his argument are like following Agatha Christie's sleuth *par excellence*, Hercule Poirot, but the bottom line is very clear. Goering makes an excellent cumulative case that Robert Pullen is the theological master behind these two manuscripts and the first to use the neologism, *transubstantio*, "transubstantiation." He concludes: "The evidence taken together permits the tentative hypothesis that the term 'transubstantiation' was first introduced at Paris around 1140, and that Robert Pullen was its inventor."[26] The term, for Pullen, describes the change that takes place in the celebration of the Eucharist, from bread and wine to the body and blood of Christ. Nothing more, but nothing less is intended by *transubstantio*. In Manuscript 32 of Corpus Christi College, Oxford, Goering's supposed author, Robert Pullen, writes: "In this consecration there is no transformation of quality but, as I might put it, a transubstantiation (*transubstantio*) or transmutation of this substance into that one."[27] It had for Pullen nothing whatever to do with the philosophy of Aristotle, but rather was Pullen's word for the eucharistic transformation witnessed throughout the tradition. The fact that he writes, "as I might put it," suggests that he realizes the novelty of the word, though not the novelty of the eucharistic conviction.

In his *Sentences* the word "transubstantiation" does not occur, but the eucharistic conviction behind it clearly does. Pullen teaches that the eucharistic presence of Christ is brought about by a conversion of the substance of the bread and wine into the body and blood of Christ:

> When the bread is changed into flesh and the wine into blood, by the power of Christ, the substance, at any rate, of wine and bread ceases to be what it was, and it becomes what before it was not. Yet the properties of both things which are being changed remain, whence it is that our five senses find after the consecration what they found before the consecration.[28]

Through the consecration the bread is not changed into Christ's blood nor the wine into his body, nor either of these into Christ's human soul or divinity. At the same time, body, blood, soul and divinity are received in holy communion, even when that communion is received under one species alone.

> Wherefore, in the blessing you must not think that the bread is changed into the blood, or the wine into the flesh, or neither into the [human] soul or the divine nature....Yet the wine is made blood, the same blood that is diffused throughout the flesh, since Christ does not have any other [body or blood].[29]

In other words, one receives the whole Christ in holy communion, because it is the integral reality of Christ that is there to be received.

When it comes to the Last Supper, Pullen insists that Christ first participated in the Jewish Passover meal before instituting the Eucharist.

> Let no one reduce the supper of the Lord, neither to the wine nor to the unleavened bread, nor to the eating of the lamb, since the Lord brought these to an end. Otherwise, one judaizes. The final part of the meal, in which the Lord distributed the sacraments of his body and blood to his own, is for the new dispensation, just as the first part was for the old dispensation.[30]

In tune with his times, a hard and fast line was to be drawn between Judaism and Christianity.

The Eucharist produces its good effects only in those who are in a fit state to receive the sacrament. "He who does not eat, does not have life. He who eats unworthily, has death."[31] Interestingly, Pullen believed that the sacrament should not be received by those condemned to death. This is how Courtney sums up Pullen's position: "By its reception a criminal will become the temple of God; yet he will not on that account be spared by his judges." Better, argues Pullen, "that the criminal should forego the consolation of Holy Communion than that men should lay violent and sacrilegious hands on the temple of God.…When the criminal has repented of his sins his salvation is not endangered."[32]

In our contemporary culture, with the ongoing debate about the morality of capital punishment, such a position as Pullen's would simply be deemed unacceptable. All Catholics who are properly disposed may receive the Eucharist. However, indirectly Pullen's theology may be thought of as subverting the practice of capital punishment on theological grounds. If a repentant sinner, condemned to die, has worthily received the Eucharist, his ongoing conformity to Christ through the sacrament makes of him a temple of God, in which God dwells. His life, in Christ, ought not to be taken.

Concerning the issue of whether people should receive under one or both species, Pullen believes that Christ left that decision up to the church. He knows, of course, that at his time circumstances were such that the laity did not receive from the chalice. From what was said above about the integral reality of the eucharistic presence, he recognized that to receive in one species only is to receive the entire Christ, since Christ's body and blood cannot be separated. He knew of the practice of intinction, dipping the host into the chalice, and was utterly opposed to it. The only person to receive bread by intinction at the Last Supper, he noted, was Judas: "'[The one who will betray me] is the one to whom I hand the morsel after I have dipped it.' So he dipped the morsel and took it and handed it to Judas, son of Simon the Iscariot" (John 13:26).

The Eucharist is the sacrifice and the salvation of the church. "The sacrifice is celebrated with this body and blood, so that the participant, whole and entire, may be vitalized by it."[33] The passion and sacrificial death of Christ is signified for Pullen by the separate reception of the elements by the priest. The very separation signifies Christ's death. "While the flesh is eaten, and the blood is poured into the mouth, the Passion of the Lord is penetrated, both by the body slain and the blood outpoured."[34]

The communion of the church is built up and signified through the communion of the Eucharist:

> Different grains come together to this sacrifice, since
> it is prepared for the different persons of the church.
> Many grains make together one bread, and the many
> persons for whom this re-making is given, are one
> church.[35]

The Eucharist is, therefore, "the principal sacrament of the church."[36]

Conclusion

Two twelfth-century Parisian teachers of theology, Hugh of St. Victor and Robert Pullen, prepared the ground for future generations to arrive at a more profound understanding of the Eucharist. The thirteenth century is the high point of the Christian Middle Ages, with the great luminaries in Paris, St. Thomas Aquinas and St. Bonaventure. The thirteenth century would not have been possible without the twelfth century and its theological teachers, and the theological syntheses and sentence commentaries of that century paved the way for the great summas of the thirteenth. In the year 1142 both Peter Abelard and Hugh of St. Victor died. Each represented a different way of studying theology. Where Hugh was more contemplative, Abelard was more rationalist in temper. St. Thomas Aquinas' way of "doing" theology combined both approaches

Hugh is much better known than Robert Pullen. When we turn to the readily available dictionaries and lexica of theology, few give any consideration to Robert Pullen. It would seem that the consensus of scholars is that Robert Pullen does not stand in the first rank. I see no good reason to argue with that consensus. Yet, the case of Robert Pullen and his appreciation of the Eucharist introduces us to the always-present fact that countless clouds of witnesses, mostly anonymous, contribute to the upbuilding of the church through their appreciation of this central sacrament. Nor are these multiple witnesses of the living tradition content simply to repeat what has been handed to them. There are those like Pullen, feeling perhaps that the older language is no longer communicating the faith with vibrancy to a new generation, who seek new language and thought forms, like *transubstantio*.

Notes

1. Gary Macy, *The Banquet's Wisdom* (New York/Mahwah, NJ: Paulist Press, 1992), 85.

2. Joseph W. Goering, "The Invention of Transubstantiation," *Traditio* 46 (1991), 158.

3. David E. Luscombe, *The School of Peter Abelard: The Influence of Abelard's Thought in the Early Scholastic Period* (Cambridge: Cambridge University Press, 1969), 184.

4. Hugh of St. Victor, "Eruditio Didascalia," in *Patrologia Latina* (Paris: Jacques-Paul Migne, 1844–55), 176, 800C.

5. ———. *Didascalion* 6.3, cited in Bernard McGinn, *The Growth of Mysticism* (New York: Crossroad, 1996), 374.

6. ———. *On the Sacraments of the Christian Faith,* trans. Roy J. Deferrari (Cambridge: The Mediaeval Academy of America, 1951).

7. Gary Macy, *The Theologies of the Eucharist in the Early Scholastic Period* (Oxford: Clarendon Press, 1984), 82.

8. Hugh of Saint Victor, *On the Sacraments of the Christian Faith,* chap. 1.

9. Ibid., chap. 3.

10. Ibid., chap. 4.

11. Ibid., chap. 5.

12. Ibid., chap. 10.

13. Ibid.

14. Ibid., chap. 6.

15. Ibid., chap. 7.

16. Macy, *The Theologies of the Eucharist in the Early Scholastic Period,* 85–86, 122.

17. Hugh of St. Victor: *On the Sacraments of the Christian Faith,* chap. 10.

18. Ibid.

19. Ibid., chap. 13.

20. Macy, *The Theologies of the Eucharist in the Early Scholastic Period,* 138.

21. Norman Tanner, ed., *Decrees of the Ecumenical Councils,* vol. 1 (London and Washington, DC: Sheed and Ward and Georgetown University Press, 1990), 230.

22. ———. "The Eucharist in the Ecumenical Councils," *Gregorianum* 82 (2001), 42.

23. Goering, "The Invention of Transubstantiation," 147–70.

24. Francis Courtney, *Cardinal Robert Pullen, An English Theologian in the Twelfth Century* (Rome: Gregorian University Press, 1954), xi.

25. Ibid., 220.

26. Goering, "The Invention of Transubstantiation," 158.

27. This eucharistic tract has been appended by Goering to his article as Appendix B, 163–68, here 165.

28. All translations from Pullen are my own, following the Latin text of Pullen's *Sentences* in Migne, *Patrologia Latina*, vol. 186: 966d.

29. Robert Pullen, *Sententiarum Theologicarum*, in *Patrologia Latina* 186:966a–b.

30. Ibid., 971a.

31. Ibid., 962d.

32. Ibid., 222.

33. Ibid., 961c.

34. Ibid., 963c–d.

35. Ibid., 961d.

36. Ibid., 963c.

8.

Eucharist in Poetry and Prose: St. Thomas Aquinas

For Thomas the Eucharist was never simply a theological problem.
Clearly his dedication to expounding its mysteries had its roots
in his own personal spirituality and in his deep sense of the role
of the Eucharist in the pastoral life of the Church.
–Raymond Moloney, SJ[1]

ST. THOMAS AQUINAS
(ca. 1225–1274)

St. Thomas Aquinas, the Angelic Doctor, was born about 1225 in the family castle at Roccasecca, near the town of Aquino, between Rome and Naples. It was also near Monte Cassino, the great Benedictine foundation. He was the youngest son of Landolfo of Aquino and his second wife, Theodora. At age five or six Thomas was given by his parents as an oblate to the Abbey of Monte Cassino, probably in the hope that he would choose the Benedictine way of life and perhaps become abbot.

In 1239 he was sent with the other oblates to the recently established University of Naples, and he remained there until 1244. Here he studied philosophy and was introduced to the philosophy of Aristotle by Peter of Ireland. Aristotelianism was an exciting, new philosophical movement in the church of the early thirteenth century, and the young Thomas Aquinas was immediately attracted to it. He was equally attracted to the Dominican way of life, a radical evangelical renewal movement in the church, and so Thomas entered the priory of San Domenico in Naples. "As an Aristotelian radical, he was opting for this world, for science, for reason, for the beauty of the senses, and as a gospel radical, he was opting for the life of the spirit, for trust, for deep faith in the love of God," says Robert Barron.[2] En route to the general chapter of the Dominicans in Bologna, he was intercepted by his brother, at his mother's request, and forcibly returned to the family home in Roccasecca. Eventually Theodora realized that Thomas was entirely serious about his Dominican vocation, and she permitted him to rejoin the community in Naples by the summer of 1245

Details remain uncertain, but shortly thereafter Thomas went north to study at Paris, the intellectual center of Christianity, and became the student of St. Albert the Great. He studied in Cologne with Albert from 1248 to 1252, and then went back to Paris for further theological studies. He became a professor of theology in Paris in 1256, and he taught, studied and wrote there until 1259. During this period he probably began work on his *Summa Contra Gentiles*, a handbook of theology for Christians working among the cultured and educated Muslims of the day.

Thomas returned to Italy in 1259, but the chronology of his stay there is unclear. He appears to have functioned as a kind of official theological consultant for the papacy in various places, but above all in Rome. During the 1260s Thomas began work on his *Summa Theologica*. He is to be found again teaching in Paris from 1269 to 1272, but in 1272 he again left for his homeland of Italy, this time to set up a Dominican house of studies in Naples. It was during this period that the work on the third part of his *Summa Theologica* was begun, and this is the section that contains most of his systematic eucharistic theology. He was in the midst of his treatment of the sacrament of penance in this third part of his *Summa* when, on December 6, 1273, he had an experience that brought his immense productivity as a theologian to an end. After Mass on that day, the feast of St. Nicholas, Thomas hung up his writing instruments, and when his secretary, Reginald, asked him why, Thomas is reputed to have answered: "I cannot go on....All that I have written seems to me like so much straw compared to what I have seen and what has been revealed to me." Summoned to the second Council of Lyons, which was to deal with the question of union between the Greek East and the Latin West, Thomas fell ill on the way and died at Fossanuova in 1274. He was not yet fifty, but few theologians in the history of the tradition can be judged to have accomplished so much.

Eucharist in Poetry: *Lauda Sion*

There is continuing debate about whether St. Thomas is the author of the hymns, readings and antiphons of the office for the Feast of Corpus Christi, and of the sequence, *Lauda Sion* for the Mass of Corpus Christi. Nevertheless, James Weisheipl, a premier biographer and scholar of Aquinas, writes of this sequence: "The sequence *Lauda Sion* in the Mass is remarkable not only for its poetry, but also for its theological content; the individual stanzas can easily be aligned with the eucharistic teaching of St. Thomas as found in the third part of his *Summa Theologica*."[3] It is the contention of the writer along with probably the majority of commentators that St. Thomas is indeed the author of this sequence, and it is from this poetic sequence that we shall begin our treatment of St. Thomas' eucharistic theology. This starting point—rather than the *Summa Theologica* with its careful, systematic, theological analysis—has the merit of showing the Angelic Doctor as a preacher and a man of prayer, with a profound sense of the Eucharist in the life of the church.[4] First, we must have the text of the sequence itself:[5]

1.
Zion, praise the Savior,
Praise the Leader and the Shepherd
In hymns and songs!

Eucharistic Doctors

Dare to praise him as much as you can,
for he is truly beyond all praising and
you will never be able to praise him adequately.

2.
A theme of special praise,
the living and life-giving bread,
is placed before us today:
the same that was given to the Twelve
at table during the holy supper.
Of this there is no doubt.

3.
Let praise be full and resounding,
a delightful and beautiful rejoicing of the soul.
For the solemn day is being observed
upon which the first of the tables of this
institution is being remembered.

4.
On this table of the new king
the new Passover of the new law
brings to an end the old.
The new puts to flight the old,
reality the shadow, and
light banishes darkness.

5.
What Christ did at the supper
this he said must be done
in memory of him.
Taught by his holy instructions,
we consecrate bread and wine in
a sacrifice of salvation.

6.
The dogma is given to Christians
that the bread is changed into flesh

and the wine into blood.
That which you cannot understand,
that which you do not see,
life-giving faith affirms.
It is beyond the ordinary course of things.

7.
Under the different species,
in the signs only and not the things themselves,
there lie hidden wonderful realities.
Flesh is food, blood is drink;
and yet the whole Christ remains
under each species.

8.
The communicant receives the complete Christ,
uncut, unbroken, undivided.
Whether one receives, or a thousand receive,
the one receives as much as the thousand.
Nor is Christ diminished by being received.

9.
The good receive him, and the bad receive him,
but with different outcomes: life or death.
To the bad it is death, to the good it is life.
Though each receives the same Christ,
the result is so different.

10.
Finally, when the sacrament is broken,
Do not doubt, but remember
that there is as much [of Christ] in a fragment
as in the whole.
There is no division of the reality.
The breaking does not diminish
the state nor the stature of the One who is signified.

11.
Look! The bread of angels has become
the food of travelers,
the true bread of sons, not to be cast to the dogs.
It is foreshadowed in figures,
when Isaac was sacrificed,
when a lamb was appointed for the Passover,
when manna was given to the fathers.

12.
Good Shepherd, true bread,
Jesus, have mercy on us.
Feed us, protect us.
Let us see good things in the land of the living.
You who know and can do all things,
who feed us here as mortals,
make us your table-guests there,
your co-heirs and companions
of the holy citizens of heaven.

Stanzas 1–3 are a summons to praise the Leader and the Shepherd who has given us the eucharistic gifts, commemorated especially on this Feast of Corpus Christi. In stanza 2 it is emphasized that the life-giving Eucharist today is the same as that first received by the twelve apostles at the Last Supper—"Of this there is no doubt." Stanzas 4 and 11 express the fulfillment in the new covenant of the types and figures of the old covenant, a common theme in patristic and medieval literature: the new Passover and Lamb, the new Isaac, the new manna. In the mention of Isaac, of course, who carried the wood for the sacrifice to Mount Moriah with his father Abraham, who was willing to sacrifice his "beloved son" (Gen 22), we have the eucharistic theme of sacrifice implied, as another Father sacrifices his beloved Son. While the Old Testament figures are but a shadow of the New, notice in stanza 11 that our Old Testament forbears are described as our fathers—"when manna was given to the fathers." For Aquinas there is no disconnect between Old and New Testaments, but rather the latter brings to fulfillment and completion the aspirations and longings of the former.

Stanzas 6, 7, 8 and 10 express the doctrine of transubstantiation, but without using the word, and express it as mystery: "That which you cannot understand....It is beyond the ordinary course of things." Thomas J. Bell comments on these stanzas as follows: "Stanzas 6 through 10 elaborate on the nature of Christ's presence....*Lauda Sion* does not only affirm that Christ himself is present in the elements but explains his presence in terms of the doctrine of transubstantiation."[6]

In stanza 7 we find St. Thomas deliberately avoiding through his understanding of transubstantiation the crude physicalism of earlier medieval authors like Paschasius. The eucharistic gifts have to do with "signs" of the glorified Christ, not Christ understood in terms of the physics of this world—"in the signs only and not the things themselves." For fear the precious blood, the transubstantiated wine, might spill when the faithful went to communion, and perhaps for other reasons, the custom grew in the thirteenth century of the laity participating in only one species. Hence, in stanza 7 Thomas also reassures us that "the whole Christ remains under each species." Stanzas 8 and 10 underscore the fact that whether one receives a broken fragment or, like the priest, a whole host, all receive the same, complete Christ. Stanza 9 picks up a theme that was important to medieval Christians: Do the bad receive Christ? Did Judas the betrayer consume the Eucharist at the Last Supper, a question that surfaced in Hugh of St. Victor's treatment of the Eucharist, noted in the last chapter? The answer is, "Yes." All receive the same Christ who never takes back his gift of self, but it is received differently, either life-giving or death-dealing.

In the latter part of stanza 11 an eschatological note is struck, as the Eucharist is described as "the food of travelers." This is the food that sustains travelers on their way to the banquet in the kingdom of heaven, the supper of the Lamb. The same eschatological theme is heard in the last stanza, where St. Thomas petitions Christ to make us his "table-guests there, your co-heirs and companions of the holy citizens of heaven." The union of the terrestrial church with the heavenly church is affirmed. The sequence in its entirety sets forth the central eucharistic doctrines, but in a poetic mode, not the systematic mode of the *Summa*. But it is to this systematic theology of St. Thomas that we must now turn.

Eucharist in Prose: *Summa Theologica*

Although St. Thomas did not write a treatise on the church as such, much of what he has to say may be gleaned from his consideration of the Eucharist. For Thomas, the Eucharist makes the church. His thought may be said in that sense to yield a eucharistic ecclesiology, though the term itself would have been foreign to Aquinas. "For Aquinas, the eucharist is the sign of what makes the church the church. It is also the reality of what constitutes the church as the church, and it is the ordinary means of growing in grace."[7] The Eucharist signals "the unity of the church into which people are drawn together through this sacrament."[8] The Eucharist is "the sacrament of the church's unity."[9] The Eucharist is, therefore, not simply one among the sacraments. It is "the summit of the spiritual life and all the sacraments are ordered to it.[10]

The Eucharist commemorates the past, celebrates the Christ who is present and anticipates the great future, when God will be all in all:

> The effect of this sacrament should be looked at first and foremost from what the sacrament holds, and this is Christ. Just as by coming visibly into the world he brought the life of grace into it, according to John, "Grace and truth came through Jesus Christ," so by coming to people sacramentally he causes the life of grace....This sacrament signifies three things. It looks back to the past: in this sense it commemorates the passion of the Lord....In regard to the pres-

ent, there is another thing to which it points. This is
the unity of the church into which people are drawn
together through this sacrament....It has a third significance with regard to the future. It prefigures that
enjoyment of God which will be ours in
heaven....Through this sacrament we take to ourselves the godhead of the Son.[11]

This emphasis on the unity of the faithful in and with
Christ harmonizes with one of the greatest themes of patristic
eucharistic thinking, and is central to eucharistic ecclesiology.
Thomas is entirely aware of this. Earlier, in the third part of the
Summa, he had written of the grace of Christ's headship in such
a fashion that it makes of Christ and his members "as though
one person."[12] His doctrine of grace in its various modes is his
scholastic expression for the divinization of human beings that
comes about through the sacraments, with the Eucharist at the
center. In the second part of the *Summa,* he cites St. Augustine's
notion of sacrifice as "any work done in order that we may
cleave to God in holy companionship,"[13] and then in the third
part he affirms that the Eucharist is the sacrifice of Christ:

The celebration of this sacrament is a definite image
representing Christ's passion, which is his true sacrifice...[and]...by this sacrament we are made sharers
in the fruit of the Lord's passion.[14]

Christ's unique sacrifice on the cross does not occur over and
over again in incessant repetition in the celebration of the
Eucharist. Rather, the celebration of the Eucharist re-presents
this unique sacrifice of Christ, that is makes it present, and so
the Eucharist in that sense may truly be called a sacrifice.[15]
However, eucharistic sacrifice is not as predominant in his
thought, neither in the *Lauda Sion* nor in the *Summa,* as is
eucharistic presence, although obviously they may not be theologically separated. Sacrifice would become a central theme

from the sixteenth century on, as Protestant denial of eucharistic sacrifice fueled Catholic defense.

In the Middle Ages, reception of the Eucharist by the faithful was so infrequent that Lateran Council IV, to remedy the situation, required the faithful to receive holy communion at least once a year. This is far from the viewpoint of St. Thomas. For Thomas, the Eucharist is something that Christians need to receive regularly to remain alive in Christ. It is the food that is "required that a person may be kept alive."[16]

Transubstantiation

The doctrine of transubstantiation found classic formulation in the teachings of St. Thomas Aquinas, though its interpretation remains in some degree controverted, theologically and historically.

The term, probably introduced by Cardinal Robert Pullen as we saw in the last chapter, first makes its way into official church teaching at Lateran Council IV in 1215. In the creed produced by the council we read the following:

> There is indeed one universal church of the faithful
> outside which no one at all is saved, and in which the
> priest himself, Jesus Christ, is also the sacrifice. His
> body and blood are truly contained in the sacrament
> of the altar under the appearances of bread and wine,
> the bread being transubstantiated into the body by
> the divine power and the wine into the blood.[17]

The creed was drawn up primarily against the Cathars, a rigorist and austere group of Christians who identified matter as evil, abstained from meat and sex and denied the value of the church's sacramental system. Transubstantiation was part of the church's response to the anti-matter, and, therefore, anti-eucharistic teachings of the Cathars. There is ongoing debate about whether Lateran IV formally intended that transubstantiation should be understood as a defined doctrine of the church.[18] It seems clear to the writer that in some sense transubstantiation had been defined by Lateran IV in order to clarify the nature of eucharistic belief, but it may not have been so understood by the theologians of the day. For example, William of Auvergne, teaching theology in Paris, concluded his discussion of transubstantiation (sometime between 1223 and 1240) as follows:

> It suffices for the piety of faith, which we intend to establish here, to believe and hold that after the priestly blessing has been correctly performed, the bread of life is placed on the altar before us in the form of material and visible bread, and the drink of life is placed before us under the form of visible wine.[19]

In other words, after the council, theologians like William continued to discuss eucharistic change as though the council had not made a definitive and binding judgment on the matter. The reason may be that, although the notion of transubstantiation had made its way into the formula of the council, it had not yet permeated the schools of theology so as to become part and parcel of normal theological discourse. St. Thomas is one of the theologians whose work made for this later clarity. He espouses transubstantiation as the clearest articulation of eucharistic change.

"[St. Thomas] does not cite the Fourth Lateran Council, nor does he use the word 'transubstantiation' to state the basic faith of the Church. He works towards it as a suitable theological term for explaining the kind of change in bread and wine that brings about the real presence," Liam Walsh points out.[20] Thomas' fullest commentary on transubstantiation occurs in *Summa Theologica* III, q. 75, a. 4. St. Thomas, of course, when he talks of transubstantiation, talks of it in language borrowed from Aristotle. He speaks of substance and accidents. However, it would be a mistake to think of Thomas using Aristotle to "explain" the Eucharist. Rather, he uses Aristotelian language because "it was the common philosophical currency of the time; but he uses it to give an account of something that simply could not happen according to Aristotle," Herbert McCabe says: "Transubstantiation, like creation or incarnation, does not make sense within the limits of the Aristotelian world-view. St. Thomas uses Aristotle's language, but it breaks down in speaking of the Eucharist."[21] In brief, there is no "explanation" of the Eucharist, but Thomas uses Aristotle to reach whatever degree of clarity concerning the mystery of faith might be possible. Transubstantiation is not for St. Thomas a matter of rational proof, but is accepted in Christian faith. "We could never know by our senses that the real body of Christ and his blood are in this sacrament, but only by our faith which is based on the authority of God," he says.[22] As with the *Lauda Sion*, "that which you cannot understand, that which you do not see, living faith affirms"; the eyes of faith behold the presence. For Thomas, transubstantiation is the plain meaning of the words of our Lord at the Last Supper: "This is my body, this is my blood," and so one may conclude: "It is not bread and wine that remain on the altar. Nor do we have sanctified bread and wine, or Christ plus bread and wine. We have no bread and wine. We just have Christ."[23] In a word, the bread and the wine in the celebration of the Eucharist turn into Christ. Transubstantiation for St. Thomas was the best possible protection against both a too physicalist understanding of that presence, and what was taken to be a purely symbolic understanding of that presence.

At the risk of being pedantic, but for the sake of those unfamiliar with Aristotle or Thomas, let us attempt to elucidate "transubstantiation" by attending further an analysis of its various elements. The first thing is the notion of "substance." A substance is that which exists independently of anything else; substance is what something is. A thing may have other components that can come and go without changing its substantial nature, and these components are known as "accidents." In fact these "accidents" are the Aristotelian categories of quantity, quality, relation, place, time, position, state, action and passion.

Substance, what a thing is, can be reached only by the intellect, by the process of reasoning and asking questions. But the accidents touch the senses. A thing or substance is not identifiable with what we experience through our senses. As Thomas puts it: "Substance cannot be seen by the bodily eye, nor is it the object of any sense, nor can it be imagined" (*Summa Theologica* III, q. 76. a.7). In colloquial language today, "substance," "substantial" and "substantially" are not used in this precise, metaphysical sense. They mean, roughly speaking, what is physical and material, what is simply "out there now." That is not Thomas' understanding of the term or its cognates.

Now Christ is an independent something, and so, in Thomas' language Christ is a substance, in fact "a substance of the thinking sort," in Latin *rationalis naturae individualis substantia.* Christ is now present in his total individual reality, with all the attributes of his being, at the right hand of the Father. Bread and wine also are independent somethings, and so bread and wine are known as substances.

Transubstantiation occurs when the substance of bread and wine is changed by God through the blessing of the priest into the substance of the body and blood of the risen and ascended Lord. Where bread and wine once were, the risen and ascended Lord now is. As Liam Walsh explains, "If bread and wine were to be changed on the level of what gives them independent existence into Christ on the level of what gives him independent existence, he, not they, would be present 'where' they had been. He would 'be there' as they had 'been there' before God changed their being there into his being there."[24]

However, it does not end at that point because the accidents, that is the sense data, of the bread and wine remain exactly as they were before. The whiteness and roundness of the bread remains, the redness of the wine remains. But it *is not* bread, and it *is not* wine. There has taken place by divine power a change of substance.

But there is a problem. The problem is that ordinarily "accidents," that is sense data, inhere in a subject or substance. They are accidents of this thing/substance or that, of X or Y. But in this particular and unique case, the previous subject/substance, that is bread and wine, no longer exist. The substance is now Christ. So, does this mean that the accidents inhere in the substance of Christ, since Christ is now the subject? No, because that would expose Christ's body to material change in a way that would contradict his glorified state. So the accidents exist without a subject. But Thomas maintains that the accident of *quantity*, one of Aristotle's categories, acts as a "quasi-subject" for the accidents. Consequently, when I bite into the host, it is this "quasi-subject" that is bitten, not strictly speaking, the body of Christ. The question then may be raised: What maintains these accidents in being since substance is what maintains accidents in being, and the substance of bread/wine is no longer present? We move further into metaphysical complexity!

"Once one reaches this degree of refinement, the person unfamiliar with Scholastic philosophy will probably withdraw in despair or derision, but the convinced scholastic presses on relentlessly," as Moloney observes.[25] For Thomas, the role previously exercised by the respective substances is now taken over by the power of God through the original miracle of transubstantiation. The accidents are maintained in being and activity through the divine action itself. This, of course, sounds very difficult to the ears of the ordinary believer, but perhaps we should be slow to disregard Thomas' point of view. This is how a contemporary eucharistic theologian puts it: "If thought about the structure of matter can issue in something as arcane as Einstein's theory of relativity, then it is hardly surprising that reflection on divine intervention in the material world should challenge our intellects in a comparable way. Generally, today people do not get to this point at all, since the basic presuppositions are no longer shared."[26]

Finally, a word about vocabulary. In Thomas' *Commentary on the Sentences*, "transubstantiation" occurs eighty-eight times, while in the *Summa Theologica* it occurs only four times. The liturgical theologian Pierre-Marie Gy detects an increasing reserve on St. Thomas' part with regard to the word. He prefers to speak of "substantial conversion." Why? Perhaps because in his mind the term "transubstantiation" was tainted by its origins in the twelfth-century notion of substance as basically material.[27]

Conclusion

In our times, there is something of a Thomistic renaissance going on, and people are reading Thomas in different ways. It seems to me that the best way to keep his eucharistic theology and vision alive in our consciousness today is *not* by espousing St. Thomas as the final word and insight in the theology of the Eucharist. Nor is it to subscribe to some formal school of thought, philosophical or theological, for its own sake. If we would cherish his achievement, we will reach out for the eucharistic God as Thomas did, using the best of thought available to us to speak the tradition. We will study his insights in their historical context and appreciate something of his genius, and then, standing on his shoulders, reach out to do for our times what he did for his.

Notes

1. Raymond Moloney, SJ, *The Eucharist* (Collegeville, MN: The Liturgical Press, 1995), 139.

2. Robert Barron, *Thomas Aquinas, Spiritual Master* (New York: Crossroad, 1996), 18.

3. James A. Weisheipl, *Friar Thomas d'Aquino: His Life, Thought and Works* (Washington, DC: Catholic University of America Press, 1974), 180–81.

4. I have found very helpful and instructive the excellent essay of Thomas J. Bell, "The Eucharistic Theologies of *Lauda Sion* and Thomas Aquinas' *Summa Theologiae*" in *The Thomist* 57 (1993), 163–85.

5. The translation of *Lauda Sion* is my own. See Roman Missal, Sequence for the Mass of Corpus Christi.

6. Bell, "The Eucharistic Theologies of *Lauda Sion* and Thomas Aquinas' *Summa Theologiae*," 168–69.

7. Brian Davies, *The Thought of St. Thomas Aquinas* (Oxford: Clarendon Press, 1992), 363.

8. St. Thomas Aquinas, *Summa Theologica* 3a.73.4. The translation followed is that of the English Dominican Province published first in 1920, most recently available as St. Thomas Aquinas, *Summa Theologica*, 5 vols. (Westminster, MD: Christian Classics, 1981).

9. Ibid., 3a.73.2.

10. Ibid., 3a.73.3.

11. Ibid., 3a.79.1 and 3a.73.4.

12. Ibid., 3a.8.2.

13. Ibid., 2a2ae.85.1ff. See St. Augustine, *City of God,* 10.28.

14. Ibid., 3a.83.1.

15. Matthew Levering, "Aquinas on the Liturgy of the Eucharist," in Thomas Weinandy, Daniel Keating and John Yocum, eds., *Aquinas on Doctrine, A Critical Introduction* (New York and London: T. & T. Clark International, 2004), 191.

16. *Summa Theologica* 3a.73.1.

17. Josef Neuner, SJ, and Jacques Dupuis, SJ, eds., *The Christian Faith in the Doctrinal Documents of the Catholic Church,* rev. ed. (London: Collins, 1983), 15.

18. This debate is amply documented in Gary Macy, "The 'Dogma of Transubstantiation' in the Middle Ages," in his *Treasures from the Storeroom: Medieval Religion and the Eucharist* (Collegeville, MN: The Liturgical Press, 1999), 81–120.

19. Ibid., 84.

20. Liam Walsh, *Sacraments of Initiation* (London: Geoffrey Chapman, 1989), 236.

21. Herbert McCabe, OP, *God Still Matters* (New York: Continuum, 2002), 116–17.

22. *Summa Theologica* 3a.75.1

23. Davies, *The Thought of St. Thomas Aquinas,* 367.

24. Walsh, *Sacraments of Initiation,* 238.

25. Moloney, *The Eucharist,* 145.

26. Ibid.

27. See Pierre-Marie Gy, OP, "L'eucharistie dans la tradition, de la priere et de la doctrine," in *La Maison Dieu* 137 (1979), 81–102, especially 95–96.

9.

Two Oxford Scholars: John Duns Scotus and John Wyclif

It was not only in virtue of the quality of his philosophy that the decision to beatify [Scotus] was taken, but all the same the philosophy was an essential part of the man beatified. I believe him to be Scotland's greatest philosopher.
–Alexander Broadie[1]

If Wyclif was the Morning Star of the Reformation, he was also the Evening Star of Scholasticism....Wyclif was the last of the great Oxford schoolmen.
–Anthony Kenny[2]

Metaphysics is the interest of but a few. Most people suffer from what might be called a metaphysical allergy. Some readers may have experienced something of that allergy as we moved through the latter part of the last chapter on St. Thomas Aquinas. Yet without some appreciation of metaphysics the eucharistic theology of the late thirteenth and fourteenth centuries remains utterly opaque. The key issue is: What is the eucharistic reality, and, behind this, what is reality? John Duns Scotus was undoubtedly the superior metaphysician, but John Wyclif was a metaphysician of the Eucharist too. One commentator writes: "The daunting sophistication of Scotus' thought helps to explain how he could be ridiculed by 16th-century humanists and reformers for pointless, nearly maniacal complexity [hence the word 'dunce'], though he wins praise in our own day as the Kant of the Middle Ages."[3] While such caricaturing comments lack the finesse and reflective accuracy of a professional philosophical devotee, they do point to Scotus as a metaphysician's metaphysician.

JOHN DUNS SCOTUS
(1265/66–1308)

Engraved on the tomb of John Duns Scotus in Cologne, Germany, one will find the following Latin summary of his short life: *Scotia me genuit* (Scotland gave me birth), *Anglia me suscepit,* (England reared me), *Gallia me docuit* (France taught me), *Colonia me tenuit* (Cologne holds my remains). Little is known of Scotus' early life. He was born probably in 1265 or 1266 in Scotland in the town of Duns, Berwickshire, near the North Sea. Entering the Franciscan Order at an early age, he may have begun his undergraduate studies in philosophy and the humanities as early as 1278 in the Franciscan Friary at Oxford. We know from the episcopal archives of the Diocese of Lincoln, the diocese in which Oxford was situated, that he was ordained a priest on March 17, 1291 by Bishop Oliver Sutton. He left Paris for Cologne in 1307, and died there on November 8 the following year. He is buried in the Minoritenkirche, Cologne.

Another Oxford priest, the poet, Gerard Manley Hopkins, has a sonnet with the title "Duns Scotus's Oxford." In the poem the beauty of the university city is described, but for Hopkins the importance of Oxford lay in the fact that Scotus had been there:

> Yet ah! This air I gather and I release
> He lived on; these weeds and waters, these walls are
> what
> He haunted who of all men most sways my spirit to
> peace.[4]

Probably Hopkins' identity with Scotus lies in Scotus' theology of the incarnation, with all the consequences, cosmological and poetic, that flow from it, but this is not the place to develop the point. Our interest is in a very specific issue, the Eucharist.

Eucharist

The translation into English of some of the medieval mystics—for example, Hildegard of Bingen, Hadewijch of Antwerp and Mechthild of Magdeburg—as well as the rendering of other sources from Latin has established that the Middle Ages were no intellectual monolith, but a period of great intellectual flourishing marked by a legitimate pluralism.[5] The Middle Ages offer in theology a rich blend of monastic, scholastic and vernacular contributions, so that in respect to Scotus and Wyclif, there was "a pregnant plurality of fourteenth-century thought."[6] The advent of the philosophy of Aristotle into the medieval West through the medium of the Arab philosophers was to transform philosophical and theological thought. Although in the second half of the thirteenth century almost all theologians and philosophers thought in Aristotelian terms, there still remained this profound diversity in philosophical reflection. For example, among various medieval authors the categories of matter and form, of hylomorphic composition, cover very different notions. And examples could be multiplied. As Aristotelian hylomorphism passed into theological conversation, it was inevitable that these categories would be used to understand the increasing refinements attached to developing eucharistic thought. Matter and form, substance and accidents became eucharistic terms, but in different ways, as different authors made different uses of Aristotle.

We have already looked at St. Thomas Aquinas and his theology of transubstantiation. Aquinas used Aristotelian categories, but the scriptured tradition of the church molded and formed his use and development of them as it did of other thinkers.[7] Scotus used Aristotelian ideas but developed them differently than Thomas did. Scotus, for example, accepted the doctrine of transubstantiation as true because he believed it to have been taught as such at the Fourth Lateran Council in 1215. In point of fact, Scotus is very clear that this doctrine is God-given:

> And if you ask why the Church chose so difficult an
> understanding of this article of faith when the words
> of Scripture can be satisfied by an understanding that
> would be easier and more true as far as appearances
> are concerned, I reply that the Scriptures are
> expounded by the same Spirit who established them.
> And so it must be supposed that the Catholic Church
> has expounded the faith passed on to us by that same
> Spirit…and therefore has chosen this understanding
> because it is true. For it is not in the power of the
> Church to make something true or false; it is in the
> power of God who ordains reality. The Church has
> expounded the understanding handed on by God
> and has done so, we believe, under God's direction.[8]

The understanding that would be easier and more true as far as the appearances are concerned is his own. In other words, as far as the appearances are concerned, consubstantiation is a less difficult doctrine to accept than transubstantiation.

Transubstantiation, as a philosophic explanation, was for him "intrinsically undesirable" because he found its metaphysical foundations unsatisfactory. "[Scotus] believes that consubstantiation—the doctrine that Christ's body comes to exist in the same place as the substance of the bread—is in principle preferable. It is simpler, it is easier to understand (because it does not involve the claim that, despite appearances, the substance of the bread has changed), and it is more scriptural," says Richard Cross.[9] Scotus would have preferred something like "substantial substitution" to "substantial change."[10] Nevertheless, Scotus recognizes and accepts and submits to the teaching of the church, since this is established by God. Here he stands in sharp contrast to John Wyclif who refuses to accept the teaching of the church. We see in Scotus a real humility.

There is a difference, too, between Thomas and Scotus in respect to the Eucharist understood as sacrifice. For St. Thomas and his followers there is but the one sacrifice of Calvary, and every Eucharist is this one sacrifice of Christ, in which Christ remains the principal offerer. Scotists develop a slightly different emphasis. The Eucharist is principally the "sacrifice of the Church." In this view there are really many sacrifices, and the immediate offerer is the church, not Christ. Scotists believe that the church is acting by deputation from Christ, who may be thought of as "the mediate offerer of the Mass."[11]

JOHN WYCLIF
(ca. 1330–1384)

John Wyclif was an Oxford scholar, reformer and heretic. He was born in Yorkshire about 1330 and was about twelve years older than Geoffrey Chaucer, with whom he had friends in common. He lived during the reigns of the last two kings of the English Plantagenet line, Edward III and his grandson Richard II. Richard succeeded to the throne while he was still a child, and the effective ruler of England during much of Wyclif's life was the regent, John of Gaunt.

Unlike other theological scholars such as Duns Scotus, Wyclif remained in England all his life, except for one brief visit in 1374 to Bruges, when he was part of an English embassy to discuss with papal representatives the vexatious question of taxation. He entered the University of Oxford, Balliol College, about 1345 and was ordained for the Diocese of Lincoln about 1361. At the time, university scholars without financial means of their own were dependent upon "provisions to livings," the assigned income of certain parishes. He received the doctorate in theology probably about 1372, after writing *On the Incarnation of the Word* (a commentary on the *Sentences* of Peter the Lombard). Though he had held a series of livings before, in

1374 he was given the parish living of Lutterworth, Leicestershire, by the king for his service on the Bruges embassy.

The Wyclif scholar Michael Wilks describes the theologian's reputation and situation in the mid-1370s this way: "Wyclif was not only acknowledged at Oxford as the outstanding teacher of his time, but was also the leader of a reform movement of 'poor priests', inspired by Franciscan ideals of apostolic poverty, for whom the obtaining of high office was not a prime consideration."[12] In 1376 Wyclif became clerical advisor to the Duke of Lancaster, John of Gaunt, the wealthiest and most influential man in England, but the following year he found himself arraigned on charges of heresy and had to appear before a group of bishops and theologians at St. Paul's, London. John of Gaunt made sure that no harm came to Wyclif. In all likelihood, the heresy had to do with his views on authority as expressed in his book *On Civil Dominion*. In Wyclif's understanding, "dominion," the right to exercise authority (and indirectly to hold property), is held from God, and is a right that God limits to those in sanctifying grace. The emphasis on sanctifying grace indicates an ecclesiological position that will come further to the fore in his theology.

In this view, both estates of the realm, civil and ecclesiastical, should fall under the authority of the king in all temporal matters. Unworthy priests, that is to say, priests reckoned not to be in a state of grace, would thereby have forfeited this right to authority and property, and lay lords could thus deprive them of their benefices. Further, Wyclif insisted that all clergy should live in poverty as had St. Peter and the other apostles. In this world, neither the saved nor the damned could be known, so that in practice the church as a visible body ceased to exist. His position may be summarized in this way:

> If only those who were chosen by God belonged to the church, and they could not be known, there was no reason for accepting any visible authority or for recognizing the claims of those who exercised it. Even more, there was no reason for such authority at

all: if those who were predestined to glory remained of the elect, regardless of temporal vicissitudes, nothing could further or detract from their final destiny. And likewise for the damned. The church in its traditional form therefore lost its *raison d'être*.[13]

This purist and elitist ecclesiology gradually brought him to view the visible church as the Antichrist. In 1379/80 he wrote the treatise, *On the Power of the Pope*. It was really designed to disprove the need for a pope at all, perhaps influenced by the ideas of Marsilius of Padua, though never acknowledged in the document. Like other reformers before and after him, Wyclif wanted a holier and purer church.

In May 1377, bulls were issued from Pope Gregory XI against the heretical teachings of Wyclif, including nineteen heretical propositions upon which he was to be examined. The examination took place in 1378, the examiners finding him "ill-sounding but not erroneous." The same year saw the completion of his *On the Truth of Holy Scripture*, in which he insisted that the Bible is the sole law of the church. Vernacular translations of the scriptures were suspect at the time and Wyclif's precise role in the production of an English Bible is far from clear.[14] At most it is possible to say that an English version of the New Testament seems to have been available by 1382, translator unknown, and in due course this was absorbed into a version by John Purvey, a member of the Wycliff circle, in the 1390s.

The year 1381, about one year after Wyclif's radical book on the Eucharist, witnessed the Peasants' Revolt. It was a protest against an unpopular tax. The rebels murdered the archbishop of Canterbury and marched on London. One of the rebel leaders, John Ball, was reported to have confessed before he was put to death "that for two years he had been a disciple of Wyclif, and had learned from him the heresies he had taught."[15] The story as it stands is probably false but the perspective on property and wealth in Wyclif's *On Civil Dominion* would have found an echo among the peasant revolutionaries. So, although Wyclif was not directly involved with the political unrest, contemporary opinion linked his revolutionary views with the "poor priests" who were his agents.

The word "Lollard" was first applied to Wyclif's followers in 1382. He did not found the Lollards as a movement, but they took over many of Wyclif's ideas and became thoroughly associated with them. In line with Wyclif's political views and his ecclesiology, Lollardy was in effect a movement that was antiestablishment, antipriest, a movement that advocated its version of righteous living. For all practical purposes, Lollardy was a form of incipient Puritanism. The name "Lollard" was a term of abuse, probably derived from "lollen," to mumble. The Lollards were judged to be mumblers of prayers. In effect, Lollard became the name for any heretic of the time in England.

Wyclif's last years are shrouded in darkness. Death followed a stroke that he suffered while hearing Mass on Holy Innocents Day, 1384. His curate tells us: "At the time of the elevation of the host he fell down smitten by a severe paralysis, especially in the tongue so that neither then nor afterwards could he speak."[16] He died on December 31, 1384, and was buried peacefully in the Lutterworth churchyard. However, the Council of Constance condemned Wyclif's writings, ordered his books burned and his body removed from consecrated ground. This last order was confirmed by the new Pope Martin V and was carried out in 1428. His body was dug up, burned and his ashes thrown in the local river.

Eucharist

Wyclif wrote his book *On the Eucharist* about 1380. It is the book that led to his expulsion from the University of Oxford. Sir Anthony Kenny, sometime master of Balliol College, Oxford, like his predecessor Wyclif (1360–61), describes the book this way:

> It is one of Wyclif's most vigorous writings, exhibiting at the same time his philosophical acumen, his

familiarity with the Bible and the Fathers, and his sweeping historical approach to questions of Church doctrine. The tone of the criticism of his adversaries is comparatively restrained, and there are comparatively few digressions on hobby horses such as clerical disendowment.[17]

One might say that it was his very clarity and in some degree persuasiveness on this one issue that brought about his downfall. Although some of his writings and his preaching had rendered him suspect in various quarters before its publication, it was the book with his eucharistic views that turned the tide distinctly against him. As a result, in 1381 he was driven from Oxford.

The book was a philosophical attack on transubstantiation. It is important to be clear about this. Wyclif was not attacking the eucharistic presence of Christ—he accepted and defended it—but rather the doctrine of transubstantiation. This now-traditional eucharistic doctrine taught that the substance of bread and wine is changed into the substance of the body and blood of Christ, but the accidents of bread and wine remained without a substance. For Wyclif, to talk of accidents without a substance was self-contradictory. An accident is a quality of something else, of a substance, and so, if one posits accidents without a substance, he felt that one was talking nonsense; one could not have accidents without a substance anymore than one could have creation without God.

Two explanations of what took place during the Mass were available from Thomas Aquinas and Duns Scotus. For the former, the substance of the bread was changed into the body of Christ, and the accidents that remained were upheld by what Aquinas called "quantity." For the latter, the substance of the bread was not changed at the consecration of the Mass, but rather the substance of bread was "annihilated" by God's power, that is to say, it simply ceased to be. But, at the level of common sense, no annihilation has taken place. We still see bread and wine. For Wyclif, the commonsense fact that we see bread and wine means, therefore, that what we see must be bread and wine, even though it is also believed that Christ is present. The Eucharist is *naturally* bread and wine and *sacramentally* Christ's body and blood. This is close to Martin Luther's idea of consubstantiation. Wyclif also attacked transubstantiation on the ground that it was an unscriptural innovation. His studies in scripture, especially in his book *On the Truth of Sacred Scripture*, were published in 1379, just one year before his eucharistic views were given public air. Transubstantiation does not occur in scripture, but faith is invited to recognize the eucharistic presence of Christ even as the eyes see bread and wine. Wyclif believed that just as in the incarnation of the Word two substances are present in the same moment, so too is the case with the Eucharist; in the Eucharist are the spiritual body of Christ, and the physical substance of bread, thus brought about by God.

What, then, happens in the celebration of the Eucharist and in the reception of holy communion? When the faithful commune with the spiritual body of Christ, something truly wonderful takes place, maintains Wyclif:

> All Christians and secular men, being one bread, may all eat of one bread, as members of one and the same Church, so that they may despise worldly honours and thus come to the supper of the Lord. When they have perfectly learned this doctrine of the sacrament of the altar, then they will begin to approach the end for which it was instituted, and will as sons of peace celebrate the Mass in truth.[18]

The real and final meaning of the Eucharist is to be found in the union of all Christ's faithful through the sacrament, a union that finally sets aside all distinctions, the distinction between priesthood and laity, the distinction of birth or class. "This is an attitude with strongly protestant overtones," says Keen, "with the priest cast in the role of the minister of the tight little group of God's elect, as he was one day to be in the high days of presbytery."[19] The morning star of the Reformation is beginning to rise.

Wyclif's denial of transubstantiation, however refined his qualifications were to academics, was "a stab at the heart of late medieval Catholicism."[20] Popular eucharistic devotion was focused on gazing at the elevated host after the consecration. It was thought of as "seeing one's Maker." To attack this notion so central to the fabric of medieval Christian faith was inevitably to put oneself in danger. After his expulsion from the University of Oxford, it seems that Wyclif made a promise not to use his offensive and heretical eucharistic ideas, accessible really only to academics and educated clergy, in public. This may have been the reason that he was permitted to live out his days in peace at his Lutterworth parish.

Conclusion

At first glance, the difference between Scotus, Wyclif and Aquinas may look like an unimportant dispute among medieval scholars—all of whom accept the reality of Christ's eucharistic presence, but comment on it using a different metaphysics, and a different theological methodology. That judgment is, I suspect, quite widespread. However, it seems to me that both Scotus and Wyclif espouse a naïve realism, that is to say, the view that reality is "already-out-there-now," and moreover, that *knowing* is pretty much the same as "taking a look." Metaphysical substance seems to be a kind of very "thin" substance underlying the physical. For Aquinas, arguably, substance is the end-product of reflection-leading-to-judgment—a very different point of view.

Sir Anthony Kenny, at the end of his fine essay on Wyclif, draws comparisons between Wyclif and John Wesley and John Henry Newman, whose eucharistic theologies are treated later in this book. All three are Oxford men. All three made names for themselves as scholars, and as pious and devout reformers of a sort. All three take steps that alienate their former theological allies and invite suspicion. "Exiled from Oxford, [each] carries on his religious missions elsewhere, tireless in preaching, writing, and controversy, casting only a rare nostalgic glance at the distant spires of the home of his youth and promise."[21]

Scotus becomes *beatus* while Wyclif is condemned as a heretic. Scotus thinks with the church, while Wyclif comes close to cutting himself off from the church. Scotus, no less than Wyclif, recognized the need of reform in the church. Both lived during a turbulent period in the church's history. During Scotus' lifetime the two Councils of Lyons took place (1245 and 1274), whose agendas were reformist and ecumenical.[22] The Great Western Schism, which was to end with the Council of Constance in 1414–18 and the decree that Wyclif was a heretic, began in 1378, six years before Wyclif died. Wyclif's witness connected more explicitly with reform, while Scotus' contribution lay primarily in the arena of scholarship.

Notes

1. Alexander Broadie, *The Shadow of Scotus: Philosophy and Faith in Pre-Reformation Scotland* (Edinburgh: T. & T. Clark, 1995), 1.

2. Anthony Kenny, *Wyclif* (New York and Oxford: Oxford University Press, 1985), v.

3. Bonnie Kent, "Franciscan Thought," in Adrian Hastings and others, eds., *The Oxford Companion to Christian Thought* (New York and Oxford: Oxford University Press, 2000), 248.

4. Gerard Manley Hopkins, *Poems of Gerard Manley Hopkins* (London: Humphrey Milford, 1918).

5. For an introduction to the women mystics in relation to the Eucharist, see Owen F. Cummings, *Mystical Women, Mystical Body* (Portland: The Pastoral Press, 2000).

6. Heiko Oberman, "Fourteenth Century Religious Thought: A Premature Profile," *Speculum* 53 (1978), 80.

7. Jaroslav Pelikan, *Reformation of Church and Dogma (1300–1700)* (Chicago and London: University of Chicago Press, 1984), 56.

8. Duns Scotus, *Opus Oxoniense*, 1.4, dist. 10, qu. 1, n. 9. I owe this reference to my colleague, Brother Ansgar Santogrossi, OSB. For a

systematic and detailed account of Scotus' eucharistic theology, see David Burr, "Scotus and Transubstantiation," in *Medieval Studies* 34 (1972), 336–60, and also Burr's *Eucharistic Presence and Conversion in Late Thirteenth-Century Franciscan Thought* (Philadelphia: The American Philosophic Society, 1984), 76–98.

9. Richard Cross, *Duns Scotus* (New York and Oxford: Oxford University Press, 1999), 141.

10. Maurice Keen, "Wyclif, the Bible, and Transubstantiation," in Anthony Kenny, ed., *Wyclif in His Times* (Oxford: Clarendon Press, 1986), 8.

11. Raymond Moloney, *The Eucharist* (Collegeville, MN: The Liturgical Press, 1995), 147.

12. Michael Wilks, *Wyclif: Political Ideas and Practice* (Oxford: Oxbow Books, 2000), 2.

13. Gordon Leff, *Heresy in the Later Middle Ages* (Manchester: Manchester University Press, one volume edition, 1999), 519.

14. Wilks, *Wyclif: Political Ideas and Practice*, 85.

15. Cited in Kenny, *Wyclif*, 92.

16. Ibid., 99.

17. Ibid., 82.

18. John Wycliff, *On the Eucharist*, 325, cited in Keen, "Wyclif, the Bible, and Transubstantiation," 15.

19. Keen, "Wyclif, the Bible, and Transubstantiation," 15.

20. Richard Rex, *The Lollards* (New York and London: Palgrave Macmillan, 2002), 42.

21. Kenny, *Wyclif*, 100.

22. See Christopher M. Bellitto, *The General Councils* (New York/Mahwah, NJ: Paulist Press, 2002), 57–61.

PART THREE:
The Reformation Age

10.

The Classical Reformers: Martin Luther, Huldrych Zwingli and John Calvin

*On the reading I will propose, there is no grand, consoling reason
for the way the Reformation turned out; the schism with which
we are living is nothing more or less than a sorry mess,
brought about by contingent human choices in a confused historical
context defined less by clear and principled theological argument
(though, of course, that was present) than by a peculiar
(and distinctively sixteenth century) combination of overheated
and ever-escalating polemics, cold-blooded Realpolitik,
and fervid apocalyptic dreaming....[The Reformation]
was a tragic chapter of accidents.*
–Lutheran theologian David S. Yeago[1]

*It has become clear that the breach of Church unity cannot be traced back
either to a lack of understanding on the part of the authorities of the
Catholic Church, or solely to Luther's lack of understanding of true
Catholicism, even if both factors played a role.*
–Catholic theologian Pope John Paul II[2]

THE REFORMATION OF THE SIXTEENTH CENTURY

Acknowledging the Reformation as "a tragic chapter of accidents" and as a breach of church unity for which both sides of the reform share responsibility is a good way to begin this chapter on the history of eucharistic theology. Both Pope John Paul II and David Yeago, in the introductory quotations, witness to the change of attitude that has come about in the study of this schismatic century. Church history and the history of doctrine are studied now not over against one another, nor from a defensive and polemical point of view, but in an effort to reach toward a more accurate understanding of what took place.

Any student of church history knows that the reform of the church was a constant concern throughout the entire medieval period. From top-down reforms imitated by popes and councils to bottom-up reforms such as the mendicant movement of the thirteenth century and even earlier, there was a clear recognition that the church was not as she was meant to be. The sixteenth-century Reformation is to be situated within these reform movements and protests, but with this difference: that, though not initially intended, it ended up splitting the church in the West, and indeed, initiating among Christians a fissiparous tendency and temptation.[3]

The sixteenth-century reforming movement was extraordinarily complex. Perhaps we may point to some of the factors that made for the complexity. The emerging consciousness of national states over against the greater powers of Europe was one such factor, leading to the formation of territorial and national churches. At the same time, it needs to be acknowledged that the Reformers passed easily from one place to another assisting in the reform of the church, without excessive awareness of national or regional boundaries. Sometimes the movement of Reformers from one place to another was motivated by persecution. Though with different emphases, we find across the spectrum of Reformed theologians a central preoccupation with the centrality of scripture, with faith and with a theological anthropology that knows humans cannot earn salvation. This brief chapter on the classical Reformers hopes to provide not a comprehensive but an accurate introductory account of their eucharistic theologies.

MARTIN LUTHER (1483–1546)

Martin Luther was the son of a miner at Mansfield, Saxony, and was educated at the University of Erfurt, where he became a member of the Augustinian Order. He became professor of biblical exegesis at Wittenberg, a position he held until his death in 1546. As a young professor at Wittenberg, he agonized for a long time over his own salvation—so much so that, when he fully grasped what he took to be the Pauline teaching of justification by faith, he felt liberated. And this liberation finds expression in his 1515–16 lectures on St. Paul's Letter to the Romans. The Reformation is conventionally dated at the point in 1517 when Luther brought his convictions to bear on the practice of indulgences, especially on the way that indulgences were being misused by the preacher Johannes Tetzel, who was not only collecting money to pay for the building of St. Peter's Basilica in Rome, but also to repay debts incurred by the Archbishop of Mainz who held three diocesan sees at the same time. Immediately both the hierarchy and the papacy were involved, for the challenge was truly systemic.

In his excellent recent book dealing with the constancy and the problems of church reform, historian Christopher Bellitto writes: "Luther's reform ideas start with many of the same complaints others voiced about the late medieval Church: arithmetical piety *in membris*, greed *in capite*. He stepped into the history of reform with his *95 Theses*."⁴ What began as a reforming impetus from within quickly gained notoriety. Charged with heresy in 1518, Luther was summoned before the learned Cardinal Cajetan at Augsburg. But Luther refused to recant, and he was protected by German princes as he continued his teaching and preaching. Between May and November 1520 he published five books in which the foundations of his new approach to Christian faith were clearly laid out: the *Treatise of Good Works*, *The Papacy at Rome*, *Address to the German Nobility*, *The Babylonian Captivity of the Church* and *The Freedom of a Christian Man*. In these books Luther attacked the papacy, liberated the sacraments from what he saw as their captivity and gave emphasis to the priesthood of all believers. He was excommunicated in 1521.

These five works met with great success and found a ready response. How is this to be explained? There was the fact that there was a growing dissatisfaction with the prevailing situation in the church in continental Europe, and there was the fact of the printing press. The former created a context for ecclesial reform, and the latter a powerful means for enabling that reform. Luther's ideas were to spread with great rapidity.

In 1524 Luther finally discarded his Augustinian habit, married the following year and continued his commitment to the reform of the church until his death in 1543. He is buried in the castle church at Wittenberg.

Eucharist

"It is a lifetime's work to read all Luther's books, pamphlets, lectures, the notes of lectures, the table talk, the letters and the rest which have come down to us, in the original German or Latin, and to master all the details of his life and achievement," comments John Todd.[5] One conclusion that can be drawn from this is that Luther was no systematic theologian; however, it is not difficult to get hold of the main lines of his thought on central doctrinal issues.

In his *The Babylonian Captivity of the Church*, Luther set out a fairly comprehensive account of the church and the sacraments, as he understood them. He held that there is no essential difference between clergy and laity, so that clergy are different in function only, to preach and to preside at the sacraments. In Luther's judgment, all share in the priesthood of Christ through baptism.

> In sum, the sacrament of ordination is the prettiest of devices for giving a firm foundation to all the ominous things hitherto done in the church, or yet to be done....Now we, who have been baptized, are all

> uniformly priests in virtue of that very fact. The only
> addition received by the priests is the office of
> preaching, and even this with our consent.[6]

The only thing that could save a person was faith, he wrote, and
so in the Eucharist the believer opens himself up in faith to
God's saving action:

> The Mass is a divine promise which can benefit no
> one, be applied to no one, intercede for no one, be
> communicated to no one, except only the believer
> himself by the sole virtue of his own faith.[7]

If the Eucharist is celebrated in true faith, it seals God's offer of
salvation by giving us the true body and blood of Christ in holy
communion, he held. Luther gives emphasis to the real presence
of Christ in the Eucharist, received in faith. This real presence
for him has nothing whatever to do with the doctrine of transubstantiation, which he regarded as a metaphysical twisting
stemming from Aristotle, not from scripture. He once said that
when scholastic theologians had to resort to Aristotelian philosophy, they turned their backs on the meaning of holy scripture; "The pagan Aristotle was not only unbaptized but
unbaptizable."[8] It is enough, he said, to trust the Word of God.

Beginning in 1525, Luther was involved in a drawn-out
controversy on the Eucharist with the Swiss reformer, Huldrych
Zwingli—leading finally, in 1529, to the Marburg Colloquy.
The Marburg Colloquy was called by the Landgraf Philip of
Hesse in order to solve the disputes among the reformers about
the Eucharist, especially those between Luther and Zwingli. At
this discussion Luther wrote with chalk on the tablecloth the
words, *"Hoc est enim corpus meum,"* "For this is my body." Then,
after a long speech about the Eucharist, he said:

> They [Zwingli and his followers] must prove that a
> body is not a body....God is above mathematics, and

his words must be received with reverence and obeyed.[9]

This is the absolute foundation of Luther's position, taking the word of the Word. We shall come to Zwingli in due course, but here we shall concentrate on Luther's famous "The Sacrament of the Body and Blood of Christ—Against the Fanatics," which presents his position against Zwingli.[10] Zwingli maintained that it was not fitting or reasonable that Christ's body and blood should be in the bread and wine. Luther recognized in this an anti-matter position, the logic of which would undermine the incarnation of the Word itself.

> To [this] point I might say equally well that it is not reasonable that God should descend from heaven and enter into the womb; that he who nourishes, sustains, and encompasses all the world should allow himself to be nourished and encompassed by the Virgin.[11]

Luther pushes back even further the logic of the real presence of Christ in the Eucharist. If one cannot accept Christ's presence in the Eucharist, a miracle of miracles, "one would be forced to allow no creature to exist." Creation itself is a miracle, in the sense that it is not necessary of itself, but is God's gift. If God condescends to create, share existence with others, and if God enters that created existence as the Incarnate Son, it is but a small step for the Incarnate Son sacramentally to be present in the bread and wine.

> As one cannot deny the fact that [Mary] thus becomes pregnant through the Word, and no one knows how it comes about, so it is in the sacrament also. For as soon as Christ says: "This is my body," his body is present through the Word and the power of the Holy Spirit. If the Word is not there, it is mere bread; but as soon as the words are added they bring with them that of which they speak.[12]

While emphasizing the mysterious nature of the transformation, Luther implies that it is no less and no more mysterious than the miracle of creation, which did not have to be, and the miracle of incarnation, which is an act of pure grace.

At the same time, Luther is powerfully eloquent about the gracious reality of Christ's presence to the believer through the preaching of the gospel:

> Again, I preach the Gospel of Christ, and with my bodily voice I bring Christ into your heart, so that you may form him within yourself....You must answer that you have the true Christ, not that he sits in there, as one sits on a chair, but as he is at the right hand of the Father. How that comes about you cannot know, but your heart truly feels his presence, and through the experience of faith you know for a certainty that he is there....Therefore, your heart is in heaven, not in an apparition or a dream, but truly. For where he is, there you are also.[13]

He draws a certain parallel between the Word in scripture and the Word in the Eucharist. "He has put himself into the Word, and through the Word he puts himself into the bread also."[14] The Word feeds the members of his ecclesial body at the twinned tables of Word and Eucharist, and this points up the importance of preaching the Word:

> There should be preaching at the mass at all times. Therefore the words, "Do this in remembrance of me" are as much as to say: "As often as you do this, preach of me," as Paul interprets it in 1 Cor. 11 when he calls it proclaiming the death of Christ.[15]

Not to accept this twinned presence of Christ for Luther is to be something of a rationalist who cannot accept the mysterious incomprehensibility of God and his action in Word and Eucharist. He fumes, with a degree of wit, against his opponents on this matter:

> For this is what they say: If I believe in Jesus Christ,
> who died for me, what need is there for me to believe
> in a baked God? Wait and see, he will bake them
> when the time comes, so that their hides will sizzle.[16]

And so Luther concluded that when the Word speaks the words, "This is my body, this is my blood," the Word, that is Christ, is truly present: "The body of Christ is present in the bread and his blood is truly present in the wine."[17]

HULDRYCH ZWINGLI
(1484–1531)

While still a parish priest at Einsiedeln, Zwingli saturated himself in the patristic authors, Greek and Latin. During a serious illness in 1519, just after his move to the minster, the principal church of Zurich, Zwingli became convinced of the absolute sovereignty of God and of the Word of God. The Zwingli scholar W. Peter Stephens maintains that most of Zwingli's eucharistic theology was in place, at least implicitly, in 1524, five years before his Marburg Colloquy with Luther.[18]

The key to Zwingli's theology is his radical separation of spirit and matter. Salvation comes about only from God, and from God as "Spirit." This clearly put him in a difficult position *vis-à-vis* creation and the incarnation—let alone the Eucharist—as being the work of God, as is suggested by these words: "Christ gave life to the world not because he is flesh, but because he is God and the Son of God."[19] We see resurrected here the christological debates of the patristic period concerning the flesh of Christ, and perhaps even an echo of gnosticism's distrust of all things created and material.

When this way of thinking is applied to the Eucharist, there can be no meaning for Christ's presence in the eucharistic gifts—which are obviously created and material—other than an utterly spiritualized meaning. That is precisely Zwingli's position. He takes up as the center of his eucharistic understanding the words of John 6:63: "The flesh is useless. The words that I have spoken to you are spirit and life." If these words are taken at face value, maintains Zwingli, there can be no real presence of Christ, of *corpus*/body, in the eucharistic gifts. It must be a spiritual experience of eating spiritually. "Eating Christ" means, and can only mean, "believing in Christ."

> For it is forever true: what is born of flesh is flesh, and on the other hand, what is born of spirit is spirit. Christ, therefore, means here a spiritual eating, but of what nature? Such that we are to say that Christ is eaten here physically? Are to eat spiritually and to eat physically one and the same thing then? Even the logician knows that it is absurd. If it is spiritual eating why do you call it physical?...Christ means, therefore, that unless we eat his flesh, that is, unless we believe that he underwent death and poured out his blood for us, we shall not attain life....But is Christ in anybody physically? By no means. Why, then, are we speaking about the body?...It is faith, therefore, not eating about which Christ is speaking here.[20]

In respect to the Latin form of the eucharistic words of Jesus, etched by Luther on the tablecloth at Marburg, "*Hoc est enim corpus meum,*" Zwingli has no difficulty. "*Est*"/is means and can only mean "*significat*"/signifies, he wrote. The bread represents or signifies Christ's body, so that when it is eaten, it calls to remembrance that Christ gave his actual body for us.

In a most lucid presentation of Zwingli's theology, building upon the more-recent work of less-accessible Reformation scholars, another Zwinglian specialist, Jacques Courvoisier, drew attention to a proposal made by Zwingli in 1525 for the liturgy of holy communion—a liturgy for which the Zurich public officials refused permission.[21] The eucharistic prayer was replaced with an exchange between the pastor and his assistants, and an antiphonal exchange between the men and women of the congregation, seated on separate sides of the nave. A simple wooden table was placed in the nave, in contrast to the altar in the chancel, and the eucharistic vessels were also wooden. The communicants were to receive communion from the servers with their own hands. Prior to communion this prayer was offered in which the entire eucharistic assembly was transformed, even transubstantiated into the body of Christ.[22] Courvoisier says of this prayer: "Transubstantiation no longer concerns the bread, but the whole congregation, and it is *this* 'body of Christ' which the congregation offers in oblation to its Lord."[23] If this line of interpretation has any degree of truth in it, there is a tension in Zwingli's thought, to say the least, between an eating and a spiritual eating, between *est* and *significat.*

JOHN CALVIN (1509–1564)

John Calvin (the Latinized form of the French surname Cauvin) was the leader of the Reformation in the Swiss city of Geneva. Born in Noyon, France, he received a number of ecclesiastical benefices from the Diocese of Noyon that enabled him to proceed to the University of Paris at fourteen years of age. At that time the university exemplified both traditional scholasticism and the new humanist learning of the sixteenth century. In Paris Calvin was introduced to nominalist theology, a style of theology that at that time in Paris was heavily under the influence of the Scottish theologian John Mair (in Latin, Major). As a result of a disagreement between his father (the diocesan fiscal agent) and the cathedral chapter at Noyon, Calvin set himself to the study of law in Orleans and Bourges from 1528 to 1531. But it was not where his heart lay. He returned to theology, plunging himself into the study of Greek, Latin and Hebrew in Paris. Speaking about a religious experience he had when he was twenty-five, he said: "God by a sudden conversion subdued my heart to teachableness." He resigned his clerical benefices, and his writings take on an unmistakably Reformed hue.

In 1536 he wrote in Basle the first edition of what was finally to become, in 1559, his *Institutes of the Christian Religion.* It is this work of dogmatic theology more than any other produced at the time of the Reformation that may be compared to St. Thomas Aquinas' *Summa Theologica.* Called to Geneva to assist in the promotion of the Reformation, he continued his study as well as preaching, teaching and counseling, as that city was shaped into a paradigm of Reformation polity. Calvin's sense of the glory of God was overwhelming, and when he died in 1564, "his wish was to be buried at an unknown place without witnesses or ceremony in the belief that the glory of God should not be overshadowed by honoring people."[24]

Eucharist

The entire *oeuvre* of John Calvin may be described as a eucharistic theology, shot through with the themes of grace and gratitude. God's abundant grace, his very being imparting himself in love is what we as creatures find all around us, and the only appropriate response is eucharistic, that is, one of sheer gratitude. Man, for Calvin, is essentially "eucharistic man." As Gerrish describes it:

> In Calvin's view, it is this that makes humans the apex
> of creation: the whole created order has its meaning
> and purpose in the praise that they alone, of all God's
> earthly creatures, can return to him, and his design in
> making the entire order of nature would be subverted
> if at any time there were no people to call upon him.[25]

If you like, eucharistic language is the proper language used by humankind prior to any consideration of the Eucharist as such.

"The gift of faith is given through the word and made visible in the sacraments."[26] In Calvin's theology, preaching the Word holds the central place of efficacy that traditionally had been held by the sacraments. The sacraments are adjuncts to the Word, signs or figures of God's grace provided in the Word.

Thus, the Eucharist is a pledge of God's continual nourishment of Christians with the bread of life.

In his teaching on the Eucharist, Calvin developed a position somewhere between those of Luther and Zwingli in their 1529 Marburg Colloquy. He did not quite accept Luther's eucharistic position. He found it conceptually difficult to explain just how communion with Christ's life-giving flesh occurred in the Eucharist. Yet, in the *Institutes* of 1543, there is a very strong statement of belief in what can only be called the "real presence" of Christ in the eucharistic gifts:

> Now if anyone asks me how, I will not be ashamed to admit that the mystery is too sublime for my intelligence to grasp or my words to declare: to speak more plainly, I experience rather than understand it. Here, then, without any arguing, I embrace the truth of God in which I may safely rest content. Christ proclaims that his flesh is the food, his blood the drink, of my soul. I offer him my soul to be fed with such food. In his sacred supper he bids me take, eat, and drink his body and blood under the symbols of bread and wine: I have no doubt that he truly proffers them and that I receive them.[27]

Calvin needs to be taken with great seriousness. The mystery of the Eucharist transcends the order of nature and may be apprehended only in faith. On one reading this position is at a considerable remove from Zwingli's *est* means *significat*, that "eating" means "believing in." On another, Calvin is unable to bring himself to say that the eating is such that Christ's flesh is conveyed to the communicant. The eating and drinking are "under the symbols," and so he seems equally unable to rid himself of Zwinglian symbolism. How is one to explain this tension? The late Max Thurian perceptively remarked:

> In his exposition of the real presence, Calvin seems to have had a too carnal conception of the body of

Christ. Despite his great emphasis on the humanity of Jesus, Calvin did not sufficiently appreciate the difference of condition between Christ living and suffering, from the Annunciation to Calvary, and Christ risen and glorified, from Easter to the Ascension and in eternity.[28]

If Zwingli espoused a position that is too anti-matter, Calvin does not sufficiently distinguish matter from glorified matter, the matter of Christ's body from the glorified matter of that body resurrected and ascended. He experienced this difficulty and yet he remained content, giving priority to faith over reason, to feel what he could not understand.

Calvin's eucharistic theology may be summarized in seven brief propositions.[29] First, the Lord's Supper is a gift. It is a gift of God, not a human work as the Catholics had it, nor a Christian confession of Christ as the Zwinglians had it. Both sides miss the mark, Calvin thought: the Eucharist is God's gracious gift.

Second, the gift is Jesus Christ himself. Calvin means here (though he finds it difficult to articulate) the whole Christ. The Eucharist is not just the benefits of Christ, but Christ, "somehow."

Third, the gift is given through the signs of bread and wine. This is opposed to both Catholic and Zwinglian beliefs. He felt the former, through the "perverted" doctrine of transubstantiation, collapsed the sign into the signified. Calvin saw this as a kind of "eucharistic monophysitism," which destroyed the necessary earthly elements of bread and wine in favor of the Lord's presence. The Catholic doctrine, for Calvin, reduced signified to sign. The "real presence" of Christ is spiritual, but the earthly sign of bread and wine is real in an ordinary empirical fashion.

In analyzing Calvin's thought, it is difficult to avoid the conclusion that one of the root problems was philosophical, and indeed epistemological, "What is the real? How is the real known?" Against the Zwinglians, the signs "present" for Calvin what they "represent," and are not mere empty signs.

Fourth, the gift is given by the Holy Spirit. The body and blood of Christ are made present by the Holy Spirit, and by this affirmation, Calvin sought to avoid the suggestion that Christ is "enclosed" within the eucharistic gifts. The Holy Spirit is the bond of union between the communicant and the life-giving flesh of Christ, present in the gifts.

Fifth, the gift is given to all who communicate, both devout believer and unbeliever. However, there is a difference. The former receive the gifts with benefit unto salvation, the latter receive them unto condemnation.

Sixth, the benefit of the gift is received by faith. Against the Catholics, Calvin considered the doctrine of *ex opere operato* to undermine the role and function of personal faith in Christ. Personal faith is necessary to receive the gift of the Eucharist as beneficial.

Seventh, the gift evokes gratitude—thanksgiving—on the part of the person and the church.

Calvin thought "the Lord's Supper" was the best name for the Eucharist. The very word "supper" indicated to him that this ritual was best understood as a meal rather than as a sacrifice in the traditional Catholic sense. He decided that the Catholic Mass, on the other hand, subverted this understanding by turning the Eucharist into a human work—something done by humans, and not a gift received by them.

Conclusion

The contemporary American Reformation scholar David Steinmetz points out how far removed in some respects the Reformers' concern about the Eucharist is from that of their heirs. "For many Protestants," he writes, "the sacraments play such a subsidiary role in their faith and piety that they are astonished to see the sixteenth century reformers attacking one another over what appears to the modern eye to be fairly minor differences in eucharistic theology."[30] Something of a slow sea change is occurring in our times. The reasons are many, but we may single out two: Catholic participation in the ecumenical movement, stemming from Vatican II, and the 1982 World Council of Churches' Faith and Order document, *Baptism, Eucharist and Ministry*. These sources are inviting serious Christians of all persuasions to reflect more deeply on the Eucharist, to read each other's eucharistic theology in the light of the classic sources, and to raise further relevant questions. When the conversation continues like this, all sides may move to regret the hardening of hearts that ought to have been more eucharistic, and a too-premature closure of eucharistic meaning in the sixteenth century and since.

Notes

1. David S. Yeago, "The Catholic Luther," in Carl E. Braaten and Robert W. Jenson, eds., *The Catholicity of the Reformation* (Grand Rapids: Eerdmans, 1996), 16–17, 33.

2. John Paul II, "Letter on the Fifth Centenary of the Birth of Martin Luther," *Information Service, The Secretariat for Promoting Christian Unity* (1983), 83.

3. See Diarmaid MacCulloch, *The Reformation* (New York and London: Viking Books, 2004).

4. Christopher M. Bellitto, *Renewing Christianity: A History of Church Reform from Day One to Vatican II* (New York/Mahwah, NJ: Paulist Press, 2001), 119.

5. John M. Todd, *Martin Luther* (New York: Paulist Press, 1964), xiii.

6. Cited from John Dillenberger, ed., *Martin Luther, Selections from His Writing* (Garden City, NY: Doubleday, 1961), 345.

7. Ibid., 283.

8. David C. Steinmetz, *Luther in Context* (Bloomington: Indiana University Press, 1986), 73.

9. Samuel Simpson, *Life of Ulrich Zwingli* (London: Hodder and Stoughton, 1903), 191.

10. The English translation followed is that of Frederick C. Ahrens, found in Helmut T. Lehmann, ed., *Luther's Works*, vol. 36, "Word and Sacrament II" (Philadelphia: Fortress Press, 1959), 335–61.

11. Lehmann, *Luther's Works*, vol. 36, 338.

12. Ibid., 341.

13. Ibid., 340.

14. Ibid., 343.

15. Ibid., 349.

16. Ibid., 344.

17. Ibid., 346.

18. W. Peter Stephens, *Zwingli, An Introduction to His Thought* (Oxford: Clarendon Press, 1992), 95.

19. H. Wayne Pipkin, ed., *Huldrych Zwingli, Writings*, vol. 2 (Allison Park, PA: Pickwick Publications, 1984), 330.

20. From Zwingli's "Letter to Matthew Alber," in Pipkin, *Huldrych Zwingli, Writings*, 2: 134.

21. Jacques Courvoisier, *Zwingli, A Reformed Theologian* (Richmond: John Knox Press, 1973), 75–77.

22. For the full text of this prayer, see Bard Thompson, ed., *Liturgies of the Western Church* (Cleveland and New York: The World Publishing Company, 1961), 149–55.

23. Courvoisier, *Zwingli, A Reformed Theologian*, 76. Not all Zwinglian scholars are in agreement with Courvoisier on this issue. See, for example, Brian A. Gerrish, *Continuing the Reformation: Essays on Modern Religious Thought* (Chicago and London: University of Chicago Press, 1993), 66–69.

24. Alexandre Ganoczy, "Calvin, John," in Hans J. Hillerbrand, ed., *The Oxford Encyclopedia of the Reformation*, vol. 1 (New York and Oxford: Oxford University Press, 1996), 237.

25. Brian A. Gerrish, *Grace and Gratitude: The Eucharistic Theology of John Calvin* (Edinburgh: T. & T. Clark, 1993), 43.

26. ———. "Calvin, John," in Adrian Hastings and others, eds., *The Oxford Companion to Christian Thought* (New York and Oxford: Oxford University Press, 2000), 92.

27. Cited in Gerrish, *Grace and Gratitude*, 174.

28. Max Thurian, *The Eucharistic Memorial*, Part 2 (Richmond: John Knox Press, 1961), 114.

29. Following Brian A. Gerrish, "Gospel and Eucharist: John Calvin on the Lord's Supper," in his *The Old Protestantism and the New* (Chicago and London: University of Chicago Press, 1982), 106–17.

30. Steinmetz, *Luther in Context*, 72.

11.

The English Reformation and the Eucharist: Bishop John Fisher of Rochester and Archbishop Thomas Cranmer of Canterbury

From a 16th century conversation on the liturgy: Thomas Cranmer, "How sad it is that the people in the nave of the church do not understand anything about what is being celebrated in the sanctuary!"
Stephen Gardiner, in response, said, "Don't worry about that, it has never occurred to them that they might want to understand it!"
–Louis Bouyer[1]

We learn to see that those who suffered and died, though deeply estranged from each other in this life, died for the one faith.
–Mark Santer[2]

ON THE EVE OF THE REFORMATION IN ENGLAND

In the introduction to the previous chapter, the reader was alerted to the dangers of an unnuanced approach to the Reformation of the sixteenth century in continental Europe.

173

The same caution must be in place as we have regard to the English Reformation, in many ways forming something of a contrast with its continental counterpart.

It is frequently assumed by historians of the period that the church in England, on the eve of the Reformation, was a church in need of a thoroughgoing reform, a church with which the majority of the English faithful were singularly dissatisfied. This seems not to have been entirely the case. More recent investigations offer an alternative reading of the situation. For example, Eamon Duffy writes:

> Late mediaeval Catholicism exerted an enormously strong, diverse and vigorous hold over the imaginations and the loyalty of the people up to the very moment of the Reformation. Traditional religion had about it no particular marks of exhaustion or decay, and indeed in a whole host of ways, from the multiplication of vernacular religious books to adaptations within the national and regional cult of the saints, was showing itself well able to meet new needs and new conditions.[3]

The ordinary people were basically satisfied and content with their inherited form of Catholic Christianity. This is in no way to deny that the "new learning" from Reformed circles on the European Continent was not making headway in English academic and ecclesiastical circles. It certainly was making a headway, and especially at the University of Cambridge. Nor is it to deny that there were issues and problems in the church that required attention. But in many ways the Reformation in England was imposed by the state.

To gain a perspective on the intricacies of the English Reformation, and especially on the theology of the Eucharist, attention will be focused on two bishops: John Fisher of Rochester and Thomas Cranmer of Canterbury. Fisher (1469–1535) represents the Catholic wing, Cranmer (1489–1556) the Reforming wing of the church in England. Both were martyrs for their sides.

JOHN FISHER (1469–1535)

St. John Fisher and St. Thomas More were both executed during the reign of King Henry VIII of England. This is how the Anglican historian and theologian Sir Henry Chadwick begins an essay on St. John Fisher, an essay in which he attempts to set Fisher's protest and martyrdom in a broad context:

> In the draft bull excommunicating King Henry VIII, of the year 1535, three themes are linked together as providing overwhelming grounds for the condemnation: the divorce of Catherine of Aragon, the claim to be supreme head of the Church of England, and the judicial murder of John Fisher. The saintly and renowned humanist Fisher, the man Henry VIII himself had been heard by [Cardinal Reginald] Pole to describe as the most learned man he knew, is a symbolic figure by his unyielding opposition to the divorce and to the king's consequent expulsion of papal authority from his realm in response to the humiliation of Pope Clement's rejection. None of the three acts was well regarded in Europe at large, and together they looked like the tyranny of a Night of the Long Knives.[4]

In this passage from Chadwick, St. John stands as the hero against King Henry VIII. He stands as a learned and holy bishop, held in high esteem throughout the continent of Europe. This positive portrait of Chadwick's contrasts with the more general image of Fisher as "a conservative medieval churchman" whose life and career have experienced at the hands of historians "continuing marginalization."[5] Who was this complex, heroic and learned man?

John Fisher was born at Beverley, Yorkshire, England, in 1469, the son of Robert Fisher, a textile dealer. His father died when John was eight, leaving his mother Agnes with four children. Agnes then married William White, and had five more children. Three of Agnes' children were to enter religion: John Fisher, and Richard and Elizabeth White. Entering Michaelhouse (later absorbed into Trinity College) at the University of Cambridge at fourteen, the young Fisher took his BA in 1488 and his MA in 1491. He was ordained a priest at twenty-two years of age. He was devoted to his *alma mater*, serving in various offices until 1501.

He became in 1502 chaplain to Lady Margaret Beaufort (1443–1509), grandmother of King Henry VIII. Undoubtedly under Fisher's influence, Lady Margaret made numerous gifts to the University of Cambridge, including founding Christ's College and St. John's. She provided for two readerships of divinity at Oxford and Cambridge, which ultimately were to become the prestigious Lady Margaret Chairs of Divinity. Fisher took his DD degree in 1501, was elected vice-chancellor of the university and chancellor three years later in 1504.

In 1504 Fisher also became bishop of Rochester. As one author describes it, it was "England's least remunerative diocese, worth a mere four hundred and eleven pounds a year. [Fisher] eschewed the pattern of his six predecessors at Rochester who had all moved on to richer sees."[6] He remained as bishop of the diocese for thirty-one years. Moreover, Fisher was a resident and an active bishop in his diocese, a bishop who preached the good news:

> At a time when the episcopal office was conceived in juridical-institutional terms, identified with the twin powers of jurisdiction and sacramental orders, when, in effect, the ministry of preaching tended to be offloaded on to the friars, and bishops were ready to admit to having never set foot in a pulpit, Bishop Fisher emerged as the foremost preacher in England.[7]

He obtained a papal bull granting the University of Cambridge the right to appoint twelve priests to preach anywhere in England. On this same subject of preaching, apparently Fisher encouraged the humanist scholar Erasmus to write a book outlining the principles of preaching. Writing from Basel to an acquaintance, Erasmus said:

> If Christ grants me the strength, I shall finish a book on the principles of preaching, which I promised long ago and am frequently asked for in letters from that best of prelates, John, bishop of Rochester, who appeals to our ancient friendship and his unfailing and continual support of me.[8]

In point of fact, not only did he espouse better preaching on his own part, but he is also widely regarded as a reforming bishop long before the Council of Trent, an "example, inspiration and the encapsulation of the 'episcopal ideal'…a 'Tridentine' before Trent."[9]

In 1511 Fisher encouraged Erasmus to come to Cambridge to teach Greek. This was part of Fisher's encouragement of the biblical languages at Cambridge, Hebrew, Greek and Latin. Fisher himself, of course, knew Latin well, as his own studies would have been conducted in that language. He did not, however, leave the advance of the new learning to others, to younger men studying at the university. Erasmus encouraged him to study Greek. He also plunged himself into the study of Hebrew in middle age. Erasmus wrote to the German humanist and Hebraist, Johannes Reuchlin that Fisher "is the best scholar of his nation and its most saintly prelate."[10]

In 1529 Fisher was named one of Catherine of Aragon's counselors and became her leading champion against King Henry VIII's attempt to divorce her. This, needless to say, did not endear him to the king. Fisher became a leading opponent of Henry's attempt to become supreme head of the church in England and to that effect defended the supremacy of the pope. He was imprisoned twice, and attempts were made on his life, yet he stayed with his position. As a result of his refusal to accept the Bill of Succession because the accompanying oath required the acknowledgment of royal supremacy in the church, St. John was arrested, imprisoned in the Tower of

London and stripped of all offices. While in prison he was named a cardinal by Pope Paul III. After ten months in prison, he was tried, convicted of treason and beheaded at Tyburn on June 22, 1535.

Church and Eucharist

The dominant conception of the church in Fisher's theology is the church as the Mystical Body of Christ. He even uses this image for the various members of the newly founded Christ's College, Cambridge. Thus, the master of Christ's College is the head, the two deans are the arms and so forth. In respect of the church he composed a beautiful prayer that gives emphasis to his membership in this Mystical Body of Christ:

> This will I seek after: that, incorporated into the Mystical Body of Christ, which is the assembly of the faithful and the house of God, I may remain in it always—that I may dwell in the house of the Lord, nor be separated nor fall therefrom by any heresy or perverse view as long as I live, all the days of my life; for, in that assembly whatever is the good pleasure of the Lord is taught most truly through the Spirit dwelling in the same, so that I may see the delight of the Lord; by adhering to her doctrines I shall dare to console myself more confidently by the contemplation of the heavenly temple.[11]

Reception of holy communion, of course, confirms and strengthens this incorporation. He uses the image of Eve to illustrate the ontological bond between Christ and the Christian incorporated into him:

> As Eve had been formed from the side of Adam so we who are the Church and the Spouse of Christ, by eating his flesh and blood, are made one Body, and

> members of the Body of Christ, and so from two is
> made one flesh.[12]

This intimate image, thoroughly traditional, makes the church his Mother, and he is ever ready to rise to her defense against reformer or king. It is not, however, a view of the church that blinds him to its imperfection and sin. In his own Tudor English he writes:

> O miserable estate of ours, O time most worthy
> bewaylyng, into the which most unfortunately our
> deare and holy Mother the Churche, the spouse of
> Christ, is fallen…and like an inchaunted woman,
> nothing regardeth nor reputeth of any moment, that
> moste excellent pryce [Christ's blood], wherewith
> she was so excedying louynglye and dearely
> redeemed.[13]

Here is a man of the church, in love with the church, but with his eyes open, bemoaning what is happening to his Mother. His hope for his Mother resides in his conviction that the soul of this maternal Mystical Body is the Holy Spirit, sent by Christ to abide with her forever.

The Eucharist was probably the occasion for more debate among Catholics and Protestants in England than any other single Reformation issue. Three of St. John Fisher's works deal with eucharistic controversy, and in roughly chronological order they are: *Defensio Regiae Assertionis* (Defense of the Royal Assertion, abbreviated to DRA), *Sacri Sacerdotii Defensio* (Defense of the Sacred Priesthood, abbreviated to SSD) and *De Veritate Corporis et Sanguinis Christi in Eucharistia* (On the Reality of the Body and Blood of Christ in the Eucharist, abbreviated to DVC).[14] The first and second works deal with the Mass as sacrifice, and the priesthood as sacrificing, against the views of Martin Luther. The third is a defense of the real presence of Christ against the Swiss Reformer John Oecolampadius. One of the most notable features of Fisher's reflection in these works is his consistent patristic approach. He certainly knows his scholastic Aristotle, and had been trained in that mold. But he is steeped in the patristic tradition, and uses it to good effect.

The sacrificial dimension of the Eucharist had been a constant aspect of Catholic teaching from the time of St. Paul's First Letter to the Corinthians (10:16–21). It had not been seriously called into question before the Reformation. In defending the sacrifice of the Mass, Fisher brought forth patristic citations describing the eucharistic liturgy in terms of sacrifice or offering. He used both the Greek and the Latin fathers, and insisted that the Mass was the sacrifice of the cross. In fact, Fisher defines the Mass as "a ceremony or action of a priest [such that] while the Eucharist is consecrated upon the altar, at the same time the sacrifice of the crucified Christ is proclaimed."[15] Sometimes it is alleged that Fisher subscribed to the view that in the sacrifice of the Mass the priest was a mediator between Christ and the congregation, but a close reading of Fisher will not support this view. For Fisher, the priest celebrating Mass is a mediator, but his action is not distinct from that of Jesus Christ. Christ is "the operative priest in the mass."[16] In giving emphasis to this teaching Fisher relies especially on the writing of St. John Chrysostom who, he notes "labours to explain how it can be that this sacrificial victim which was offered for us upon the cross is altogether the same as that which we offer daily."[17] To take the sacrifice of the Mass away from the church, as he understood Luther to do, is like snatching the sun from the world.[18] It would take the light out of life. It would be the end of life.

The doctrine of eucharistic sacrifice is necessarily bound up with the idea of the priesthood and the priest as the one offering the sacrifice of the Mass. Since the Reformers attacked the former, they also rejected the latter. It is not surprising, therefore, that Fisher wrote his *Defense of the Sacred Priesthood*. Again, his approach is not in the first place that of traditional scholasticism, but is thoroughly patristic. Richard Rex indicates that in the *Defense of the Sacred Priesthood 1*, Fisher cites Augustine, Jerome, Ambrose, Hilary, Arnobius, Cyprian, Tertullian, John of

Damascus, Gennadius, Cyril, John Chrysostom, Gregory of Nazianzus, Basil, Eusebius, Origen, Ignatius, Polycarp and Pseudo-Dionysius.[19]

Fisher's patristic expertise does not rest with a catena of citations from the fathers. The medieval scholastic theology of ordination assumed that the medieval rite of ordination was the same as that of the early church. Developing their theology of the sacraments in terms of "matter" and "form," the scholastics further assumed that the "matter" of ordination lay in the *porrectio instrumentorum*, the tradition of the implements, that is to say, the handing over of the book of the gospels to a deacon, and the handing over of the chalice and paten to a priest. Fisher, on the other hand, concentrates on the laying on of hands in his defense of ordination. For this he cites the New Testament—the laying on of hands in the Acts of the Apostles and the Pauline letters—and also St. Jerome. Admittedly, Jerome is the only one of the fathers he cites in this regard, but, given Fisher's patristic knowledge, he cannot have been unaware of the laying on of hands in ordination mentioned by writers throughout the patristic period.

The Reformed theologian John Oecolampadius had been on the side of Huldrych Zwingli at the Marburg Colloquy in which Luther defended the real presence of Christ in the Eucharist against the Swiss reformer's symbolic sense of that presence. Oecolampadius wrote a book in 1525 with the title *On the Genuine Interpretation*. In this essay he set out to show that the "realist" eucharistic language of the fathers of the church ought to be understood in a "symbolic" fashion. It would not be difficult to show that the fathers used what might be loosely called "symbolic" language of the Eucharist in their quest for a "eucharistic epistemology," a way of knowing and articulating Christ's presence in the elements. However, as we have seen in earlier chapters, the dominant understanding of the patristic period is that Christ is really and truly present, else the church cannot be the Body of Christ. Although various other Catholic theologians attempted to refute this symbolist interpretation of Oecolampadius, Fisher's was the most comprehensive and successful. His *On the Reality of the Body and Blood of Christ in the Eucharist* (DVC) is divided into five sections, each beginning with its own preface that sets out the main lines of his approach.

Here we shall simply draw attention to some of Fisher's emphases in these remarkable prefaces. In the first preface, Fisher sees the internal dissension about the Eucharist, and especially the eucharistic presence, in the Reformed camp as an indication of God's judgment on those who had fractured the unity of the church.[20] The Catholic Church is one because of Christ's continual real eucharistic presence. In the second preface he focuses on the many different names given to the Eucharist throughout the tradition. His conviction is that just as the nature of God cannot be definitively described by the many names given to him—God is sheer mystery—so too the Eucharist cannot be exhausted by the many names and titles used of it: the body of the Lord, the sacrament of the body and blood of Christ, the mysteries, the synaxis, communion, sacrifice, supersubstantial bread, the food of the Lord, banquet, mystical blessing and so forth. The sacrament like God is ineffable, because the sacrament communicates the life of the ineffable God to the communicant. In the fourth preface, claims Richard Rex, "we are presented with Fisher's patristic scholarship at its best."[21] He traces with finesse the constancy of the tradition, through the fathers, of the eucharistic presence of Christ. The interesting thing is that he begins this historical trajectory not from the beginning, but starts with the later fathers and goes back to the earlier. The implication is clear. The Reformers, especially Oecolampadius, are departing from what has been the clear eucharistic tradition of the church, which is being upheld by the Catholic Church.

When he comes to the fifth preface, Fisher pays particular attention to the words of St. John in the sixth chapter of his gospel. The Zwingli-Oecolampadius line of thought had real trouble with the dominical words "Unless you eat the flesh of the Son of Man and drink his blood, you have no life in you" (John 6:54). Here is eucharistic realism *par excellence*. The named reformers had resorted to an artificially contrived symbolist interpretation to get around the rather obvious meaning of these words. If the realism of these words is not accepted, argues Fisher, is not the realism of the incarnation immediately undermined? "The Word became flesh," says St. John, in the prologue to the gospel (John 1:14). The same word for flesh in the prologue, *sarx*, is used in the sixth chapter. This is a long way from seeing the eucharistic gifts as "reminders" of Christ that confirm our faith in him. Oecolampadius argued that our souls are fed on the Word of God, by hearing and believing the Word of God in holy scripture. Fisher agreed with that. The Word of God is spiritual food. But that same Word of God, expressed in scripture, has been enfleshed in Jesus of Nazareth——his life, death and resurrection——and is now sacramentally available in the Eucharist. In the last analysis, Oecolampadius' theology of the Eucharist is excessively intellectual, that is to say, it is an act in which the communicant is spiritually reminded of Christ, and so chooses to deepen his/her commitment to that Christ. Fisher, on the other hand, experiences the Eucharist not only as the sacramental presence of Christ, but experiences it emotionally. The frequent tears he shed at Mass are evidence of this, as also is the passage in DVC near the end of Book III: in holy communion, "the whole person is taken up and transformed into Christ; the minds of the faithful are filled by the presence of this flesh with a sort of cream or oil of devotion, and are fattened with a sweetness beyond words."

Finally, Fisher's emphasis on the importance of frequent communion needs to be recognized, especially when frequent communion was not the order of the day. Most Christians would have received communion only once a year, at Easter. In DVC Fisher recommends frequent and regular communion. "It is indeed true," he writes, "that we eat spiritually through faith and love [of the Lord]; but his faith, unless it is strengthened frequently by eating his body, will weaken and vanish."[22] In some of Fisher's earlier writing he had warned of the dangers of unworthy reception of holy communion, but, faced with the

Reformers' position, he enters wholeheartedly into commending frequent reception.

FROM HENRY VIII TO ELIZABETH I

John Fisher was executed under King Henry VIII, and something, albeit briefly, must be said about the Henrician Reform. There can be little doubt that the Reformation in England was inextricably knit into the constitutional problem of King Henry VIII (1509–47) having no male heir to his throne. Henry's desire to divorce his wife Catherine of Aragon (the wife of his dead brother Arthur, whom he had married with papal dispensation) had reached a canonical *impasse* with Rome. Henry then sought an annulment of the marriage from the English clergy, and, in 1534, in the Act of Supremacy, he proclaimed himself the supreme head of the church in England. Between 1535 (the year of Fisher's execution) and 1540 Henry suppressed all the monasteries and convents, distributing their lands and properties to his nobles.

The paradox is that while these events were taking place, Henry himself was not especially receptive to the ideas of the continental Reformers. In point of fact, before all this happened, Pope Leo X had conferred on Henry in 1521 the title *Defensor Fidei*, "Defender of the Faith," for a treatise he had written against Martin Luther entitled *The Defense of the Seven Sacraments*. Probably not too much should be made either of Henry's theological competence or of this title, which Henry valued more for its political statement than for its religious implications.[23] It gave status similar to that of the honorific titles of the emperor and the king of France, "Most Catholic" and "Most Christian." The church of which Henry had declared himself the head thirteen years later was really Catholicism without the papacy. However, the spread of Lutheran ideas was enabled in England, especially through a number of clerical figures who became associated with the University of Cambridge from at least as early as 1520. Henry may not have favored such Protestant ideas personally, but he was aware of their power not only in terms of doctrinal revision but also politically. When Henry died in 1546, he was pretty much committed to Catholic doctrine and practice, but the fact that he left his son, Edward VI, still a minor, in the hands of those who had definite Reformed sympathies and leanings shows that he was aware of the need to speak to and to satisfy both camps, Catholic and Protestant. In that basic sense Henry anticipated the Elizabethan religious settlement that was yet to come, a settlement that sat between Catholicism on the one hand and Protestantism on the other, and sat somewhat uncomfortably and uneasily. One who tried to ease the religious situation in the direction of the reform was the archbishop of Canterbury, Thomas Cranmer.

THOMAS CRANMER(1489–1556)

Thomas Cranmer was born in Aslockton, Nottinghamshire, England, July 2, 1489. He was educated and ordained at Jesus College, Cambridge, his studies including the new humanism of Erasmus as well the traditional scholasticism, and the biblical languages—Latin, Greek and Hebrew. However, it should be noted that Cranmer took no part in the emerging Lutheran controversy at Cambridge. Indeed, "the more one pieces together the scraps of evidence concerning Cranmer's religious outlook in his Cambridge years, the less these seem to point to the later reformer," says Diarmaid MacCulloch.[24] The comments made in his own hand in the margin of his personal copy of Bishop John Fisher's *Confutation of the Lutheran Assertion* show Cranmer often in agreement with Fisher. Cranmer, however, was more of a conciliarist than a papalist. It is perhaps not always adequately recalled that the reform-minded but conciliarist Council of Constance (1414–18) was but one hundred years before the Reformation. Shocked as he was at some of Luther's denunciations of the papacy, Cranmer was even more concerned over his attitude toward the councils of the church. He was deeply attached to the principles of conciliarism.

Probably because he spoke publicly of finding a solution to the matter of Henry VIII's divorce through consultation with faculties of theology in the universities rather than through the various ecclesiastical courts, Cranmer was rapidly promoted, being consecrated archbishop of Canterbury in 1533. In that same year, he annulled Catherine's marriage to Henry as contrary to the law of God, and crowned Anne Boleyn as his queen. After Henry's death in 1547, Cranmer's thinking advanced rapidly in a Protestant direction. On his initiative a number of Reformed theologians were invited to England, including Peter Martyr Vermigli and Martin Bucer. The former became Regius Professor of Divinity at Oxford (1548) and the latter Regius Professor at Cambridge (1549). Their eucharistic theologies tended in a Zwinglian direction, and this was to be the mark of Cranmer's also.

When Edward VI died in 1553, his Catholic sister, Mary, succeeded him. Peter Martyr, Martin Bucer and Thomas Cranmer were to suffer under Mary. Peter Martyr was imprisoned for six months, but then was released to return to Strasbourg, and later to Zurich where he became a professor of Hebrew. Martin Bucer died in 1551, but the queen had his body exhumed and publicly burnt in 1557. Finally, in 1554, Cranmer was brought to trial for heresy under Queen Mary. Under pressure, Cranmer wrote out several recantations of his supposed heretical positions, but on the day of his burning at Oxford, March 21, 1556, he recanted his recantations, and thrust his hand into the flames, crying out, "This hand had offended."

Eucharist

With the accession of King Edward VI after Henry VIII's death, Thomas Cranmer moved speedily to produce his first edition of *The Book of Common Prayer* in 1549, containing an outline of the Mass in English and provision for communion under both kinds. Partly under the influence of Peter Martyr and Martin Bucer, Cranmer had developed a more Zwinglian eucharistic theology, but it did not come to liturgical expression all at once. In producing this first *Book of Common Prayer* Cranmer chose to adapt, to paraphrase and to transform the Sarum (or Salisbury) rite, the rite most in use in England at the time. Very probably, Cranmer did not intend absolutely to exclude any particular doctrinal position on the Eucharist in the canon of the 1549 book. "It was a first step, following the precedent of the older Reformers, who all began with a conservative revision, and gave full liturgical expression to their opinions only when they felt the time to be ripe," says Geoffrey Cuming.[25] However, it must be said that Cranmer's second edition of the *Book of Common Prayer* of 1552 was to go much further in the promotion of Protestant eucharistic ideas. If one tries to relate the clear eucharistic differences between the first and second editions of the *Book of Common Prayer*, the best way is probably to regard the first edition as preparatory for the more radical revision represented by the second edition.

Some examples from the revised eucharistic liturgy will establish the point. Traditionally, at the reception of communion, the communicant was met with words about the eucharistic gifts preserving their bodies and souls unto everlasting life. That was changed in 1552 to:

> Take and eat this in remembrance that Christ died for thee, and feed on him in thy heart by faith, with thanksgiving....Drink this in remembrance that Christ's blood was shed for thee, and be thankful.[26]

This is a radical departure from traditional eucharistic understanding. Anything that smacked of the traditional Catholic doctrine of transubstantiation was eliminated. Should there be any doubt, a sentence in the rubrics for the communion service reads as follows: "And if any of the bread or wine remain, the Curate shall have it to his own use." MacCulloch comments:

Bread and wine there had been at the beginning of the service, and bread and wine there had been at the end of it. Once they had served their purpose, and treated with the reverence which the solemnity of the service demanded, they could be taken home to the parsonage and used as the human creations which they were.[27]

TWO SISTERS: MARY AND ELIZABETH

Despite his evident revisionist eucharistic theology, Cranmer's 1552 service did not please those who were further to his left in terms of their reformist tendencies. Within months King Edward VI died and was succeeded by Mary Tudor who was a devout Catholic. Often Mary's attempt to restore Catholicism is understood only in purely reactionary terms—and it cannot be denied that, like others of the time, she used violence and death to deal with perceived heresy. But there is also evidence that the Marian authorities' program was not entirely reactionary but creatively reconstructive, absorbing what they interpreted as positive during the reigns of Henry and Edward.[28] Thus, the revived interest in preaching was retained by the Marian authorities; the possession of Bibles and Bible reading by the people were never condemned. At the same time, there was a distinct push to regain the power of sacrament, typical of Catholicism, alongside word, typical of the Reform. The restoration sent a series of reform-minded theologians into exile on the continent of Europe, and there liturgical revision continued to be discussed and debated. Some advocated more or less the eucharistic celebration of Cranmer's 1552 book—the Prayer Book party—and their basic theological position was ultimately to prevail, while the more radical reformers such as John Knox argued for a ritually and theologically slimmer Eucharist, what might be described as a merely commemorative meal.

Mary's attempt at restoration was not to last very long. In November 1558, Elizabeth came to the throne and immediately set about the rehabilitation of the reforms. She was not to have an entirely free hand at liturgical revision because, as the exiles returned home, so did their debates about the prayer book and, most especially, the Eucharist. Eventually, in 1559, Elizabeth restored the Prayer Book of 1552 with a few alterations, changes that were all in a conservative mold. But, even so, "no one really wanted the Prayer Book they had been given."[29] It satisfied neither the more Catholic wing of the church nor the more Puritan-Reformed wing of the church. This 1559 *Book of Common Prayer* remained in constant use until 1604 when some very minor changes were made. Again, some further changes were made with the 1661–62 revision when the monarchy was restored in England after the Puritan commonwealth period. These latter changes were of no great substance, so that "the Restoration Book maintained the tradition established in the sixteenth century and represented a defeat for both the High Churchmen…and for the Puritans."[30] It is this Elizabethan 1559 book, based on the 1552 book, that has remained in place in Anglican worship until the Prayer Book revisions of the late twentieth century.

Conclusion

Fisher and Cranmer—both bishops, both martyrs, but with significantly contrasting theologies. In the final chapter of his excellent book *The Theology of John Fisher*, Richard Rex summarizes his years of reading Fisher's theology and examining accounts of his life with these words:

> More than anything, however, it was Fisher's vocation as a bishop that dominated his theological as well as his ecclesiastical career. The main implication of this was that his interest in theology was practical rather than speculative….His own writings were

designed either to defend the doctrines of Catholicism or else to encourage Christians in their devotions.[31]

While in some quarters this might seem to be a negative judgment on Fisher, it is to me a very high accolade. Bishop John Fisher models good *episkope*, not only for the sixteenth century but also for our own times. Both in his own life and throughout his sphere of influence he fostered the conditions for a genuinely ecclesial theology. Thomas More and John Fisher share the same feast day, June 22. If Thomas More is a man for all seasons, in Robert Bolt's famous description, John Fisher is a bishop for all seasons.

Toward the end of his magisterial biography of Cranmer, Diarmaid MacCulloch writes:

> To define Cranmer as a reformed Catholic is to define all the great Continental reformers in the same way: for they too sought to build up the Catholic Church anew on the same foundations of Bible, creeds and the great councils of the early Church....Cranmer was guiding the Church of England to a renewed Catholicity.[32]

No less than St. John Fisher, Cranmer was committed to the church, but he understood that commitment to lie in a somewhat different direction. Where would Fisher and Cranmer stand now, given the ecumenical dialogue and discussion that has taken place between Canterbury and Rome? Perhaps we may look to the inscription on the tomb of the two royal sisters, Queen Mary and Queen Elizabeth, in Westminster Abbey. The inscription reads: "Sharing the same throne and tomb, here we sleep, Elizabeth and Mary, in the hope of the resurrection." The question and the inscription are surely worth pondering for their descendants in both ecclesial traditions, since resurrected life begins *now* in the Christian tradition. The *now* of the ongoing ecumenical dialogue between Canterbury and Rome surely augurs well for the healing of this sixteenth-century ecclesial wound.

Notes

1. Louis Bouyer, *Liturgical Piety* (Notre Dame: University of Notre Dame Press, 1955), 2.

2. Mark Santer, "The Reconciliation of Memories," in Mark Santer, ed., *Their Lord and Ours* (London: SPCK, 1982), 158.

3. Eamon Duffy, *The Stripping of the Altars* (New Haven and London: Yale University Press, 1992), 4.

4. Henry Chadwick, "Royal Ecclesiastical Supremacy," in his *Tradition and Exploration* (Norwich: The Canterbury Press, 1994), 229.

5. Brendan Bradshaw, "Bishop John Fisher, 1469–1535: The Man and His Work," in Brendan Bradshaw and Eamon Duffy, eds., *Humanism, Reform and the Reformation* (Cambridge: Cambridge University Press, 1989), 1.

6. Michael A. Mullett, *The Catholic Reformation* (London and New York: Routledge, 1999), 20.

7. Bradshaw, "Bishop John Fisher, 1469–1535: The Man and His Work," 4.

8. Desiderius Erasmus, *The Correspondence of Erasmus*, in *The Collected Works of Erasmus*, vol. 9 (Toronto: University of Toronto Press, 1988), 229.

9. Mullett, *The Catholic Reformation*, 19–20.

10. St. John Fisher, "Sermons on the Seven Penitential Psalms." Cited in Edward Surtz, SJ, *The Works and Days of John Fisher* (Cambridge, MA: Harvard University Press, 1967), 143.

11. Ibid., 36–37.

12. Ibid., 37.

13. St. John Fisher, "Treatise on Prayer," in Surtz, *The Works and Days of John Fisher*, 37.

14. All translations of and references to these works are taken from Richard Rex, *The Theology of John Fisher* (Cambridge: Cambridge University Press, 1991), unless otherwise noted.

15. St. John Fisher, *Defensio Regiae Assertionis* (DRA), 6.

16. ————., *De Veritate Corporis et Sanguinis Christi in Eucharistia* (DVC), 3.2.

17. Ibid., 2.17.

18. Surtz, *The Works and Days of John Fisher*, 321.

19. Rex, *The Theology of John Fisher*, 251.

20. DVC 1, preface.

21. Rex, *The Theology of John Fisher*, 140.

22. DVC 5.17.

23. See E. G. Rupp, *Studies in the Making of the English Protestant Tradition* (Cambridge: Cambridge University Press, 1966), 89–90.

24. Diarmaid MacCulloch, *Thomas Cranmer, A Life* (New Haven: Yale University Press, 1996), 24–25.

25. Geoffrey J. Cuming, *A History of Anglican Liturgy*, 2nd ed. (London: Macmillan, 1982), 57.

26. Cited from MacCulloch, *Thomas Cranmer, A Life*, 506.

27. Ibid.

28. Duffy, *The Stripping of the Altars*, 526.

29. Cuming, *A History of Anglican Liturgy*, 98.

30. John E. Booty, ed., *The Book of Common Prayer 1559: The Elizabethan Prayer Book* (Charlottesville: The University of Virginia Press, 1976), 329.

31. Rex, *The Theology of John Fisher*, 190–91.

32. MacCulloch, *Thomas Cranmer, A Life*, 617.

PART FOUR:
After the Reformation

George Herbert, Cardinal Robert Bellarmine and Jeremy Taylor

Although the polemical stance of the theologians in the seventeenth century compelled all of them to emphasize their theological differences, they did have much in common both theologically and philosophically.
Jaroslav Pelikan[1]

Anglicanism forms a middle ground between Catholicism on the one hand, and the Reformation on the other. In this chapter we shall look at the eucharistic theology of three thinkers: the Anglican George Herbert (1593–1633), the Catholic Robert Bellarmine (1542–1621) and the Anglican Jeremy Taylor (1613–67). It is no part of my concern here to wade into the complex and thorny issue of the validity of Anglican orders, but rather to limit myself to an exploration of eucharistic reflection, and to show how the Catholic tradition of eucharistic thought perdured in the English reformation tradition. We are dealing with the eucharistic "wisdom of the ancients," to use a term of Jeremy Taylor's, on both sides of the divide, Catholic and Reformed. Jeremy Taylor, bishop in the "Reformed Catholic Church," as it were, uses this telling phrase in connection with John Fisher, bishop of Rochester, bishop in the Roman Catholic Church and the subject of our last essay, over a century after Fisher's death:

But thus the Enemy of Mankind hath prevailed upon us while we were earnest in disputations about things less concerning. Then he was watchfull and busie to interweave evil and uncertain principles into our Moral institutions, to intangle what was plain, to divide what was simple, to make an art of what was written in the tables of our hearts with the finger of God. When a gentleman was commending Dr. Fisher Bishop of Rochester his great pains in the confutation of Luther's books, the wise Prelate said heartily, that he wish'd he had spent all that time in prayer and meditation which he threw away upon such useless wranglings. For that was the wisdom of the Ancients.[2]

GEORGE HERBERT (1593–1633)

George Herbert was the younger brother of Lord Herbert of Cherbury—the same Lord Herbert who is commonly regarded as the father of deism. George was born of an aristocratic family in Montgomeryshire, in the Welsh borders in 1593. Like John Fisher before him, he was a Cambridge man. After his studies at the University of Cambridge, Trinity College, Herbert followed various secular callings before finally becoming a deacon in 1624. Herbert married Jane Danvers in 1629, and the following year was ordained priest in Salisbury Cathedral. He became rector of Bemerton, near Salisbury in the southwest of England, and he remained there for the rest of his short life. Herbert has left us some of the most remarkable poetry in the English language, poetry that "is shot through with sheer delight in God."[3]

Eucharist

The point has been made by one Herbert scholar that there is a constant temptation for readers of George Herbert to remake him in their own image.[4] It is not my intention here to make Herbert into a Catholic eucharistic theologian, but rather to advert to some of his writing in which a strong resonance with the Catholic tradition may be recognized.

In the Anglican Church of Herbert's day the Eucharist only would have been celebrated perhaps five or six times a year, though it is most probable that Herbert himself would have preferred a more frequent celebration. This is what he has to say on the matter:

> Touching the frequency of communion, the Parson celebrates it, if not duly once a month, yet at least five or six times in the year; as, at Easter, Christmas, Whitsuntide, afore and after Harvest, and the beginning of Lent.[5]

While communion services might be expected in Lent, at Easter, Pentecost and Christmas, the celebration before and after the harvest is interesting. Herbert believed the celebration expressed our ultimate dependence on God's graceful providence. He is entirely clear that at the times of celebration it is his responsibility to prepare his flock adequately for "receiving God," and he notes the major issues that need to be attended to at those times:

> [The Parson] considers and looks into the ignorance, or carelessness of his flock, and accordingly applies himself with Catechizings, and lively exhortations, not on the Sunday of the Communion only (for then it is too late) but the Sunday, or Sundays before the Communion, or on the Eves of all those days. If there be any, who having not received yet, is to enter into this great work, he takes the more pains with them, that he may lay the foundations of future Blessings. The time of everyone's first receiving is not so much by years, as by understanding: particularly, the rule may be this: When anyone can distinguish the Sacrament from common bread, knowing the Institution, and the difference, he ought to receive,

of what age soever. Children and youths are usually deferred too long, under pretense of devotion to the Sacrament, but it is for want of Instruction; their understandings being ripe enough for ill things, and why not then for better?[6]

Herbert's catechetical concern for his congregation, both before they receive the Eucharist for the first time, and before they receive it thereafter, is fueled by his love for and belief in the sacrament. Age of first reception is to be determined by a person's basic awareness of the narrative of the institution of the sacrament at the Last Supper, and his or her ability to distinguish the eucharistic gift from ordinary bread. Recipients should prepare with great care to receive the Lord in holy communion. Of course, attendance at prayer is expected to be ongoing. The regular offices of morning and evening prayer would have been celebrated by Herbert daily in his church.

Herbert has a powerful sense of his unworthiness as a priest and of Christ's en-worthing him through his presence, and this comes to expression in his poem "Aaron":

> Holiness on the head,
> Light and perfections on the breast,
> Harmonious bells below, raising the dead
> To lead them unto life and rest.
> Thus are true Aarons drest.
>
> Profaneness in my head,
> Defects and darkness in my breast,
> A noise of passions ringing me for dead
> Unto a place where is no rest.
> Poor priest thus am I drest.
>
> Only another head
> I have, another heart and breast,
> Another music, making live not dead,
> Without whom I could have no rest:
> In him I am well drest.

Christ is my only head,
My alone only heart and breast,
My only music, striking me ev'n dead;
That to the old man I may rest,
And be in him new drest.

So holy in my head,
Perfect and light in my dear breast,
My doctrine tun'd by Christ (who is not dead,
But lives in me while I do rest)
Come people; Aaron's drest.

In the first stanza Aaron is presented as the idea priest, and Herbert is following the elaborate vestments of Aaron, including bells, which rang as he moved into the sanctuary.[7] In the second stanza Herbert realizes that in his own life he does not measure up to this high ideal of what a priest should be. That realization, however, does not lead him to despair because in stanzas three and four he recognizes his absolute dependence upon Jesus Christ, who is his only head, heart and breast. He recalls the ontological character of his priesthood, that, by grace, he is a sign/representation/icon of Christ. Calling upon the Pauline passages of Colossians 3:9–10 and Galatians 2:20 (the passages about stripping off the old man, dying to the old man and putting on Christ), he accepts that it is no longer he who lives but Christ who lives in him. And so he is ready to celebrate Eucharist with his people, "Come, people, Aaron's drest." The liturgy may now begin because its reality depends not on the presiding priest and his personal qualities, but on Christ the High Priest.

In the collection known as "The Church" we find this poem entitled "The Holy Communion":

Not in rich furniture, or fine array,
Nor in a wedge of gold,
Thou, who from me wast sold,
To me dost now thyself convey;

For so thou should'st without me still have been,
Leaving within me sin:

But by the way of nourishment and strength
Thou creep'st into my breast;
Making thy way my rest,
And thy small quantities my length;
Which spread their forces into every part,
Meeting sin's force and art.

Yet can these not get over to my soul,
Leaping the wall that parts
Our souls and fleshly hearts;
But as th' outworks, they may control
My rebel flesh, and carrying thy name,
Affright both sin and shame.

Only thy grace, which with these elements comes,
Knoweth the ready way,
And hath the privy key,
Op'ning the soul's most subtle rooms;
While those to spirits refin'd, at door attend
Dispatches from their friend.

The first stanza expresses clearly Christ's coming to the communicant, "To me dost now thyself convey." The reality of Christ's eucharistic presence lies behind "thyself." The stanza may also contain a contrast between the Anglican Rite and the Roman Catholic Rite. Christ's coming is "Not in rich furniture, or fine array, Nor in a wedge of gold." Herbert may be implying that the rich ornamentation of the Catholic Eucharist in the paten or the chalice is not the necessary foundation for Christ's presence. The simplicity of the Anglican ritual is every bit as good. No one, of course, would contest the theological principle as such, but it may be that Herbert betrays here some influence of a more nude Calvinism in matters ecclesial. The real presence of Christ within the communicant, within the eucharistic host, may be small—"thy small quantities"—but it does not thereby lack power. Christ makes his way into the communicant, spreading his healing grace "into every part." In fact, the grace that "these elements" brings opens up, in the last stanza, "the soul's most subtle rooms."

Also in "The Church" we find one of Herbert's best-known poems, "Love," a poem through which the twentieth-century French thinker Simone Weil had her decisive experience of God:

> *Love bade me welcome: yet my soul drew back,*
> *Guilty of dust and sin.*
> *But quick-ey'd Love, observing me grow slack*
> *From my first entrance in,*
> *Drew nearer to me, sweetly questioning,*
> *If I lack'd anything.*
>
> *A guest, I answer'd, worthy to be here:*
> *Love said, You shall be he.*
> *I the unkind, ungrateful? Ah my dear,*
> *I cannot look on thee.*
> *Love took my hand, and smiling did reply,*
> *Who made the eyes but I?*
>
> *Truth Lord, but I have marr'd them: let my shame*
> *Go where it doth deserve.*
> *And know you not, says Love, who bore the blame?*
> *My dear, then I will serve.*
> *You must sit down, says Love, and taste my meat:*
> *So I did sit and eat.*

Strictly speaking, this is not an explicitly eucharistic text for Herbert. The poem is the very last one in "The Church." There is something of a linear movement in the collection toward the last things, and the last four poems but one are titled after the four traditional last things: death, doomsday, judgment, heaven. However, there are verbal echoes of this poem in a passage where Herbert is speaking of the Eucharist: "He that comes to the sacrament, hath the confidence of a Guest, and he that kneels, confesseth himself an unworthy one, and therefore different from other Feasters...."[8]

However, even without this verbal resonance it is very easy to read the text eucharistically, and I believe entirely in line with Herbert's theology. The first stanza tells us God's name, Love, the host who welcomes to the banquet. The soul, however, realizes its unworthiness, "Guilty of dust and sin." Love tells the soul that the soul is "a guest worthy to be here," and, as so often in the tradition of eucharistic reflection, it is affirmed that the worth of the soul comes from the en-worthing action of God, "You shall be he....Who made the eyes but I?" After a fairly traditional soteriological affirmation in the third stanza, "And know you not, says Love, who bore the blame?", the God who is Love invites the soul to "sit down...and taste my meat." What could God's meat be but the eucharistic gift of God's self in Christ through the Holy Spirit?

In Herbert's poem, "The Pearl," based on the parable of the pearl of great price in St. Matthew's gospel (Matt 13:45–46), there is a beautiful line operating like a refrain: "Yet I love Thee." That really sums up for Herbert what Christian faith is about, loving God. And his eucharistic reflections, perhaps less prolific than other authors because of his reformed context in sixteenth-century England, nevertheless retain the main contours of the tradition, the whole purpose of which is "to love [Him.]"

ROBERT BELLARMINE
(1542–1621)

Robert Bellarmine was born in Tuscany in 1542. He became a member of the newly established Society of Jesus in 1560, entering the Jesuits' Roman College for studies in philosophy. Ordained in 1570, Bellarmine became the first Jesuit professor of theology at Louvain. There he taught from Aquinas' *Summa Theologica* and began to lay the groundwork for what was later to become his *Controversies*. During his seven years in Louvain,

Bellarmine steeped himself in the study of scripture, church history and patristic theology, as well as developing his very considerable preaching skills. As Brodrick tells us,

> Robert in the pulpit and Robert on the ground appeared to be two different people. When preaching he looked a tall, striking figure and, as most men saw him only at such times, the story got about in Louvain that a young giant had come forth from Italy to instruct them in the word of God. In reality he was undersized, and would have been quite lost in the huge, enveloping pulpits of Flanders had he not by taking thought found a simple means of adding inches to his stature. He stood upon a stool.[9]

To further his scriptural knowledge, he began the study of Hebrew at Louvain. He even produced an introductory Hebrew grammar, running to some 334 pages.

Called back to Italy in 1576 to the Roman College—later to become the Gregorian University—he was appointed to take up the new chair in "controversial theology"; he remained a professor there until 1588. It was there that Bellarmine produced the three volumes of his *Controversies*, a synthesis of Catholic and Protestant theology. They were to be most influential. A work of apologetic theology, nonetheless the method and the content of the *Controversies* shows Bellarmine trying to be fair and to avoid the abuse that can so easily mar this genre. It is in this work that we find his famous apologetic definition of the church against the perceived errors of the Reformers' "invisible Church":

> The assembly of people bound by the same faith and communion of the same sacraments under the government of legitimate pastors and especially the Roman Pontiff....The Church is as visible and palpable as the assembly of the Roman people, or the kingdom of France, or the republic of Venice.[10]

His ecclesiology, however, goes well beyond the important but limited apologetic affirmation of the church's visibility. He draws into his discussion of the church, for example, the theology of the Body of Christ, the Holy Spirit, the papacy and the ecumenical councils, so much so that he has been described as "the first comprehensive exponent of Catholic ecclesiology."[11]

Made a cardinal in 1599, Bellarmine was ordained archbishop of Capua in 1602. Pope Clement VIII, in making Bellarmine a cardinal, marked the occasion with these words: "We elect this man because the Church of God has not his equal in learning."[12] With the conclave after Clement's death in 1605, he returned to Rome where he remained in the service of the church for the rest of his life.

Eucharist

The eucharistic theology Robert Bellarmine received and taught was that of the Council of Trent (1545–63). The centerpiece of this conciliar eucharistic teaching in respect to the presence of Christ is the doctrine of transubstantiation. As the conciliar decree stated, the change of bread and wine into the body and blood of Christ "fittingly and properly has been named *transubstantiation*."[13] Bellarmine, of course, in his *Controversies* defended this teaching. It was a standard Catholic presentation.

In 1609 he published anonymously a pamphlet attacking the oath of loyalty that King James I required of his subjects. This oath, as Bellarmine understood it, involved a rejection of the papacy and of certain elements of Catholic doctrine. Because of political circumstances in England at the time—the aftermath of the "Gunpowder Plot" of 1605—the king enjoined the Anglican theologian and bishop Lancelot Andrewes (1555–1626), a friend of George Herbert, to respond to Cardinal Bellarmine. Thus, the year 1610 saw Andrewes' *Response to the Apology of Cardinal Bellarmine*. To the cardinal, Bishop Andrewes wrote in respect of the Eucharist: "We believe no less than you that the presence [of Christ] is real. Concerning the method of this presence, we define nothing rashly."[14] "Transubstantiation" works for Cardinal Bellarmine, but for Bishop Andrewes it is not possible to define exactly how Christ is present. An established authority on Bellarmine comments on both men embroiled in this controversy:

> [Lancelot Andrewes] was the one man then living in England who most resembled Bellarmine in knowledge and piety....What a strange contradictory world it is that set those two men, Andrewes and Bellarmine, so much alike in the very texture of their minds and hearts, at loggerheads.[15]

The Council of Trent, while it underscored the sacrificial nature of the Mass, did not define "sacrifice" precisely. That definition was left to the development of individual theologians. What emerged as central in the development was the idea of the destruction of a victim. This notion arose from what it was possible to glean from the study of religions as such, and not immediately from the *donnée* of the New Testament documents. "One did not look to the Christ-event in order to understand the central meaning of the sacrifice of the Mass," Robert Daly comments. "One looked to the history-of-religions phenomenology of sacrifice—specifically, was there, and in what way was there a destruction of the victim?—in order to prove or disprove that the Mass was a sacrifice."[16] This formed Bellarmine's context for thinking about the Mass as a sacrifice. The sacrifice consisted in both the consecration of the elements and in the communion. In rendering Christ present sacramentally, the consecration must, therefore, render Christ's sacrifice present. It is the Christ, sacrificed and risen, with whom we are dealing. But, we might say, the consecration is not so *obviously* significant of sacrifice. Where is the destruction of the victim in the consecration? Thus, Bellarmine was led to believe that the communion of the priest constituted the consummation of the sacrifice, while the communion of the assembly was the eating of the victim. In the *Controversies* we find this stated very clearly:

> The consumption of the sacrament, as done by the people, is not a part of the sacrifice. As done by the sacrificing priest, however, it is an essential part, but not the whole essence....For the consumption carried out by the sacrificing priest is not so much the eating of the victim [what the people do] as it is the consummation of the sacrifice. It is seen as properly corresponding to the combustion of the holocaust.[17]

Clearly the cardinal is intent upon defending not only the Eucharist understood sacrificially, but also the notion of a sacrificing priesthood, a doctrine under attack by the Reformers. This explains the apparent distance between priest and people on the issue. Along with all scholars of his day, the methodology was flawed. It would have been better to take the definition of sacrifice from the New Testament, and not immediately from religion in general, as it were.

The Eucharist is the twelfth rule of Bellarmine's "the art of dying well" in his book of that title. There he tells us that the Eucharist is "the greatest of all the sacraments," and a Christian needs to receive it and to receive it worthily. He reiterates the eucharistic theme initiated by Ignatius of Antioch, that the Eucharist is medicinal, healing the sin-sick, "the best and most effective medicine against all the diseases of the vices." Frequent reception of the sacrament, therefore, is encouraged:

> For annual communion was prescribed by the ecumenical council not as at most an annual event, but as at least an annual occurrence, if one does not want to be thrown out of the Church and handed over to Satan.[18]

Eucharistic reception should emerge in the devout Catholic marked by the love of a son and not by the fear of a slave.[19] Such a loving and fruitful reception of the sacrament becomes more possible in the context of a celebration that is slow, dignified and reverent. And so the cardinal takes to task those priests

> who celebrate and perform something so holy with such unbelievable haste that they do not seem to know what they are doing and do not allow others to consider a little more attentively so great a reality.[20]

Later in *The Art of Dying Well*, Bellarmine turns his attention to those who are gravely ill and commends the Eucharist specifically to them. "The sacrament of the Lord's Body is the conclusion and, so to speak, the seal of all the sacraments."[21] As a Christian prepares to make his or her way out of this world, there could be no better way than to be sealed with this seal of all the sacraments. Those who are ill should take to heart the sentiments of Aquinas' *O Sacrum Convivium*, especially the line that affirms the Eucharist as "the pledge of future glory." He comments on the hymn as follows:

> The Holy Eucharist is offered to us on our pilgrimage as food so that we do not faint on the path to the fatherland, especially at that time when, tired by a long journey, our forces are apt to wane....The Lord left his Body in the Eucharist as a pledge of heavenly beatitude.[22]

This feels like the considered judgment of one who is not only a theologian but a pastor.

JEREMY TAYLOR (1613–1667)

Another Cambridge man, like Herbert, is Jeremy Taylor, educated at Gonville and Caius College. Ordained in the Church of England in 1633, Taylor came to the attention of the archbishop of Canterbury, William Laud, and was nominated to a fellowship at All Souls College, Oxford, in 1635. During his time at Oxford Taylor read widely in the Greek and Latin fathers of the church, and it was at Oxford too that he came into contact with Christopher Davenport. He developed a friendship with Davenport, which brought him into suspicion of having Roman Catholic tendencies, a suspicion that had some foundation. Davenport, it would appear, attempted to win Taylor over to Rome. One Taylor biographer describes Taylor's situation in this fashion: "His omnivorous reading would make him a Catholic in the widest sense of the word, and to his opponents in the heated feeling of the time, scarcely distinguishable from a Papist."[23]

Davenport was appointed chaplain to the Catholic wife of King Charles I, Queen Henrietta Maria. He was on good terms with many Anglican clergy, and in fact, tried to show that the Thirty-Nine Articles of the Anglican Church were compatible with Roman Catholicism. It seems most unlikely that Taylor experienced any real temptation to go over to Rome, and he finally cleared himself of any Catholic associations through his "Gunpowder Sermon" at St. Mary's Church, Oxford, in 1638. In the same year he was appointed rector of Uppingham in the Diocese of London.

The year 1641 saw the abolition of the episcopate by the English Parliament, and the following years witnessed the civil war. "Thus politics and religion combined," notes Carroll, "and the pastor of Uppingham became a pilgrim whose wanderings for the next few years are difficult to trace."[24] These difficult years saw some of Taylor's best writing, especially his spiritual classic, *Holy Living, Holy Dying*. After the Commonwealth years under Oliver Cromwell, and the Restoration under King Charles II, Taylor in 1660 was appointed bishop of Down and Connor in Ireland and vice-chancellor of the University of Dublin. In 1661 he was appointed to the further see of Dromore. His time as a bishop in Ireland was far from happy, as he faced the constant opposition of the Presbyterian ministers in his diocese. After witnessing the death of his seventh child and only surviving son on August 2, 1667, Taylor himself died eleven days later on August

13. He was buried in the cathedral at Dromore. Though at times Taylor engaged in very strong anti-Catholic invective, he entertained eucharistic reflections not far distant from the Catholic tradition.

Eucharist

There is a purple passage in Taylor's treatise *Great Exemplar* that gives us a fine sense of the centrality of the Eucharist in his life and thinking:

> As the sun among the stars, and man among the sub-lunary creatures, is the most eminent and noble, the prince of the inferiors, and their measure, or their guide; so is this action among all the instances of religion; it is the most perfect and consummate, it is an union of mysteries, and a consolidation of duties; it joins God and man, and confederates all the societies of men in mutual complexions, and the entertainments of an excellent charity, it actually performs all that could be necessary for man, and it presents to man as great a thing as God could give; for it is impossible any thing should be greater than Himself.[25]

The Eucharist is the holiest thing in the universe, the holiest thing in creation because it simply is the gift of God himself to us. It is the fulfillment of what it means to be human—"it actually performs all that could be necessary for man." It binds together God and humankind, and all people among themselves—"it joins God and man, and confederates all the societies of men in mutual complexions." The Eucharist unites with God, the vertical aspect, and with all others, the horizontal aspect. His choice of the verb "confederates" is not without interest. As a man of great classical and patristic learning, Taylor knew that the Latin word for "covenant" was *foedus*. The Eucharist, in our Lord's own words, has to do with "the new covenant," and therefore, has the power to bind in covenant, to "confederate" people of all societies. In that sense the Eucharist is the center of Catholicism, that is to say, it has the power to confederate all people everywhere, of any time. It transcends the particularities of time, space and culture, to unite humankind as one in and with Christ.

The Eucharist is intimately connected with the incarnation, God's unique presence among us, and the church becomes in grace the unique manifestation of Christ. This comes to fine expression in his *The Worthy Communicant:*

> For God descended and came into the tabernacle invested with a cloud, so Christ comes to meet us clothed with a mystery: He hath a house below as well as above; here is His dwelling and here are His provisions, here is His fire and here His meat; hither God sends His Son, and here His Son manifests Himself: the church and the holy table of the Lord, the assemblies of the saints, and the devotions of His people, the word and the sacrament, the oblation of bread and wine and the offering of ourselves, the consecration and the communion, are the things of God and of Jesus Christ, and he that is employed in these is there where God loves to be, and where Christ is to be found; in the employments in which God delights, in the ministries of His own choice, in the work of the gospel and the methods of grace, in the economy of heaven and the dispensations of eternal happiness.[26]

Here is the tradition of eucharistic reflection at its best, but it is not couched in scholastic terms. Its expression is almost entirely patristic. In fact, throughout this text, *The Worthy Communicant*, the references are all patristic or medieval, and there are none from the Reformation.[27] At the same time, one can glimpse more than a hint of personal piety and devotion. When one is employed in the celebration of the Eucharist, one is "there where God loves to be." Out of love God creates and redeems, and out of love God makes himself accessible and available in Eucharist. God makes himself available in order to make us like God himself.

> [The sacraments] are instruments in the hands of God, and by these His Holy Spirit changes our hearts and translates us into a divine nature; therefore the whole work is attributed to them by a synec-doche; that is, they do in their manner the work for which God ordained them, and they are placed there for our sakes, and speak God's language in our accent, and they appear in the outside; we receive the benefit of their ministry and God receives the glory.[28]

Needless to say, Taylor is aware of the Reformation cri-tiques of Christ's eucharistic presence in the gifts, but he pro-vides an induction into the eucharistic appreciation noted in the above paragraphs through an appreciation of God's presence in creation, and especially in the human heart. This inductive approach is very clear in his *On the Reverence Due the Altar*. In this text he takes issue with those of a Puritan frame of mind who lay all the emphasis on an interior disposition for worship, as if externals did not count, and as if the eucharistic gifts were only *aides-mémoires*. Equally he asserts God's holy presence every-where:

> For although God bee present in all places alike in respect of his essence, yet he exhibits the issues, and effects of his presence more in some than in others. And that thither the addresses of our adorations must bee where God is specially present, nature teaches us. We looke men in the face when we speake to them, and if we may any where pray to God, and adore him because he is every where present and heares us, then by the same reason we must specially adore him where he is specially present...that is in

Heaven, and in all Holy places; and therefore the gen-
erall addresse of our devotion is towards heaven.[29]

Put briefly, God is indeed present everywhere, but especially in
heaven, which is the proper "place" of God. Yet there is an
intensity of God's presence in some places in this world that are
designated specifically for awareness and worship of God. The
Temple of Solomon is cited as an example of such a place where
God may be especially encountered. Again, a very special place
of God's presence is the human heart:

God is especially present in the hearts of his people,
by his Holy Spirit: and indeed the hearts of holy men
are temples in the truth of things, and in type and
shadow they are heaven itself....[The human heart]
is heaven in a looking-glass, dark but yet true, representing the beauties of the soul, and the graces of
God, and the images of his eternal glory, by the reality of a special presence.[30]

Conclusion

George Herbert, Robert Bellarmine and Jeremy Taylor
were indeed much alike in the very texture of their eucharistic
minds and hearts. Nonetheless, it goes without saying that this
quick perusal of some aspects of their eucharistic theology does
not eliminate all differences between them, nor between Catholic
and Anglican eucharistic traditions. But the claim is being made
that Catholics are largely ignorant of this period of Anglican
eucharistic reflection, and we are the poorer for it. In the Second
Vatican Council's *Decree on Ecumenism* we read: "Among those
[communions] in which some Catholic traditions and institutions
continue to exist, the Anglican Communion occupies a special
place."[31] It is easy today to point to the serious divisions between
the Catholic Church and the Anglican Communion—for example, validity of orders, and the ordination of women to the priesthood and the episcopate. It is more difficult and more time-

consuming to work at understanding and retrieval for ourselves of the Anglican eucharistic tradition. But, if we believe in the cause of Christian unity, so recently emphasized for us by Pope John Paul II in his encyclical letter *Ut Unum Sint,* and if we accept with Vatican II that Catholic traditions and institutions in part continue to exist in the Anglican Communion, we need to set our minds to this more difficult and time-consuming work.

Notes

1. Jaroslav J. Pelikan, *Reformation of Church and Dogma* (Chicago and London: University of Chicago Press, 1984), 337.

2. Cited in Edward Surtz, *The Works and Days of John Fisher* (Cambridge, MA: Harvard University Press, 1967), 349–50.

3. David F. Ford, "George Herbert: The Centrality of God," *Theology* 96 (1992), 360.

4. Elizabeth Clarke, "George Herbert's *The Temple*: The Genius of Anglicanism and the Inspiration for Poetry," in Geoffrey Rowell, ed., *The English Religious Tradition and the Genius of Anglicanism* (Nashville: Abingdon Press, 1992), 128.

5. George Herbert, "The Country Parson," 22. There are many editions and anthologies of Herbert's works available.

6. Ibid.

7. See Exodus 29:34.

8. Herbert, "The Country Parson," 22.

9. James Brodrick, *Robert Bellarmine, Saint and Scholar* (Westminster, MD: The Newman Press, 1961), 26.

10. Robert Bellarmine, *De Controversiis: De conciliis et ecclesia* 3.2.

11. John A. Hardon, "Robert Bellarmine's Concept of the Church," *Studies in Medieval Culture* 2 (1966), 120.

12. Cited in Bernard McGinn, *The Doctors of the Church* (New York: Crossroad, 1999), 153.

13. The Council of Trent, "Decree Concerning the Most Holy Sacrament of the Eucharist," 1551, chapter 4.

14. Cited in Kenneth Stevenson, *The Covenant of Grace Renewed: A Vision of the Eucharist in the Seventeenth Century* (London: Darton, Longman and Todd, 1994), 45.

15. Brodrick, *Robert Bellarmine, Saint and Scholar,* 286–87.

16. Robert J. Daly, "Robert Bellarmine and Post-Tridentine Eucharistic Theology," *Theological Studies* 61 (2000), 248.

17. Cited in Daly, "Robert Bellarmine and Post-Tridentine Eucharistic Theology," 253.

18. Robert Bellarmine, *The Art of Dying Well,* Book 1, Chapter 12. The text is readily available in English in John P. Donnelly and Roland J. Teske, eds., *Robert Bellarmine, Spiritual Writings* (New York/Mahwah, NJ: Paulist Press, 1989).

19. Donnelly and Teske, *Robert Bellarmine: Spiritual Writings,* 287–88.

20. Ibid., 289.

21. Ibid., 344.

22. Ibid., 345–47.

23. George Worley, cited in Thomas K. Carroll, ed., *Jeremy Taylor: Selected Works* (New York/Mahwah, NJ: Paulist Press, 1990), 18.

24. Carroll, *Jeremy Taylor: Selected Works,* 20.

25. Jeremy Taylor in *The Whole Works of Jeremy Taylor,* ed. Reginald Heber, revised and corrected by Charles Eden, vol. 2 (London: Longmans, 1852), Discourse 19, Section 1.

26. Ibid., vol. 8:6.

27. Stevenson, *The Covenant of Grace Renewed,* 119.

28. Ibid., 121–22.

29. Cited in Carroll, *Jeremy Taylor: Selected Works,* 222.

30. Taylor, *Holy Living and Holy Dying,* 1.3.5, cited in Carroll, *Jeremy Taylor: Selected Works,* 447.

31. Second Vatican Council, *Decree on Ecumenism (Unitatis Redintegratio),* par. 13. In Walter M. Abbott and Joseph Gallagher, eds., *The Documents of Vatican II* (New York: America Press, 1966), 356.

13.

John Wesley

It is not commonly known today either by Anglicans or by Methodists that the Wesleyan revival was as much a eucharistic revival as it was an evangelical revival. The genius of the Wesleys lies precisely in the unity that they saw between a sacramental and an evangelical vision of Christianity.
–William R. Crockett[1]

JOHN WESLEY
(1703–1791)

There needs to be a note of caution about idealizing John Wesley in our contemporary ecumenical climate, a note sounded by the Methodist ecumenical and liturgical theologian Geoffrey Wainwright:

> Franz Hildebrand, who came to Methodism from a Lutheran background, brings Wesley close to Luther. Maximin Piette and Michael Hurley, Belgian Franciscan and Irish Jesuit respectively, emphasize his Catholic sympathies. Gordon Rupp, who is interested in the "making of English religion," reminds us that Wesley was after all an Anglican, and the figure that tends to emerge is what the nineteenth century would have called "the Churchman's Wesley." Albert Outler, who comes from Texas, turns Wesley into an early Desert Father.[2]

Who was this man who could mean so much to so many?

He was the fifteenth child of an Anglican priest, Samuel Wesley, and his wife, Susanna. Their Anglican faith, with a strong and constant sense of ecclesial service, provided the fertile soil in which John's soul was to grow. John Wesley came of four generations of clergy in the Church of England. His domestic Anglican piety was a blend of both High Anglican and Puritan spirituality. From the Caroline tradition, Jeremy Taylor's *Holy Living and Holy Dying* (1650–51) awakened in him a longing for a deeply personal piety. The Nonjuror William Law's *A Serious Call to a Devout and Holy Life* (1728) exercised a profound influence not only upon John but also upon his brother Charles. From his Puritan ancestry he absorbed such practices as "the making of rules of life both for individuals and for societies, in a service for renewing the covenant with God, in the keeping of a journal, in the strict observance of the Lord's Day, in simplicity of life and in regular examination of conscience."

The devotional practices of the Epworth Rectory, Lincolnshire, where he was born and reared, and in which daily Bible reading and the Book of Common Prayer featured prominently, created the ethos in which his spiritual sensibilities were formed. This was true especially of the Eucharist. William Crockett notes Susanna Wesley's influence on both John and Charles: "Susanna, their mother, was also deeply formed in seventeenth-century eucharistic spirituality and, along with their father, implanted in her sons a high regard for the sacrament, which never left them."[3]

Educated in theology at the University of Oxford, Wesley gathered around him a group of ardent young Christian men who became known as "the Holy Club" or "Methodists." Sometimes they were known as "Sacramentarians," because of their emphasis on frequent communion, as well as their disciplined approach to spirituality. In 1735, along with his brother Charles, John set out for the new world colony of Georgia as a missionary. Both his antislavery and anti-gin preaching made him somewhat unwelcome among the colonists, and he returned home to England in 1737, feeling something of a failure. Wesley said he found "true" faith in Christ on May 24,

1738, when he attended a Moravian meeting in a room in Aldersgate Street, London:

> In the evening I went very unwillingly to a society in Aldersgate Street, London where one was reading Luther's preface to the Epistle to the Romans. About a quarter before nine, while he was describing the change which God works in the heart through faith in Christ, I felt my heart strangely warmed. I felt I did trust in Christ, Christ alone, for salvation; and an assurance was given me, that he had taken away *my* sins, even *mine,* and saved *me* from the law of sin and death. I began to pray with all my might for those who had in a more especial manner despitefully used me. I then testified openly to all there what I now first felt in my heart.[4]

Not finding favor among the Anglican clergy nor in the churches of his day, in large measure due to his revivalist preaching methods, Wesley saw his "Methodism" as a renewal movement within the Church of England. Wesley took to preaching in the fields, and took as his congregations the working men and families of the newly industrialized cities in the land. Though he made trips both to Ireland and Scotland, it was largely in England and in the industrialized zones that his "Methodist" approach to Christianity took firm root. Wesley's achievement in reaching out to the urbanized masses is well described by Louis Bouyer:

> The ecclesiastics responsible had by and large done nothing for these uprooted masses, overwhelmed by poverty and alcoholism and the worst degradations. Wesley...was the first churchman whether Protestant or Catholic to become aware of the need for a mission to the new pagans of the modern world, a mission no less urgent than the one he had been previously engaged on in distant lands.[5]

Wesley never wished to leave the Church of England, but his passion for the renewal of the church along his "Methodist" lines led him to seek ordination for his preachers. When that was not forthcoming from the authorities of the church, he turned to ordaining candidates himself. However, these ordinations took place as he saw it our of dire necessity rather than out of personal wish or desire.

In 1749 Wesley wrote his famous "Letter to a Roman Catholic."[6] In paragraph seventeen he lays out four principles for mutual regard between Catholic and Methodist, ahead of their time in ecumenical sentiment. They are not to hurt each other but to be kind and friendly in a Christian fashion. They are to speak nothing harsh or unkind of each other, but to use only the language of love consistent with truth and sincerity. No unkind thought is to be harbored, no disposition "which is contrary to tender affection." They are to "endeavor to help each other on in whatever [they] are agreed leads to the Kingdom." Not only was Wesley the first to reach out to the industrialized poor in a new evangelization, but he also takes the lead in practicing what might be termed an immensely practical ecumenism.

Eucharist

To underscore the eucharistic revival that is part and parcel of John Wesley's gift to the church at large, I wish to begin and end this treatment of his eucharistic theology with a particular sermon. In 1733 John Wesley published a sermon that came to be well-known, entitled "The Duty of Constant Communion." The title reveals the content, that is to say, an exhortation to frequent and devout eucharistic communion. He republished this sermon in 1787, just four years before his death, and he noted in the preface that he had seen no reason to change his position on the matter.[7] Wesley favored regular and frequent eucharistic communion.

It is not possible to separate the eucharistic theology of John Wesley from the eucharistic hymnody of his brother,

Charles. John Wesley's eucharistic theology, apart from occasional and incidental references, may be found in a condensation he made in 1745 of a tract by Daniel Brevint, dean of Lincoln, entitled *The Christian Sacrament and Sacrifice*, originally published by Brevint at Oxford in 1673, and in the *Hymns on the Lord's Supper*. The music in the hymns is the work of John's brother, Charles, but there can be no doubt that John was most closely associated with the theological sentiments and convictions set forth in the verses. The division of hymns corresponds, albeit not with complete exactness, to the section headings of Brevint's tract, as John's eucharistic theology finds expression in Charles' eucharistic hymnody. In these hymns the Eucharist is described as, among other things, a memorial of the sufferings and death of Christ, a sign and a means of grace, a pledge of heaven. And it implies a sacrifice. By way of summary, "The Sacrament ordained by Christ the night before He suffered, which St. Paul calls the Lord's Supper, is without doubt one of the greatest mysteries of godliness, and *the most solemn feast of the Christian religion.*"[8] In these descriptions we can see themes that mark the entire tradition of reflection on the Eucharist.

Hymn 92 includes these words:

> We need not now go up to heaven,
> To bring the long-sought savior down;
> Thou are to all already given,
> Thou dost even now thy banquet crown:
> To every faithful soul appear,
> And show thy real presence here.

The words "real presence" are intriguing here. They do not appear to be in any sense polemical, but simply affirm the reality of Christ's presence in and at the Lord's Supper. However, the words had become by this time a code or cipher, as it were, for the defining mark of Catholic eucharistic theology, and there can be no doubt that Wesley knew this. Now and again in the hymns we find expressions that signify the work of the Holy Spirit in the Eucharist, an emphasis on epiclesis that the

Wesleys may have picked up from their patristic studies. Thus in Hymn 85, the Spirit is invoked:

> Come Holy Ghost, thine influence shed,
> And realize the sign;
> Thy life infuse into the bread,
> Thy power into the wine.

Wesley and Anglicans of his day generally were opposed to the Catholic doctrine of transubstantiation, but again, as with Anglicans generally of his time, it remains unclear that they understood the Catholic doctrine with accuracy. John M. Todd points out that "there is a phrase in one of the hymns, 'no local deity,' which indicates that Charles had not mastered the scholastic terms, and it seems most probable that John also did not know that the doctrine of transubstantiation specifically excludes the confinement of God to place."[9] Having said this, however, Todd goes on to point out that the Wesleys' eucharistic hymns brought "the whole doctrine back in other language."[10] Some of the hymns will bear this out.

In Hymn 153 we read:

> Father, Thy feeble children meet,
> And make thy faithful mercies known;
> Give us through faith the flesh to eat,
> And drink the blood of Christ Thy Son;
> Honor Thine own mysterious ways
> Thy sacramental presence show,
> And all the fullness of Thy grace,
> With Jesus on our souls bestow.

"Flesh to eat" and "blood to drink" as "the sacramental presence" is just what the Catholic doctrine of transubstantiation was designed to say, and opens the question whether the mutual confessional polemics of the time prevented that being seen.

Wesley also rejects what he takes to be the Catholic understanding of the Mass as a sacrifice. He understands the

Catholic position on the Mass as a repetition of the unique sacrifice of Christ on the cross, and rejects the notion of regular repetition. Such a repetition would detract from the one necessary and unique sacrifice of the Lord upon the Cross. Daniel Brevint (1616–95), of whose eucharistic theology John had made a *précis*, had written of the sacrifice:

> The main intention of Christ was not here to propose a bare image of his passion once suffered, in order to a bare remembrance; but, over and above, to enrich this memorial with such an effectual and real presence of continuing Atonement and strength, as may both evidently set forth Christ Himself crucified before our eyes (Gal. 3.1) and invite us to his sacrifice, not as done and gone many years since, but, as to expiating grace and mercy, still lasting, still new, still the same that it was when it first was offered for us.[11]

Brevint's understanding of eucharistic sacrifice is beautiful and lucid, but finds its most euphonic expression in the Wesleyan Hymn 122.3, where we read:

> Still the wounds are open wide,
> The blood doth freely flow
> As when first His sacred side
> Received the deadly blow:
> Still, O God, the blood is warm,
> Cover'd with the blood we are;
> Find a part it doth not arm,
> And strike the sinner there!

Similar thoughts are found in Hymn 140.1–2:

> He dies, as now for us He dies!
> That all-sufficient sacrifice
> Subsists, eternal as the Lamb,
> In every time and place the same;

To all alike it co-extends,
Its saving virtue never ends.
He lives for us to intercede,
For us He doth this moment plead,
And all who could not see Him die
May now with faith's interior eye
Behold Him stand as slaughter'd there,
And feel the answer to His prayer.

It may be useful to compare Wesley's sense of Christ "slaughter'd there" in the Eucharist with expressions from the 1994 *Catechism of the Catholic Church*.[12] There we are told that the Eucharist is "the making present and the sacramental offering [of Christ's] unique sacrifice." The Eucharist is sacrificial "because it re-presents [makes present] the unique sacrifice of the cross," and because the liturgical celebration applies the fruit of that sacrifice to the participants. There does not appear to be any great doctrinal distance between Wesley and the *Catechism* on these points.

At the same time, Wesley took great care not to isolate the Eucharist from the other means of grace: prayer (private and corporate), searching the scriptures, fasting, Christian conference (gathering together for fellowship/nurture), the preaching service, watch nights (vigils), the love feast and the covenant service. It was the center of Christian life and practice, but he believed that a center only found significance when it was surrounded by an apparatus of prayer and devotion, and Wesley was keen to see that such was in place.

As already noted, in 1787 Wesley republished a sermon, "The Duty of Constant Communion," which he had written some fifty-five years before. There he writes: "It is the duty of every Christian to receive the Lord's Supper as often as he can." The reasons for frequent reception are given. As both "a command of God" and as "a mercy to man," constant reception of communion is a means through which "we may be assisted to attain those blessings which he hath prepared for us; that we may obtain holiness on earth, and everlasting glory in heaven."

Frequent reception was his own personal practice. He makes a striking contrast with Herbert's infrequent celebration but profound theology, as he has both. The average Anglican parish of the time celebrated the Eucharist four or five times a year. Wesley, however, communicated on an average every three or four days.[13] Introducing an anthology of the Wesleys' works, the Methodist theologian Frank Whaling makes the important point that Methodism departed from this central idea of constant communion when he writes: "The American Methodists remain to this day more liturgical than the British Methodists, and both bodies have strayed from Wesley's ideal of constant communion."[14] Wesley's eucharistic vision and theology remain an invitation to his latter-day disciples and followers in the Methodist tradition. The warmth of his vision and his ecumenical outreach in his *Letter to a Roman Catholic* invite Catholics to a fresh, ecumenical appreciation of this ecclesial tradition and the eucharistic renaissance that lies at its base. Indeed, Whaling goes on to say: "In [the hymns] Charles managed to combine an evangelical passion with a sacramental stress, and in so doing, he held together elements that have so often, in the history of the Church, been put asunder."[15]

Conclusion

For Wesley, worship is central to Christian life, and there is a vital interconnection between worship, life and theology; and even though he does not use this terminology as such, at the center is the Eucharist making the church, until the final consummation in heaven. This is eucharistic ecclesiology in theory. Describing the spirituality of Wesley and the early Methodists, one scholar writes beautifully:

> There was also the spiritual fabric of the Methodists, the intimate bands which were almost lay confessionals, the class meeting which was the essential cell, or koinonia, the love feasts and the occasional

splendid eucharistic solemnities when thousands gathered at the Lord's table and when Wesley and his ordained Anglican friends administered.[16]

Here is a description of the Eucharist making the church that is second to none. It is, if you like, eucharistic ecclesiology in practice. In a subsequent chapter we shall find in the contemporary contribution of Geoffrey Wainwright, Methodist theologian, liturgical scholar and passionate ecumenist the same inspiring eucharistic vision of John Wesley

Notes

1. William R. Crockett, *Eucharist, Symbol of Transformation* (New York: Pueblo Publishing Company, 1989), 199.

2. Geoffrey Wainwright, *Wesley and Calvin: Sources for Theology, Liturgy and Spirituality* (Melbourne: Uniting Church Press, 1987), 14.

3. Crockett, *Eucharist, Symbol of Transformation,* 199.

4. From *The Journal of John Wesley*, May 24, 1738.

5. Louis Bouyer, *Orthodox Spirituality and Protestant and Anglican Spirituality* (London: Burns and Oates, 1969), 190.

6. See Michael Hurley, ed., *John Wesley's Letter to a Roman Catholic* (London: Geoffrey Chapman, 1968).

7. For the complete text of the sermon, see Albert C. Outler, ed., *John Wesley* (New York: Oxford University Press, 1964), 332–44.

8. J. Ernest Rattenbury, *The Eucharistic Hymns of John and Charles Wesley,* 2nd American edition (Akron, OH: Order of St. Luke Publications, 1996), 130. Citation of hymns in this chapter is from Rattenbury.

9. John M. Todd, *John Wesley and the Catholic Church* (London: Hodder and Stoughton, 1958), 148.

10. Ibid.

11. Daniel Brevint, *The Christian Sacrament and Sacrifice,* rev. ed. (Oxford and London: Hatchard and Son, 1847), 11.

12. *Catechism of the Catholic Church* (Washington, DC: United States Conference of Catholic Bishops, 1994), 1362, 1366.

13. J. Munsey Turner, "John Wesley, People's Theologian," *One in Christ* 14 (1978), 338.

14. Frank Whaling, "Introduction," in *John and Charles Wesley, Selected Writings and Hymns*, ed. Frank Whaling (New York/Mahwah, NJ: Paulist Press, 1981), 15.

15. Ibid., 33.

16. Gordon Rupp, "John Wesley, Christian Prophet," *Concilium* 37 (1968), 48.

PART FIVE:

The Modern Age

14.

Friedrich Schleiermacher and Johann Adam Möhler

Vatican II was an event of ecclesial renewal, and the thinking of Möhler stood behind many of the German and French theologians who fashioned the Council's change of direction....In Schleiermacher Möhler found a theologian lecturing upon the social dimensions of the history of Christian dogmas.
–Thomas F. O'Meara, OP[1]

Neither Friedrich Schleiermacher nor Johann Möhler wrote a separate and discrete treatise on the Eucharist, nor did they in their works of dogmatics write very much about the Eucharist as such. However, each represents in his own way a new approach to theology, to ecclesiology and so to the Eucharist. In each we find a reaction against the hard, rational dogmatism of the Enlightenment, and a desire to return to a more holistic way of doing theology. They represent in their own ways a return to a corporate sense of the church, and a corporate understanding of Christian doctrine. A useful description of both theologians is provided by Dennis Doyle:

> Both Schleiermacher and the early Möhler con-
> structed their ecclesiologies over against what they
> took to be a medieval, juridical view of the Church
> that focused too much or even exclusively on the
> Church's institutional aspects to the neglect of its
> communal and personal aspects. Both approached

the Church as being most basically a fellowship or communion carrying forth in history the relationship between Jesus and his disciples. In comparison with what they cast as the juridical view, their own views were personal, historical, and grounded in human experience.[2]

Extrapolating from the possible inference that medieval ecclesiology may be construed as entirely juridical, this description of Doyle's is quite fair to both theologians. Their theological contributions went beyond the arid dogmatics and polemics that tended to mark both Protestant and Catholic approaches of the time. Nonetheless, their individual appreciations of the Eucharist stand in striking contrast.

FRIEDRICH SCHLEIERMACHER
(1768–1834)

Friedrich Daniel Ernst Schleiermacher, often referred to as the "father of modern theology," was born and brought up in a family of Reformed preachers. He is called the father of modern theology because the major expressions of modern theology— for example, immanentism, humanism, an anthropological starting-point, the stress on experience—are already found in his work. He received his education initially at a Moravian school, and absorbed the pietism of that environment. Going on to a Moravian seminary, he experienced doubt, and went on to the University of Halle. Having completed his studies for ministry in the Reformed Church, he seems to have rediscovered something of his former Moravian piety.

Schleiermacher's first book, *On Religion, Speeches to Its Cultured Despisers*, was published in 1799 while he was working as a chaplain at the Charite Hospital in Berlin. It was written as an apologetic work to respond to those who were disdainful of the church and its traditional Christian teachings. To reach the cultured disdainers of religion, Schleiermacher came at an understanding of religion as "a universal, if elusive element in every human consciousness."[3] This is a "sense and taste for the Infinite," the unifying One that lies behind everything that is. "The One in the All is accessible only to feeling. To be religious, then, is to feel that everything that affects us is, at bottom, one: which is to say, that our being and living are a being and living through God."[4] "Feeling," however, is not the polar opposite of "thought" for Schleiermacher. Feeling is what we might call "immediate self-consciousness," that is to say a form of consciousness. Since this immediate self-consciousness is a consciousness of our being and living through God, the One, it may rightly be thought of as "a kind of mystical vision," an innate orientation to the divine.[5] As he develops his *apologia*, Schleiermacher moves to the conclusion that Christianity is the highest expression of this universal, innate feeling.

In 1809 Schleiermacher became the Reformed pastor at the Trinity Church in Berlin, and the following year he was appointed professor of theology at the newly established University of Berlin. His major work, *The Christian Faith*, appeared between 1821 and 1822. In this book he attempts to ground all Christian doctrine in feeling, as understood above. "Christian doctrines are accounts of the Christian religious affections set forth in speech," he writes.[6] On the surface a statement like that looks very subjective, but, in fact, for Schleiermacher, it is not for doctrine points beyond itself, and therefore beyond the human subject, to God, the One.

Jesus Christ is the Redeemer because in him alone there is found a life of "unbroken communion with God in total commitment to God's Kingdom."[7] Jesus is perfectly conscious of God, and is therefore human. The perfection, the unbroken constancy and intensity of that consciousness point to his divinity, such that what God is, he is. Christ the Redeemer brings into existence a new corporate life, assuming believers into the power of his unique God-consciousness. This new corporate life is, of course, the church. Schleiermacher is "pre-eminently a theologian of the Church, in which, as he puts it, the redemptive forces of the Incarnation are implanted."[8]

Eucharist

The church periodically needs nourishment and strengthening of its fellowship in Christ, of its common Christian consciousness, and "it is the satisfaction of this need that believers seek in the sacrament of the altar."[9] These words reveal the essence of Schleiermacher's eucharistic theology. He does not shirk from using the language of "presence" concerning the Eucharist, but it is a very diminished presence indeed. "While it is a presenting of Himself," that "presenting" strengthens fellowship with him and with all in the church. Really, that "presenting" strengthens the God-Christ-consciousness already present, so to speak, in the believer. It is an epistemological or convictional confirmation of Christian consciousness, rather than an ontological bond with Christ. Because the Lord's Supper comes from Christ himself, the supper is "the most intimate bond of all" with Christ, but only because "it is simply the whole redeeming love of Christ to which we are pointed there."[10] The Eucharist enhances our awareness of Christ, and so of God, but it does not effect anything more. Perhaps, better, we may say that the Eucharist for Schleiermacher *affects* but does not *effect*.

Of course, Schleiermacher is aware of the eucharistic differences in respect to Christ's presence within the Protestant tradition, compared to the Roman Catholic tradition. There is little or no harmony of understanding: "Even if different parties did not protest that the Supper as celebrated by others than themselves was no Supper at all, the variety of eucharistic practice within the Church sufficiently declares that on this point no agreement has so far been reached."[11] He knew that within ecclesial traditions there was a measure of agreement. Thus, for the Lutherans the body and blood of Christ are received corporeally along with the bread and wine, in what is known as "consubstantiation." Schleiermacher outright rejects this Lutheran position as being too close to what he held was the erroneous Roman position. He felt that the Zwinglian view represented the eucharistic gifts as tokens of our spiritual conjunction to Christ, and the Calvinist view, nicely expressed by Schleiermacher, lay somewhere in between: "While it is true that Christ conjoined something exclusively with the action of eating and drinking, this was not merely spiritual participation, available quite apart from the sacrament; it was a real presence of His body and blood not to be had anywhere else."[12]

He seems to have found this Calvinist perspective the most acceptable in that it lacked "the over-intellectual bareness of the Zwinglian view" and "the mysterious sensuousness of the Lutheran," yet for him it, too, did not possess a satisfying clarity. He believed that the central issue was one's union with Christ and fellowship with one another, and that came into being by the emergence and deepening of one's awareness. It is the depth of consequent awareness that is the criterion of "real presence," nothing more, nothing less. This becomes very clear when he states that there can be no eucharistic action "for those whose mental condition is defective or whose consciousness is obscured or on the point of disappearing."[13] If anything betrays a lack of eucharistic ontology in Schleiermacher, this does.

Schleiermacher is equally disappointing when it comes to the Eucharist as sacrifice:

> The evasive suggestion that such sacrifice [of the Eucharist] is not different from but identical with that accomplished on the cross has for us no value whatever, for in that case we should have to separate altogether the sacrifice in the death of Christ from the obedience in His life, and His original sacrifice would then be just as arbitrary a transaction and just as magical as the sacrifice of the Mass. In any case, this latter sacrifice would have to be regarded as supplementary to Christ's original sacrifice.[14]

There is no appreciation here of the unique sacrifice of Christ on the cross being represented in the Eucharist, nor even any sense of connection of the entire event of Christ as being morally and ontologically one with the sacrificial death.

JOHANN ADAM MÖHLER
(1796–1838)

Johann Adam Möhler was born on May 6, 1796, in the little town of Igersheim, Wurttemberg, in southwest Germany. In 1815 he began the study of theology in the local seminary, which moved to Tübingen in 1817, and brought him into contact with the wider world of theology at the university. The ambience of Catholic theology at Tübingen was not scholastic but organic and dynamic, best described in these words of Alexander Dru:

> Revelation is an organic plan unfolded in history. Tradition is not a fixed code, but a complex, living whole. Heresy spells death because it "fixes" one element in isolation from others. It was in Tübingen that Catholic theology rose from the ashes of enlightened indifference and, transcending romantic relativism and aestheticism, attained to a full doctrine of the Church.[15]

This was the context for Möhler's organic and dynamic theology, and especially his ecclesiology and sacramental theology.

Johann Adam Möhler was the pupil of Sebastian Drey. He still remains insufficiently known in the theological community. Perhaps a number of accolades he has received from twentieth-century theologians will establish something of his influence. For Alexander Dru, Möhler was "the light of the [Tübingen] school, neither a dry-as-dust nor an inflated metaphysical balloon."[16] The late Cardinal Yves Congar (1904–95), perhaps the premier Catholic ecclesiologist of the twentieth-century, pays Möhler the highest of compliments: "In Möhler I found a source, the source which I needed. What Möhler had done in the 19th century became for me an ideal toward which would inspire and lead me to my own theology in the 20th century."[17] Congar's ecclesiology, developed through careful historical studies ranging especially through the second millennium, has all the feel of Möhler's organic and dynamic approach. Pope Benedict XVI, when still a cardinal, referred to Möhler as "the great reviver of Catholic theology after the ravages of the Enlightenment."[18]

In 1825 Möhler published *The Unity in the Church,* and in 1832, *Symbolism,* which became something of a classic and an answer to Hegel's adversarial attitude to Catholicism. One of the first things Möhler did to prepare himself to teach theology was to tour the German universities for a period of several months. He visited both Catholic and Protestant faculties of theology. Like Edward Bouverie Pusey, the Anglican subject of our next chapter, he found himself taken with the historical methodology and theology of Joachim Neander at the University of Berlin. He wrote: "Learning reveals itself [in Berlin] in its proper form: it embraces thought and life. I admired Planck [in Göttingen] but what is Planck compared with Neander."[19] In *The Unity in the Church* Möhler shows that he had fallen under the influence of Friedrich Schleiermacher (who was also at the University of Berlin), but not totally. There were real differences between them.

Eucharist

The Eucharist pointed to the essential communion of the church. In a passage that has become well known in its own right, we find a fine distillation of Möhler's ecclesiology:

> Thus, the visible Church, from the point of view here taken, is the Son of God himself, everlastingly manifesting himself among men in a human form, perpetually renovated, and eternally young—the permanent incarnation of the same, as in Holy Writ, even the faithful are called "the body of Christ." Hence it is evident that the Church, though composed of men, is yet not purely human.[20]

The passage provides in miniature the panoramic, organic vision of his ecclesiology, closely linked to his Christology. At the center of this "perpetual renovation" of the Son of God is, of course, the Eucharist.

As if to anticipate, almost literally, his treatment of the church somewhat later in *Symbolism*, Möhler writes of the Eucharist:

> The Church, considered in one point of view, is the living figure of Christ, manifesting himself and working through all ages, whose atoning and redeeming acts, it, in consequence, eternally repeats, and uninterruptedly continues. The Redeemer not merely lived eighteen hundred years ago, so that he hath since disappeared, and we retain but a historical remembrance of him, as of a deceased man: but he is, on the contrary, eternally living in his Church; and in the sacrament of the altar he hath manifested this in a sensible manner to creatures endowed with sense.[21]

The Eucharist is the heart of the church for Möhler, for it is nothing more than Christ made manifest through sacramental signs.

If Schleiermacher lacked a eucharistic ontology, Möhler has it in a plenary fashion. Where Schleiermacher displays no explicit appreciation of the Eucharist as sacrifice, Möhler affirms its sacrificial character, and, moreover, connects this sacrificial character with the entire *donnée* of the Lord's life:

> The sacrifice of Christ on the cross is put only as a part for an organic whole. For his whole life on earth—his ministry and his sufferings, as well as his perpetual condescension to our infirmity in the Eucharist—constitute one great sacrificial act, one mighty action undertaken out of love for us, and expiatory of our sins.[22]

Furthermore, while Schleiermacher finds the notion of the Eucharist as representing the unique sacrifice of Christ "evasive," Möhler recognizes that "without that presence, the solemnity of the Lord's Supper is a mere reminiscence of the sacrifice of Christ, exactly in the same way as the celebration by any society of the anniversary of some esteemed individual."[23]

The reality of the Eucharist, of Christ's presence with the believer, is such that a bond of ontological intimacy is established that is almost ineffable. When Möhler tries to put it into words, he seems to fall back on a poetic rendition of biblical passages and allusions:

> The believer has thrown off himself, excommunicated himself, if I may so speak, in his existence, as separated from Christ, in order to live only by him, and in him. Hence he is in a state to enter into the most intimate fellowship with Christ, to commune with him, and with his whole being to be entirely absorbed in him.[24]

Why is it that the Reformers, and perhaps he also has Schleiermacher in mind at this point, failed to grasp this organic, ontological union with Christ through the Eucharist? Möhler suggests that it may be the poor performance of the celebration of the Eucharist in the church that is partly to blame. He writes:

> It ought not to be overlooked, that the Reformers might be led into error through various, and some extremely scandalous, abuses, especially an unspiritual, dry, mechanical performance and participation in this most mysterious function.[25]

The suggestion is that if the Eucharist were celebrated with all the due solemnity and dignity consequent upon a real recognition of its meaning, the ontology of the Eucharist would be spoken with a clear voice to the Reformed world. Mechanical and habitual practice speaks a contrary message.

His concern with the Eucharist went well beyond the brief exposé in *Symbolism*. Möhler campaigned for active participation of the laity in the liturgy, especially in the Eucharist. In an article published in the Tübingen Catholic periodical, *Theologische Quartalschrift*, he advocated the vernacular language for the celebration of Mass. He could not accept the argument that Latin was the language of unity and catholicity, but rather wrote:

> Such a unity! A unity based on ignorance and as for antiquity, why not use Hebrew in the liturgy?...Let the people understand their prayers....The celebration of the Eucharist is the supreme action by which each Christian comes into her or his own as a member of Christ's body.[26]

For reasons such as these, and also to eliminate what he considered to be artificial barriers between laity and clergy, Möhler recommended the restoration of the chalice to the laity. The entire community should share in both eucharistic gifts. Möhler anticipated the liturgical reforms consequent upon Vatican Council II, as well as elements of its ecclesiology.

Conclusion

Both Schleiermacher and Möhler recognize the centrality of the Eucharist, but from different vantage points. While both eschew what might be called a sacramental extrinsicism, in which the Eucharist is understood as outside and alongside the experience of the Christian, Schleiermacher lacks a eucharistic ontology, while Möhler sees in such an ontology the heart and mechanism of communion with Jesus Christ.

Notes

1. Thomas F. O'Meara, *Romantic Idealism and Roman Catholicism: Schelling and the Theologians* (Notre Dame and London: University of Notre Dame Press, 1982), 146, 148.

2. Dennis M. Doyle, *Communion Ecclesiology* (Maryknoll, NY: Orbis Books, 2000), 24.

3. Brian A. Gerrish, "Schleiermacher, Friedrich Daniel Ernst," in Adrian Hastings and others, eds., *The Oxford Companion to Christian Thought* (New York and Oxford: Oxford University Press, 2000), 644.

4. Ibid.

5. John Macquarrie, "Schleiermacher Reconsidered," in his *Thinking About God* (London: SCM Press, 1975), 161.

6. Friedrich Schleiermacher, *The Christian Faith*, trans H. R. Mackintosh and J. S. Stewart (Edinburgh: T. & T. Clark, 1928), 76.

7. Gerrish, "Schleiermacher, Friedrich Daniel Ernst," 645.

8. Ibid., 646.

9. Schleiermacher, *The Christian Faith*, 638.

10. Ibid., 640.

11. Ibid., 642.

12. Ibid., 649.

13. Ibid., 654.

14. Ibid.

15. Alexander Dru, *The Contribution of German Catholicism* (New York: Hawthorn Books, 1963), 59.

16. Ibid., 60.

17. Cited in Thomas F. O'Meara, OP, "Beyond 'Hierarchology': Johann Adam Möhler and Yves Congar," in Donald J. Dietrich and Michael J. Himes, eds., *The Legacy of the Tübingen School* (New York: Crossroad, 1997), 173.

18. Joseph Ratzinger, *Church, Ecumenism and Politics* (New York: Crossroad, 1988), 4.

19. Cited in Dru, *The Contribution of German Catholicism*, 62.

20. Johann Adam Möhler, *Symbolism*, trans. James Burton Robertson, introduction by Michael J. Himes (New York: Crossroad, 1997), 259.

21. Ibid., 236.

22. Ibid., 238.

23. Ibid., 240.

24. Ibid., 242.

25. Ibid., 245.

26. Cited in R. William Franklin, "Tradition as a Point of Contact between Anglicans and Roman Catholics," in Kenneth Hagen, ed., *The Quadrilog, Tradition and the Future of Ecumenism* (Collegeville, MN: The Liturgical Press, 1994), 148.

15.

Cardinal John Henry Newman and Edward Bouverie Pusey

It would be too sharp a dissection, but not therefore without its truth, to say that Newman represented the moral and intellectual force in the Oxford Movement...Pusey the moral and devotional.
–Owen Chadwick[1]

The nineteenth century in England witnessed what has come to be known as the Oxford movement, an ecclesial renewal movement beginning at Oxford University and associated with some of the faculty, and tending in what might be called a Catholicizing direction. The Oxford movement is complex, both historically and theologically, but fundamental to it was "an appeal to the Fathers as interpreters of Scripture, and a sacramentalism of nature and the world, into which the sacraments of the Church fitted easily."[2] This is certainly true of two of the movement's best-known characters, John Henry Newman and Edward Bouverie Pusey, almost exact contemporaries and close friends. While Newman became a Catholic and Pusey remained an Anglican, in so many ways their eucharistic appreciation was very close. This is an important consideration because, in the Church of England in the nineteenth century, the Eucharist was not always understood as the sacrament of unity. "In the Church of England Anglo-Catholics and 'Ritualists' were sharply divided from other groups of churchmen on this issue of the sacraments in general and of the Eucharist in particular, "as Alf Haerdelin notes.[3]

JOHN HENRY NEWMAN
(1801–1890)

The eldest of six children, John Henry Newman was born in London, England, on February 21, 1801. Unlike his friend of later years, Edward Pusey, Newman was not born into the High Church tradition of Anglicanism, whose sacramental and ecclesial positions leaned toward Rome. Newman's family was described by his brother Francis as being quite evangelical and "somewhat free-thoughted, fond of seeing what different people had to say for their opinions."[4] John attended Trinity College at Oxford and was elected a fellow of Oriel College, where he met Pusey and others involved in what came to be known as the Oxford or the Tractarian movement. Pusey was also elected to a fellowship of Oriel College in 1823, the year after Newman, and Newman has left us a description of his first meeting with Pusey:

> His light, curly head of hair was damp with the cold water which his headaches made necessary for comfort; he walked fast with a young manner of carrying himself, and stood rather bowed, looking up from under his eye-brows, his shoulders rounded, and his bachelor's gown not buttoned at the elbow, but hanging loose over his wrists. His countenance was very sweet, and he spoke little.[5]

Newman was most impressed with Pusey's theological learning, and referred to him as *ho megas*, Greek for "the great one."[6]

Ordained as an Anglican priest on May 29, 1825, Newman served as a lecturer, examiner and select preacher at the university church, St. Mary's, the setting for his famous *Parochial and Plain Sermons.*

Newman was censured for his Catholicizing tendencies, as Pusey was to be later, and retired to Littlemore in 1841. There, with several companions, he built rudimentary living quarters and adhered to a rule of life, including the regular disciplines of prayer and fasting, so that his perceptions of the Catholic Church could be clarified. The Italian Passionist Dominic Barberi received Newman into the Catholic Church on October 9, 1845. When Edward Pusey heard of Newman's conversion, he wrote to a mutual friend, John Keble, "Our Church has not known how to use him."[7]

It was a most perceptive insight on Pusey's part, and in many ways it was to remain true also of the positions given Newman by the Roman Catholic Church. Though Newman was to influence so many in later generations, at the time the English Catholic Church was unsure how to use him. Indeed, in a church so dominated by medieval and scholastic thought,

> Newman repeatedly repudiated any suggestion that he was a theologian or that he was qualified to write on theological subjects. Compared with his profound knowledge of Scripture and the Fathers his familiarity with St. Thomas Aquinas and the scholastic tradition was much more modest.[8]

In terms of this book on the Eucharist it may be of interest to note that much later, in 1855, when Newman had been appointed rector of the newly established Catholic University in Dublin, he appointed James Burton Robertson as professor of modern history and geography. It was this scholar who in 1843 had translated Johann Adam Möhler's *Symbolik* into English.

Eucharist

As O'Carroll has noted, "Newman presents the interesting case of a man of genius, with immense spiritual potential, expressing his thought on the Eucharist from within two different Christian communions, in the successive phases of his religious pilgrimage," from Canterbury to Rome.[9] Though this contrast can be too easily overdrawn, it is helpful as an entry into Newman's thought. As an Anglican, Newman accepted the central aspect of eucharistic doctrine: the real presence of Christ—in point of fact, Newman speaks of having as an Anglican "an absolute and overpowering sense of the Real Presence"[10]—and the Eucharist as sacrifice. However, as an Anglican he does not accept the doctrine of transubstantiation, and while he accepts the Eucharist as sacrifice, there is no articulation of a sacrificial theology as such. He is content to affirm that the eucharistic sacrifice is not a new sacrifice, but rather "a mysterious representation of [Christ's] meritorious sacrifice in the sight of Almighty God."[11] There is no speculation with *how* the Eucharist is sacrificial, but its ontological connection with Christ's unique sacrifice on the cross is underscored.

Newman's Anglican approach on eucharistic presence does not differ significantly from that of Bishop Lancelot Andrewes in his reply to Cardinal Robert Bellarmine. This is what Newman has to say:

> Our Church argues that a body cannot be in two places at once; and that the Body of Christ is not locally present, in the sense in which we speak of the Bread as being locally present. On the other hand she determines, as I have already said, that the Body of Christ is in some unknown way, though not locally, yet really present, so that we after some ineffable manner, partake of it. Whereas then the objection stands, Christ is not really here, because he is not locally here, she answers, he is really here, yet not locally.[12]

Newman's movement into the Catholic Church involved obviously an assent to the eucharistic doctrine of that church. It comes, therefore, as no surprise that he did not write a great deal about the Eucharist. The grammar of eucharistic doctrine had been clearly set out in the decrees of the Council of Trent, and Catholic theologians saw it as their task to teach, to preach and to clarify this doctrine. That Newman did on an *ad hoc* basis. However, on the personal level he had a deep appreciation of the Eucharist, not only in public, liturgical celebration, but in his private devotional practice. This was something that developed after he became a Catholic. Dom Placid Murray points out with reference to a number of Newman texts that as an Anglican he had little or no idea of the eucharistic presence in the Reserved Sacrament.[13] This was to change enormously in the direction of a really intense devotion. In one of his letters in 1846 to Mrs. John Bowden, a letter written from Milan, Newman writes finely of the Blessed Sacrament and what it means to him:

> Here a score of churches which are open to the passer-by...in each of which...the Blessed Sacrament is ready for the worshipper even before he enters. There is nothing which has brought home to me the Unity of the Church, as the Presence of its Divine Founder and Life wherever I go—All places are, as it were, one[14]

Unity and catholicity through the Eucharist blend together in this comment, and the sheer physical presence of so many Catholic churches compared with England made a very deep impression on him. A later letter to the same Mrs. Bowden has Newman telling her that "an intense devotion to the Blessed Sacrament will overcome every trial."[15] Mrs. Bowden herself was received into the church in July 1846.

In this letter Newman is revealing the depths of his own soul. He found solace and comfort before the Blessed Sacrament. In 1860, he writes in his personal journal concerning his lack of appreciation by his ecclesiastical superiors, Rome not knowing how to use him any better than Canterbury:

> This has naturally made me shrink into myself, or rather it has made me think of turning more to God,

if it has not actually turned me. It has me feel that in the Blessed Sacrament is my great consolation, and that while I have him who lives in the Church, the separate members of the Church, my Superiors, though they may claim my obedience, have no claim on my admiration, and offer nothing for my inward trust....[16]

It is not difficult to hear the misunderstanding and the hurt in these words, but equally his love of the Eucharist shines through. It is his great consolation, even as he also recognizes that this consoling Christ lives in the entire church.

EDWARD BOUVERIE PUSEY
(1800–1882)

The Anglican theologian Edward Bouverie Pusey was born in Berkshire, England, August 22, 1800, and educated at Eton and at Christ Church, Oxford. Further theological pursuits took him to Germany, where he met, among many other theologians, Friedrich Schleiermacher, and the great patristic scholar and historian Johann August Wilhelm Neander, as Johann Adam Möhler had done. It may be that Schleiermacher's emphasis on religion as a feeling of absolute dependence upon God had some influence on Pusey's own growing devotional life. Pusey was also a student of Arabic and Syriac, as well as Hebrew, and in 1826 he wrote to Newman from Berlin where he was studying: "I rejoice that you are learning Hebrew, and that you already relish it."[17] In 1828 Pusey was married and ordained, and the following year he was appointed to the Regius Chair of Hebrew at Oxford.

Pusey, John Henry Newman, John Keble and Richard Hurrell Froude were all key players in the Oxford movement, which had been established to revive the Catholic tradition in the Church of England. Pusey, as Regius Professor of Hebrew, and reputed for great learning and holiness, was an invaluable asset influencing serious church considerations. Newman apparently thought that Pusey would follow him into the Roman Catholic Church, but that was never to happen. "I think that the year can hardly be named," wrote Newman to Pusey, "which you ended with the same view of the Roman Catholic religion as you began with. And every change has been an approximation to that religion."[18] Eventually, Pusey assumed leadership of the Oxford movement, in part to try to keep others from following Newman into the Catholic Church, not so much in an adversarial fashion as to encourage them to stay committed to the renewal of the Church of England. They remained friends and continued to correspond until Pusey's death in 1882.

In 1843 the Oxford authorities took Pusey to task for his mildly Catholic sermon on the Eucharist, and he was suspended from preaching for two years. The Anglican ecclesiastical historian Sir Owen Chadwick comments: "In 1846 the name of Pusey stank in the Church. At least half the Church, and more than half the university, regarded him as a heretic and the leader of heretics."[19] The Oxford movement and Pusey in particular were considerable threats to the establishment of the established church. They were not in favor of the disestablishment of the church, but they were opposed to the careerism of clergy, to liturgical minimalism, to the lack of pastoral care. They were reformers in the best sense of the word, and those most in need of reform did not appreciate it. Pusey's somewhat tedious treatises, *The Real Presence in the Fathers* (1855) and *The Real Presence* (1857), defended the High Church, that is, the Catholic position. He attempted to check the spread of liberalism in the church, thinking reunion with Rome the most effective means to that end.

Pusey was fully aware of the doctrinal and practical issues that seemed to keep Canterbury and Rome separate. In his first *Eirenicon* (1865), he described the obstacles to reunion as "unofficial doctrines respecting the Blessed Mother, purgatory, and indulgences"; in his second *Eirenicon* (1869), he cited "Anglican objections to the Immaculate Conception."

Newman's discouraging reply to Pusey's appeals, followed by the definition of papal infallibility in 1870 by the First Vatican Council, ended his hopes.

Eucharist

Temperamentally, Pusey was a retiring man, not popular in the sense of a party leader. In fact, Owen Chadwick says of him that "if he had thought a party to be following him, he would have shut himself in his house, said his prayers and continued with his studies."[20] Chadwick goes much further in his description of Pusey. He was the *doctor mysticus* of the Oxford movement, the one who constantly underscored the dwelling of the Christian in Christ, the Christian as the very Body of Christ.[21] We get a fine sense of mystical union with God in a letter he wrote to a friend in the last weeks of his life:

> You, I hope, are ripening continually. God ripen you more and more. Each day is a day of growth. God says to you, "Open thy mouth and I will fill it." Only long. He does not want our words. The parched soil, by its cracks, opens itself for the rain from heaven and invites it. The parched soil cries out for the living God. Oh! Then long and long and long, and God will fill thee. More love, more love, more love![22]

It is in the vibrant context of this deep longing for God and of this being filled up by the God who longs for us that Pusey thought of the Eucharist as the central gate through which the Lord came to take up his habitation within us, and to draw us into the communion of the Trinity.

A sermon from 1853 gives us a clear indication of Pusey's eucharistic theology, especially his understanding of the eucharistic presence of Christ. In that year Pusey preached:

> The presence of which our Lord speaks has been termed sacramental, supernatural, mystical, ineffable,

as opposed *not* to what is real, but to what is natural....We know not the manner of his presence...but it is a presence without us, not within us only; a presence by virtue of our Lord's words, although to us it becomes a saving presence, received to our salvation, through our faith....But, while the consecrated elements...remain in their natural substances, still, since our Lord says, "This is my body,'" "This is my blood," the Church of England believes that "under the form of bread and wine," so consecrated, we "receive the body and blood of our Saviour Christ." And since we receive them, they must be there, in order that we may receive them.[23]

A Catholic would say, perhaps, that the affirmation that "the body and blood of Christ must *be* there in order that we may receive them," is precisely what is intended by the doctrine of transubstantiation. But not Pusey. He explicitly rejected transubstantiation as such. Indeed, he wrote in *Tract 67:* "The error of Transubstantiation has modified other true doctrine, so as to cast into the shade the one oblation once offered upon the Cross."[24] And yet his sermon was understood to be so closely connected with doctrine contrary to the Church of England, especially its Thirty-Nine Articles, that he was suspended from preaching before the University of Oxford for two years. Despite Pusey's rejection, one must conclude that the university authorities were indeed correct. Pusey's strong statement of the real presence of Christ in the Eucharist, with all the learned patristic support that he brought in its defense, is quite simply what is intended by the doctrine of transubstantiation. He rejected what he referred to as "a physical and carnal transubstantiation" but was happy to accept a "sacramental and mystical" transubstantiation.[25] At times he goes so far as to insinuate that the difficulties between Rome and Canterbury concerning transubstantiation are but a matter of words.

Why, one may ask, was there such vehement rejection of transubstantiation and yet such warm acceptance of the real eucharistic presence of Christ, indeed a "sacramental and mystical" transubstantiation? It is a puzzle. Part of the answer is to be found in the very term "transubstantiation" as an ecclesial and polemical term with several centuries of history behind it by that time. The term trails many unhealed memories and misunderstood meanings. Part of the answer is also to be found in a lack of awareness of its real meaning and of its originating context. Gabriel O'Donnell comments: "Tractarian negligence of the medieval theological synthesis and their inexperience of the Catholic counter-Reformation created a lacuna in their understanding of what post-Tridentine Catholicism and its spirituality really meant."[26] Because of their explicit desire to renew the church through the patristic period—its writings and its liturgy and its tradition—the Oxford divines tended to pass over the entire medieval period prior to the Reformation as being of no great significance. For all practical purposes they lacked the conceptual apparatus to appreciate the philosophical value and theological insight afforded by transubstantiation, especially as taught by St. Thomas Aquinas.

Pusey was well aware that the Council of Trent did not teach that the Mass added to the sacrifice of Christ on the Cross, but rather re-presented that unique sacrifice. He is so clear about this that he can write:

> I am persuaded that, on this point, the two Churches might be reconciled by explanation of the terms used. The Council of Trent, in laying down the doctrine of the sacrifice of the Mass, claims nothing for the Holy Eucharist but an *application* of the one meritorious sacrifice of the Cross. An *application* of that sacrifice the Church of England believes also.[27]

This is identical, almost verbally, with Newman's understanding. Of course, this way of thinking also found resonance in the High Church, but, as discussion around the time of the Windsor Agreed Statement on the Eucharist of the Anglican-

Roman Catholic International Commission showed, this was far from being the Low Church or Evangelical perception.

Pusey's eucharistic appreciation did not remain at the level of academic theology. In 1833 he launched a campaign to establish "eucharistic" parishes in the new industrial conurbations of England, and remained interested in this project until his death. He advocated that the weekly celebration in parishes should be the Eucharist, and not simply Morning Prayer. It is estimated that by his death in 1882 in excess of five hundred parishes, out of a total of fourteen thousand in England and Wales, had been won over to the weekly celebration of the Eucharist.[28]

Conclusion

"The genius of the Oxford Movement and the secret of its influence was in its rediscovery of the wholeness of patristic theology, of the reality of sacramental grace, and a refusal...to confine theology to the domain of the speculative,"[29] says Geoffrey Rowell. This is evident in both Newman and Pusey. The nonscholastic, patristic-steeped Newman pushed out the horizons of ecclesial and theological renewal especially but not only in the English-speaking world. The equally patristic Pusey did the same for the Church of England, and had more of an immediate influence than Newman at the level of pastoral, eucharistic practice. The ecclesial and theological vision of both friends would have found fulfillment in the renewal consequent upon Vatican Council II. R. William Franklin reaches this judgment: "As a result of the process initiated within Anglicanism by E. B. Pusey and from the perspective of the change to a vernacular Roman Catholic liturgy at Vatican II, at last the English liturgy derived from Thomas Cranmer and the Catholic liturgy of the Council of Trent were hardly to be distinguished."[30] It may be that the liturgy in both communions is hard to distinguish in our times, but Anglicans and Catholics remain separate, and so the work for unity must go on.

Notes

1. Owen Chadwick, *The Spirit of the Oxford Movement* (Cambridge: Cambridge University Press, 1990), 39.

2. Ibid., 9.

3. Alf Haerdelin, "The Eucharist in the Theology of the Nineteenth Century," in *Eucharistic Theology Then and Now* (London: SPCK, 1968), 76.

4. Cited in Geoffrey Rowell, *The Vision Glorious* (Oxford and New York: Oxford University Press, 1983), 45.

5. John Henry Newman, *John Henry Newman, Autobiographical Writings,* ed. Henry Tristram (New York: Sheed and Ward, 1957), 74.

6. Rowell, *The Vision Glorious,* 74.

7. Ibid., 70.

8. Ian Ker, *Newman the Theologian, A Reader* (Notre Dame and London: University of Notre Dame Press, 1990), 41.

9. Michael O'Carroll, *Corpus Christi* (Wilmington, DE: Michael Glazier, 1988), 144.

10. John Henry Newman, Letter to Henry Wilberforce, quoted in Placid Murray, *Newman the Oratorian* (Dublin: Gill and Macmillan, 1969), 43.

11. ———. *Lectures on the Doctrine of Justification,* cited in Haerdelin, "The Eucharist in the Theology of the Nineteenth Century," 83.

12. ———. *Tracts for the Times,* 90, cited in O'Carroll, *Corpus Christi,* 144.

13. Placid Murray, *Newman the Oratorian* (Dublin: Gill and Macmillan, 1969), 48.

14. C. S. Dessain, ed., *The Letters and Diaries of John Henry Newman,* vol. 11 (London and Edinburgh: Thomas Nelson, 1961), 254.

15. Ibid., vol. 14, 307.

16. Tristram, *John Henry Newman, Autobiographical Writings,* 252.

17. Cited in Alan Livesley, "Regius Professor of Hebrew," in Perry Butler, ed., *Pusey Rediscovered* (London: SPCK, 1983), 95.

18. Quoted from Robert H. Greenfield, SSJE, "Such a Friend to the Pope," in Butler, *Pusey Rediscovered,* 174–75.

19. Chadwick, *The Spirit of the Oxford Movement,* 215.

20. Ibid., 37.

21. The title *doctor mysticus* was first given to Pusey by Yngve Brilioth. See Brilioth's *The Anglican Revival* (London and New York: Longmans Green, 1925), 296.

22. A. M. Allchin, "Pusey: the Servant of God," in Butler, *Pusey Rediscovered*, 388.

23. Edward Bouverie Pusey, *The Presence of Christ in the Holy Eucharist*, 1853, cited in Rowell, *The Vision Glorious*, 19.

24. Cited by Greenfield, "Such a Friend to the Pope," in Butler, *Pusey Rediscovered*, 168.

25. See Edward Bouverie Pusey, *An Eirenicon* (London: Gilbert and Rivington, 1865), 25.

26. Gabriel O'Donnell, "The Spirituality of E. B. Pusey," in Butler, *Pusey Rediscovered*, 248.

27. Pusey, *An Eirenicon*, 28.

28. R. William Franklin, "Tradition as a Point of Contact between Anglicans and Roman Catholics in the Nineteenth Century: the Case of Johann Adam Möhler and Edward Bouverie Pusey," in Kenneth Hagen, ed., *The Quadrilog: Tradition and the Future of Ecumenism* (Collegeville, MN: The Liturgical Press, 1994), 159.

29. Rowell, *The Vision Glorious*, 96.

30. Franklin, "Tradition as a Point of Contact between Anglicans and Roman Catholics in the Nineteenth Century: the Case of Johann Adam Möhler and Edward Bouverie Pusey," 152.

16.

The Eucharist in Our Times: An Irish Catholic, David N. Power, and an English Methodist, Geoffrey Wainwright

This love of and for God events in the community of faith and in the presence of this community in time and place and event, even in the midst of discontinuities and ambiguities to which there is no intelligible pattern.
–David N. Power[1]

The Church's worship assembly is an expression and a school of faith; its liturgical celebration enacts, in ritual mode, the love toward God and neighbor in which true religion consists.
–Geoffrey Wainwright[2]

Vatican Council II (1962–65) brought about a scriptural renewal in the Catholic Church, finding its key expression in the Constitution on Revelation (*Dei Verbum*), and a liturgical renewal, expressed centrally in the Constitution on the Sacred Liturgy (*Sacrosanctum Concilium*). Add to this the Constitution on the Church (*Lumen Gentium*) and the Decree on Ecumenism (*Unitatis Redintegratio*), and all the ingredients are present for a Spirit-given moment of ecclesial growth, a moment in which

254

we continue to share. To focus these aspects of church renewal, we could not do better than turn to the contributions of David N. Power, an Irish Catholic who has spent the greater part of his working life in the United States, and Geoffrey Wainwright, an English Methodist who has taught in the United States for more than two decades. Each is a passionate churchman combining a love for the Word and for the Eucharist in an ecumenical outreach. The contributions of each will be examined quite deliberately—in the case of Power, with the primary emphasis on Word, and with Wainwright on Eucharist. The intention is both to point out that the inaccurate but widespread caricature of the Reformation tradition as "Word" and the Catholic tradition as "Eucharist" will not be found in either of these contemporary theologians, and, more particularly, to underscore the ecumenical lineaments of eucharistic theology today.

DAVID NOEL POWER
(b. 1932)

Born in Dublin, Ireland, in 1932, David Power made religious profession as an oblate of Mary Immaculate in 1950. He studied philosophy and theology at the Gregorian University in Rome, and was ordained a priest in 1956. After ordination he was assigned to teach systematic theology at his religious congregation's scholasticate in Ireland, where for seven years he taught the cycle of dogmatics. From 1964 to 1968 Power was back in Rome, this time at Sant'Anselmo where he was awarded the STD for his dissertation, *Ministers of Christ and His Church*.[3] A confrere, commenting on the dissertation as showing the qualities that would mark Power's lifework, says: "By training and inclination, David Power is first of all a systematic theologian who takes the liturgy, traditions and texts, as the particular field of his inquiry."[4] He returned to Ireland to teach until 1971 but then went back to Rome. Among other assignments he taught liturgical and sacramental theology at the Gregorian and Angelicum universities until 1977, when he accepted a position in systematic theology and liturgy at the Catholic University of America in Washington, DC. Power remained there until his formal retirement in 2000 as the Shakespeare Caldwell-Duval Professor of Theology. Needless to say, retirement has not ended his theological and liturgical research and teaching. David Power contributed an essay, "Koinonia, Oikumene, and Eucharist in Ecumenical Conversations," to the *Festschrift* honoring Geoffrey Wainwright.[5]

Word

A former student of David Power's, Michael Downey, provides a good, orienting description of what Power has tried to do in his liturgical theology: He has opened up

> the discourse about liturgy and sacrament to include other fields, as well as by the nature of his probings, the types of needs he addresses, the kinds of questions he engages, and the way he brings the Christian sacramental tradition to bear on the pressing needs and urgent demands of our age.[6]

This is a very fair description of Power. When one reads through his liturgical output, one is struck not only by the width of his historical knowledge and interpretation, but also by the way in which he engages with other disciplines and authors in the humanities to reach fresh readings of worship and sacrament. This is true of his collected volumes of theological articles, *Unsearchable Riches: The Symbolic Nature of Liturgy*[7] and *Worship: Culture and Theology*.[8] It is even more true, however, of his more recent systematic works on sacrament and the Eucharist. In his earlier work it is possible to note especially his engagement with the philosophical theology of the Canadian Jesuit, Bernard J. F. Lonergan, in particular Lonergan's version of transcendental Thomism.[9] Power's later work sees a similar engagement with such diverse thinkers as Paul Ricoeur, Hans-Georg Gadamer, Louis-Marie Chauvet and various postmodernist thinkers. Liturgical theology never becomes for him a self-enclosed circle, but must always find points of reflective connection in the wider horizon of thought. At the same time, his close awareness of the history of eucharistic theology from the time the scriptures were written down through our own times unfolds for him, as one author notes, "twenty centuries of plurality in unity," a plurality in unity that is both practical and doctrinal as well as legitimate.[10]

In a similar fashion, one finds in Power the "option for praxis." This is a desire to locate the ethical, social and political dimensions of the liturgy, both for and beyond the church. In this respect he has shown himself sensitive to the voices of those on the margins, so to speak. Again, Michael Downey proves an effective guide:

> Whether it be his sustained attention to the emergence of base Christian communities as clear expression of the Spirit's voice in the churches, his continuing commitment to the development and support of lay ministries in the Church, his attentiveness to the emergent consciousness of women in Church and society, his commitment to the mission of evangelization of and by the poor, or even his efforts to assure that the often facilely villainized Tridentine theology of sacrifice be given a fair hearing, his concern is to give attention to those experiences and to those voices which speak a different word from what the prevailing social and ecclesial orders maintain is the way things are and must be.[11]

The upshot is that, when we come to look at Word and Eucharist in Power's theology, there is no neat and tidy package. There is no traditional, analytic treatment of the various themes one would expect for these doctrinal issues. Power's liturgical theology is really an invitation to agonize over what Word and

Eucharist have meant, to imagine what Word and Eucharist could mean, but—most of all—to commit oneself to the disciplined performance of Word and Eucharist. Conversion, personal and ecclesial, is at the heart of Power's liturgical theology.

The canon of scripture that the lectionary represents is marked by a variety of literary genres. Power points especially to narrative, prophecy, hymn and wisdom literature. Let's consider narrative first. Narrative itself may be distinguished as institution narrative, foundational story, foundational myth and parable. An *institution* narrative is one that provides a story of a beginning or foundation, such as the Passover seder or the Last Supper. Beneath or behind the institution narrative lies a foundational story that offers an account of the beginnings of what is celebrated in sacrament. Thus, behind the Passover seder lies the Exodus event, the stories of the Patriarchs, going back to the founding narrative of Abraham's call by God. For Christians this *foundational* word from the past is addressed to the present, not in its storied purity, but—in Power's words—"wrapped in the testimony of all those witnesses to Christ who have translated this story into their own lives."[12] While a foundational narrative is rooted in some historical event, even though its precise nature may now be impossible to recover, a *foundational myth* such as creation or the flood calls out to be demythologized. It may seem to be historical because of its shape, but in reality it is best understood as a poetic expression of a deeper theological conviction. The *creation* narrative points to everything having its origin in God, while the flood story points to the enigma of moral evil, and how humans have the capacity to infect their environment. While some *parables* of Jesus are stories intended for moral exhortation or instruction, like the parable of the sower and the seed, others are intended to subvert our false and inauthentic moral or religious presuppositions, like the parable of the Good Samaritan.

Prophecy reflects on the covenantal relationship between God and his people, highlighting "God's loving care and a constant maternal and spousal readiness to renew the covenant."[13] Whether the prophet is Isaiah or Hosea or Ezekiel, here too the covenantal invitation is not simply extended to its initial hearers, but to us as well. This emerges with clarity when it comes to the prophetic messages that speak of justice, peace and righteous living for God's people. While prophecy evokes a true and right confidence in God's covenantal love, it also demands repentance from all that disfigures our covenantal response.

"Wisdom literature offers a practical avenue for integrating the reality and the wonder of creation into sacramental memorial," Power says.[14] God's good creation is celebrated as also is his providential governance of the world and its affairs. The themes of the Wisdom authors invite those in the community to recognize God's continuing governance of their own lives, and to see in Jesus wisdom enfleshed. Finally, the omnipresent psalms and canticles of the liturgy, "in their variety and poetic quality, serve as an address to the God who first addresses us."[15]

Although the genre of narrative bears all these distinctions and more, they share something in common:

> They are always heard as an irruption into life, as an interruption of the tempo of life and the sequence of happenings that go on within the ordinary efforts of managing time. While they are stories for all who believe, they are always an address to this particular assembly, gathered within this rite and in this place.[16]

Narratives reach out to the liturgical assembly not in the first instance to provide them with historical information about a remote past, albeit the remote past of their ancestors in faith. Narratives function as an invitation to configure or re-configure one's own Christian life in the light of this salvific event here and now. The narrative enscripts the gracious event of God's saving action now, in this congregation, in this congregant. This is a paschal or cruciform enscription, because the Word/word has to be accompanied "by a willingness to be disturbed."[17] Being conformed to the Word of God means, in the last analysis, letting the Word perform the paschal mystery in our own persons, being disturbed out of complacency, being literally "excited" by the Word, stirred up into ever-fresher levels of response.

Given the profile of Power's theology offered so far, it should come as no surprise that he is not content simply to articulate the eucharistic ontology of the Catholic tradition. He takes that as given, and it finds fine summary toward the end of his book *The Eucharistic Mystery: Revitalizing the Tradition*:

> All the words and rites of celebration lead to the still moment of communion, when at last in the gift of Christ's body and blood the invitation to contemplation is heard and accepted. The words and the rites gather into one a diversity of persons and cultures, the living and the dead, human events past and present, lives rich and impoverished, earth and its cycles and its inner yearnings. All these are gathered into the Pasch of Christ and into the promise that it offers. In the hope of that promise, the church receives the covenant of an abiding being in God that eye has not seen and ear has not heard. Groping for a name, it can only proclaim the hope of glory. Even amid the ruins.[18]

What a splendid passage! The entire eucharistic celebration, words and ritual gestures, is rightly seen as reaching its climax in the moment of receiving holy communion, "the still moment of communion" brought about by Christ's body and blood. Changed by grace into Christ, all peoples and cultures are made one. The communion of all explicitly is made to include our sainted dead as well as the living, every human person irrespective of status or fulfillment in this life. The eucharistic life trails the only completion and fulfillment that really counts, "the hope of glory." The cosmos too, "earth and its cycles and its inner yearnings," is caught up in this eucharistic fulfillment. In the Eucharist we have the promise, God-given, of an ineffable "abiding being in God." All of this occurs really and truly, "even amid the ruins" of history, personal, national, universal. This is Power at his best, indeed, this is our tradition at its best.

Nevertheless, Power wishes to probe further and beyond this eucharistic ontology. His probings may be seen as articulating a solidarity with others. The Catholicity and inclusiveness of the passage cited above must be verified in right practice, orthopraxis:

> The orthodoxy of the eucharistic canon is verified by the orthopraxis of solidarity with victims and with those who hope and serve the fullness of human life, even in the midst of suffering and injustice.[19]

He exemplifies as victims the Jewish people—the Holocaust is an important theme in Power's theology—and women, whose concerns and identity still remain insufficiently recognized and appreciated in both church and world. We must be disturbed into appropriate action for victims by Eucharist as well as Word.[20]

GEOFFREY WAINWRIGHT
(b. 1939)

Born at Monk Bretton in the West Riding, Yorkshire, England, in 1939, Geoffrey Wainwright completed his undergraduate studies in modern languages and theology at the University of Cambridge. Accepted as a candidate for the British Methodist ministry in 1961, he studied at Wesley College, Leeds, and then served his probationary circuit years in the Liverpool area from 1964 to 1966. Wainwright's doctoral studies proceeded in Geneva, his dissertation being published as *Eucharist and Eschatology*.[21] Ordination took place in 1967, after which he served as professor of systematic theology at the Protestant Faculty of Theology at Yaounde, Cameroon, from 1967 to 1973.

Wainwright's ecumenical activities have been central throughout his entire life of teaching, serving the World Council of Churches in various respects, as well as his own Methodist tradition. In 1973 the British Methodist Conference called him back to teach systematics in the Queen's College, Birmingham, an Anglican-Methodist ecumenical seminary. He remained there until 1979, and then took up an appointment as Roosevelt Professor of Systematic Theology at Union Theological Seminary, New York City. In 1983 Wainwright moved to the Cushman Chair of Christian Theology at the Divinity School of Duke University, Durham, North Carolina. Geoffrey Wainwright contributed an essay, "The Roman Catholic Response to *Baptism, Eucharist and Ministry*: The Ecclesiological Dimension," to the *Festschrift* honoring David Power.[22]

Eucharist

The most obvious feature of Geoffrey Wainwright's eucharistic theology is the emphasis on eschatology. This was the focus of his doctoral work. He moves through the biblical and patristic and liturgical material, including the competing hypotheses of contemporary interpreters, gradually developing the eschatological dimension of the Eucharist. The conclusion is clear: the Eucharist brings heaven to earth, the Eucharist is the antepast of heaven.

> The eucharistic table is the heavenly table at which
> is enjoyed the heavenly banquet of the heavenly gifts
> of the heavenly bread and the heavenly cup, the
> whole being a heavenly mystery.[23]

He recognizes the diminution of this eschatological aspect of the Eucharist especially in the West, perhaps especially during the polemics consequent upon the Reformation. At least in part, its retrieval came with his own Methodist tradition through the insights of the Wesley Brothers. Wainwright wrote:

> It was not until the Wesleys' *Hymns on the Lord's Supper*
> (1745) that the Western Church achieved a rich
> appreciation of the Eucharist as the sign of the future
> banquet of the heavenly kingdom.[24]

The Lord's Supper *now* is the promise of the great Kingdom *to
come*.

The eschatological theme is pursued into the difficult
context of ecumenical relations between the churches. After
surveying various possible positions on the relation between
sacraments and church, Wainwright's own position is eminently
clear: "There *can* be no satisfactory account of the relation
between sacraments and Church as long as there is disunity
among Christians."[25] The Eucharist must be seen as not only
expressing church unity, but also as creating church unity. This
is not a plea for open eucharistic commensality on his part, but
it is a clear recognition of the power of the Eucharist to build
unity, an edification that should be entered into in given circumstances:

> When a state of Christian disunity obliges us to
> choose between the Eucharist's value as expressive of
> existing unity and its value as creative of deeper
> unity, eschatology then impels us to choose the
> Eucharist's *creative value*, and that means intercommu-
> nion.[26]

In my judgment, the most exciting contribution of
Geoffrey Wainwright to liturgical theology is his *Doxology: A
Systematic Theology*.[27] It is one of the most complete attempts in
English to produce what might be termed a liturgical systematics. At every point in this one volume summa the *lex orandi* comes
into play, and comes into play across confessional boundaries. In
this major work Wainwright further develops his views on
eucharistic sharing, noting that "it is when it is celebrated ecu-
menically that the Eucharist can most truly fulfill its character as
an effective sacrament of reconciliation and renewal."[28] He offers

some examples of how this could happen in a limited but real fashion: in "mixed marriages," considered as domestic churches; when Christians due to travel are visiting some other part of the world; when Christians of different traditions come together specifically to promote the cause of Christian unity; finally, between churches that have covenanted toward unity. Such eucharistic sharing, in Wainwright's judgment, would increase—slowly but really—the impetus toward Christian unity. Though this is not the case with the Roman Catholic Church for complex but defensible reasons, other ecclesial communities and traditions that take the Eucharist seriously have found in proposals like these great promise.

The Eucharist as sacrament of reconciliation helps to heal the fractures between Christians of different traditions. While the Eucharist is at the center of "the vertical reconciliation of humanity to God," it also features in "the horizontal reconciliation of human beings among themselves."[29] The Eucharist can aid in the healing of old divisions, and help to carry the Christian witness with greater vigor where it is most needed:

> The gathering, when it is allowed to happen, of the separated but penitent brothers and sisters around the one table of the one Lord exemplifies before the world the holiness which consists in the overcoming of sin and in the growth of love.[30]

Wainwright in one particular essay is very specific about the reconciliatory potential of the Eucharist. He has had a long association with the cause of ecumenism in Ireland, and especially with the Irish School of Ecumenics, based in Dublin. In an essay penned in 1993 the following words will be found:

> My bet is that water, bread and wine are more potent symbols than sashes, berets and flags. Hands lifted in prayer or laid on heads in forgiveness and healing are closer to reality than hands that plant bombs or squeeze triggers. The kiss of peace is more signifi-

cant than a political pact, for which, however, it may
lay the ground. If these things are not the case, then
ultimately we are all losers.[31]

Wainwright is surely right, and not only about Ireland.

The Eucharist as the center of Christian life gives rise
also to what Wainwright describes as a "eucharistic ethics." As
we are conjoined with Christ in and through the Eucharist so
that his life flows into ours, our moral lives may be said to take
on a eucharistic shape.

> As grateful response to what God has already done
> for us, and as thankful cooperation with what God
> continues to do in us, our self-offering to God is
> removed from Pelagianism or works-righteousness.[32]

"Pelagianism" or "works-righteousness" is an ethical perspective
in which the primary player is the autonomous human subject
doing the right thing. Eucharistic ethics stems from the Christ-
life flowing within us, giving rise to the right thing. If you like,
there is a eucharistic ontology behind the human act.

Conclusion

Power shows us a theology of the Word, rediscovered
by Catholics in the reformed rites mandated by Vatican II. He
demonstrates for us that liturgy must be able somehow to speak
to the outsider by using his/her language, and not just the in-
house language of the church. He offers us a disturbing
eucharistic vision that refuses to permit the marginalization of
any in the church. Wainwright pleads an ecumenical vision of
the Eucharist that will not simply salve our ecclesial wounds but
heal them and make the united church's witness so much more
real. This Eucharist as eschatological can raise us up to heaven,
if we but let its power be unleashed in our lives.

The theology of David Power and Geoffrey Wainwright
shows us what a long way we have come as Christians in the last

four decades to heal the wounds that have been some five centuries old. Much still needs to be done. This Irish Catholic and this English Methodist show us just what is possible and encourage us to take up their example, an example that is both eucharistic and ecumenical.

Notes

1. "Sacrament: Event Eventing," in Michael Downey and Richard Fragomeni, eds., *A Promise of Presence, Studies in Honor of David N. Power, OMI* (Washington, DC: The Pastoral Press, 1992), 296.

2. Geoffrey Wainwright, *Worship with One Accord: Where Liturgy and Ecumenism Embrace* (New York and Oxford: Oxford University Press, 1997), vii.

3. Published under this title by Geoffrey Chapman of London in 1969.

4. Kenneth Hannon, OMI, "David N. Power, OMI: Biographical Note," in Downey and Fragomeni, *A Promise of Presence*, 310.

5. In David S. Cunningham, Ralph Del Colle and Lucas Lamadrid, eds., *Ecumenical Theology in Worship, Doctrine and Life—Essays Presented to Geoffrey Wainwright on his Sixtieth Birthday* (New York and Oxford: Oxford University Press, 1999), 116–26.

6. Michael Downey, "*Lex Orandi, Lex Credendi*: Taking It Seriously in Systematic Theology," in Downey and Fragomeni, *A Promise of Presence*, 4.

7. David N. Power, *Unsearchable Riches: The Symbolic Nature of Liturgy* (New York: Pueblo Publishing Company, 1984).

8. ———. *Worship: Culture and Theology* (Washington, DC: The Pastoral Press, 1990).

9. See Downey, "*Lex Orandi, Lex Credendi*," in Downey and Fragomeni, *A Promise of Presence*, 10–11.

10. "Eucharist," in Francis Schüssler Fiorenza and John P. Galvin, eds., *Systematic Theology, Roman Catholic Perspectives*, vol. 2 (Minneapolis: Fortress Press, 1991), 262, 265.

11. Downey, "*Lex Orandi, Lex Credendi*," Downey and Fragomeni, *A Promise of Presence*, 17.

12. David N. Power, *Sacrament, The Language of God's Giving* (New York: Crossroad, 1999), 155.

13. Ibid., 160.

14. Ibid., 162.

15. Ibid., 164.

16. Ibid., 152.

17. ————. *"The Word of the Lord": The Liturgy's Use of Scripture* (Maryknoll, NY: Orbis Books, 2001), 16.

18. ————. *The Eucharistic Mystery: Revitalizing the Tradition* (New York: Crossroad, 1992), 349.

19. Ibid., 348.

20. See David N. Power, "Vatican II and the Liturgical Future," *Antiphon, A Journal for Liturgical Renewal* 5 (2000), 10–18.

21. Geoffrey Wainwright. *Eucharist and Eschatology* (London: Epworth Press, 1971, second edition 1978).

22. Downey and Fragomeni, *A Promise of Presence*, 187–206.

23. Wainwright, *Eucharist and Eschatology*, 51.

24. Ibid., 56.

25. Ibid., 140–41.

26. Ibid., 143.

27. ————. *Doxology: A Systematic Theology* (New York and London: Oxford University Press, 1980).

28. Ibid., 319.

29. Adapted from the essay, "Eucharist, Reconciliation and Renewal," in Geoffrey Wainwright, *The Ecumenical Moment* (Grand Rapids: Eerdmans, 1983), 54–55.

30. Ibid., 69–70.

31. Wainwright, *Worship with One Accord*, 197.

32. Ibid., 205.

Epilogue

We have made our way through a selection of eucharistic witnesses of the two millennia of Christianity. They represent different geographical locations: from Ignatius-the-Syrian bishop in Antioch to Jeremy Taylor, the Anglo-Irish-Caroline bishop. They exemplify different time periods: from Justin in the early second century to David Power in the twenty-first century. They speak and write in different languages: from the Syriac of Ephrem and the Latin of Ambrose and Augustine, to the polished English of George Herbert. They demonstrate different Christian traditions attempting to articulate the meaning of the mystery of the Eucharist, the very heart of Christian faith.

Each of these men recognized the Eucharist as central. The Eucharist was of the *esse* of the church; the Eucharist made the church. Ours is a time of sadness and tragedy. The Eucharist remains the bond of unity, but, because of ecclesial separation, it cannot be shared. Perhaps the ecumenical cause is served not only through official dialogue between the churches, but also through this kind of ecumenical retrieval. Knowing the tradition of eucharistic thought and identity provides all Christians with a strong base for moving ahead into greater unity.

Index of Names